TWILIGHT NATIONALISM

TWILIGHT NATIONALISM

Politics of Existence at Life's End

DANIEL MONTERESCU and HAIM HAZAN

STANFORD UNIVERSITY PRESS

Stanford, California

Stanford University Press
Stanford, California

Printed in the United States of America on acid-free, archival-quality paper

Library of Congress Cataloging-in-Publication Data

Names: Monterescu, Daniel, author. | Hazan, Haim, author.
Title: Twilight nationalism : politics of existence at life's end / Daniel Monterescu and Haim Hazan.
Description: Stanford, California : Stanford University Press, 2018. | Includes bibliographical references and index.
Identifiers: LCCN 2017061059 (print) | LCCN 2017058111 (ebook) | ISBN 9781503604322 (cloth : alk. paper) | ISBN 9781503605633 (pbk. : alk. paper) | ISBN 9781503605640 (e-book)
Subjects: LCSH: Jaffa (Tel Aviv, Israel)—Biography. | Nationalism—Israel—Tel Aviv. | Older people—Israel—Tel Aviv—Biography. | Jews—Israel—Tel Aviv—Biography. | Palestinian Arabs—Israel—Tel Aviv—Biography. | Jaffa (Tel Aviv, Israel)—Ethnic relations. | LCGFT: Biographies.
Classification: LCC DS110.J3 M66 2018 (ebook) | LCC DS110.J3 (print) | DDC 305.80095694/8--dc23
LC record available at https://lccn.loc.gov/2017061059

Typeset by Bruce Lundquist in 10.25/15 Adobe Caslon Pro

This land is a traitor
and can't be trusted.
This land doesn't remember love.
This land is a whore
holding out a hand to the years,
as it manages a ballroom
on the harbor pier—
it laughs in every language
and bit by bit, with its hip,
feeds all who come to it.

Taha Muhammad Ali, "Ambergris"

CONTENTS

PART III: NIGHTFALL

ACKNOWLEDGMENTS

This book stems out of a long personal, intellectual, and political fascination with the time of life, the time of the nation, and the time of the city. Speaking of and for the city, however, is a chronicle of foretold failure. As Italo Calvino notes in his *Invisible Cities*, "The city does not tell its past, but contains it like the lines of a hand, written in the corners of the streets, the gratings of the windows, the banisters of the steps, the antennae of the lightning rods, the poles of the flags, every segment marked in turn with scratches, indentations, scrolls." We therefore have attempted to read the city and its citizens as a palimpsest of successive owners, subjects, and bystanders. The violently divergent histories of Jaffa, a binational city of contention, cannot be erased from memory and place; rather, they are impregnated in uncanny manners. The return of the repressed springs out with a vengeance from the interstices. However, the voice of the repressed is commonly silenced by hegemonic narratives of self and nation and by identity politics in public discourse and academic scholarship. When heard, this voice is often faint and feeble, cracked and incoherent. In this book we seek to recoup the incongruities of these narratives and tell the tale of these historical scratches, indentations, and scrolls.

Following the lead of reflexive anthropology, oral history, postcolonial studies, critical nationalism studies, and memory studies, we sought to listen to the inchoate orally transmitted knowledge that is fast disappearing right before our eyes, as the Nakba generation and the cohort of elderly Jewish immigrants wither away. Our only working assumption was that they have a significant story to tell and that they speak truth to power, regardless of its factual historical falsifiability. Jaffa's elderly from all walks of life—Jewish, Palestinian, Muslim, Christian, Ashkenazi, Mizrahi, rich, poor—appear to us as oracles of the city and prophets of rage of the nation. They are, as we see them, alchemists of culture, turning the narrative stuff of life into golden memory and stories of resilience.

The resulting life story accounts are iconoclastic and at times baffling and disturbing. Idiosyncratic as they are, though, they encapsulate a whole world of lifelong projects, themes, and tribulations. By turning microhistorical glimpses into macrohistorical insights, they produce minor literature consisting of fragmented rhythms of life. This kind of research prescribes a unique methodological sensibility. Our interlocutors and their families all had a say in its making. We took heed of their interpretation of times past, present, and future and did our best to faithfully and humbly transmit it to the reader.

Any study of everyday binationalism is by necessity transcultural and oftentimes bilingual. The interviews with the Palestinian interlocutors were conducted in Arabic by us but in the presence of other Palestinian interviewers (Moussa abu-Ramadan or Mai Masalha-Chabaita), which generated a narrative triangle between Jewish researchers, Palestinian storytellers, and Palestinian participant listeners-*cum*-observers who conversed together. Cultural intimacy and analytical externality were thus constantly evoked. Each interview was subsequently transcribed in Arabic and then translated. Likewise, the interviews with the Jewish subjects were conducted by the authors in Hebrew.

We conducted the interviews using the open-ended, qualitative research method we call participant conversation. We adhered to several guiding themes, so the interviews took the form of informal exchange and for the most part evolved according to the narrator's associative flow. Most of our questions were framed during the course of the conversation in response to the narrators' words. The original recordings and their transcriptions have been archived at the Central European University and at Tel Aviv University's Herczeg Institute on Aging in order to serve as raw material for further study.

This project of documentation, preservation, and distribution of the life stories of elderly Jewish and Arab Jaffaites was made possible primarily thanks to a research grant from the Price-Brody Initiative at Tel Aviv University, which we received in 2002. The material gathered during the course of the project serves academic and educational purposes and is available to anyone interested in Jewish-Arab relations and the life of Arabs and Jews in a mixed city. A research stipend from the Central European University in Budapest and the European University Institute in Florence (the European Commission's Marie Curie Fellowship) enabled Daniel Monterescu to devote the time required to complete the research. We thank the Israel Center for Digital Art and the Autobiography of a City project, run by the Ayam Association—Recognition and Dialogue (RA) and led by Eyal Danon and Sami Bukhari, for a grant that allowed us to complete the processing of the material.

The Tel Aviv University Herczeg Institute on Aging offered us a welcoming home throughout our work on the project. In particular, we thank the institute's staff, especially Meira Berger and Nitza Eyal, for their valuable help and collegial collaboration. We wish to express our appreciation to Professor Jiska Cohen-Mansfield, head of the Herczeg Institute, for her generous support in preparing the manuscript. We thank Professor Shimon Spiro, who encouraged us and the project from the very beginning.

Special thanks are due to Moussa abu-Ramadan and Mai Masalha-Chabaita, who assisted in the interviewing process, and to Hicham Chabaita, who served as the project's photographer. We are grateful to 'Ayush Kheil of the 'Ajami club for the elderly, who welcomed us to the club and introduced us to its patrons. We thank Pnina Steinberg for skillfully editing the Hebrew manuscript and Avner Greenberg and Ami Asher for their invaluable assistance in preparing the English version. Further thanks go to Nisrin Siksik, Raneen Jeries, and Yaakov Nahmias, and the staff of the Tamlil office, who all assisted in transcribing the interviews.

Without the munificent contribution made by the Van Leer Jerusalem Institute toward the preparation of the manuscript for publication, this project could not have been accomplished. We are grateful to Professor Gabriel Motzkin, director of the Van Leer Jerusalem Institute, and particularly to Dr. Tal Kohavi, the head of the publication division, whose dedicated commitment both to the Hebrew edition and to the English version made this volume possible. Special thanks are due to Professor Yehouda Shenhav, of the Van Leer Jerusalem Institute, under whose conscientious editorship the Hebrew edition of this book first appeared.

The Minerva Center of the Interdisciplinary Study of the End of Life was highly instrumental in facilitating the publication of the book, and our thanks are extended to the directors and colleagues who spared no effort to lend an ear and to offer constructive advice.

Last but not least in the order of thanksgiving are our partners Roni Dorot and Mercia Hazan for bearing with us throughout this treacherous way and for their steadfast engagement in good spirit, sound advice, and unflinching faith in our Sisyphean pursuit of the eclipse.

This book is a tribute to our protagonists, both living and dead.

TWILIGHT NATIONALISM

TOWARD TWILIGHT NATIONALISM

"Me or him"—
That's how the war begins. But it
Ends in an awkward encounter:
"Me and him."

Mahmoud Darwish, "State of Siege"

Performing Identity: Narratives of Disenchantment

Since the 1990s, Gabi 'Abed, social worker, amateur dramatist, and Jaffa Arab activist, has been staging a one-man show: the story of an elderly Palestinian called Samed 'abd al-Baqi al-Maslub (literally, "the crucified who remains steadfast").[1] The old man is dressed in a traditional Arab robe, with his head covered by a large skullcap and his chest bearing a wooden cross. He waves a stout walking stick as he addresses the audience: "Once we were landlords, and now we are no more than protected tenants." The personal testimony he shares with the audience in both Hebrew and Arabic offers a glimpse into the tragic annals of the entire Palestinian community.

> I remember that in 1948 our peace of mind vanished all at once. There was shooting and bombing all around us. . . . They began to scare people; they gave out pictures of rape, of murder, of blood. Mayhem broke out; people didn't know what to do. . . . They wanted to escape and didn't know where. The Arab leaders came [laughs sardonically]—Arab leaders, my foot! They told the people, "Brothers, fear not. These are only a handful of Jewish gangs. We shall eliminate them. Leave Jaffa, only for a fortnight, no longer." The people trusted them; they were naïve. They abandoned everything . . . and took the key with them [laughs bitterly]. They keep the keys to this day . . . and fifty-five years have now passed and they still hope to return.[2]

Dwelling on the past glory of Jaffa, 'Abed's character binds past and present together as he proceeds to lament:

> Jaffa, *Yafa*, was Palestine's cultural, political, and commercial center. Is there anyone who doesn't know the Jaffa port? They used to call Jaffa *umm al-gharib*, which means "Mother of the Stranger," because foreigners of all places and religions would come there to work. When the Jews came [in 1948], they made us share houses with them. We lived together, but the Jaffa of old is no more. When Jaffa was built up, they called her *'arus al-bahr*, "Bride of the Sea." She really was very beautiful. Not as you see her today, but nonetheless, she remains enchanting.

The street actor personifies the ethos of Palestinian Jaffa's collective memory, portraying its people as the innocent victims of the perfidious Arab elites, Jewish violence and cunning, and historical and economic forces that they could not control. Palestinian Jaffa of the dramatic ethos is an earthly paradise, the Fertile Crescent's crown jewel. But no more. This mythical, romantic, utopian Bride of the Sea is inaccessible to the young audience, who are fed only secondhand reports and rumors. 'Abed, the old witness, offers a momentary glimpse into the memory zone that is Jaffa, at once close at hand and illusive.

The choice of an old man is of course no coincidence. The Palestinian elder is traditionally considered an agent and a guardian of memory capable of providing a firsthand testimonial. The old man appears as the ultimate victim, yet he is also Samed—a survivor who clings to his town and heritage. To this cultural bedrock, 'Abed adds a further layer of Christian iconography, portraying the elderly witness as the bearer of the collective cross.[3] *Sumud*, or "persistence," however, is hard to live by. As a principle of steadfast communal survival, it paradoxically evokes "fortitude in the occupied and frailty in the occupier . . . a tragic sensibility that claims an ethical form of power (and freedom) through powerlessness."[4] This tragic irony could account for the popularity of 'Abed's play in Palestinian communities in Israel, Palestine, and beyond. The power of the play thus derives from the shadow that memory casts over the hardships of the mundane. The momentary solace and acute identification it offers to its audience accentuates the gulf between the dreamt-of and the lived-in, thereby safeguarding Palestinian national memory. However, in a city marked by the copresence of the political Other, how can the lived experience of Palestinian Jaffa residents be reconciled with that transcendental image? How does one cope with such irreconcilable tension between the memory of past life and the exigencies of everyday living, between myth and reality?

The binational city forges a shared arena of interaction, communication, and conflict far removed from the ideals of what Edward Said dubbed "the myths of imagination."[5] The following vignette invites the reader to get acquainted with such an encounter. Safiyya Dabbah and Hanna Swissa, two elderly neighbors living in the Jaffa C (Yafo Gimel) neighborhood, meet daily over breakfast. Safiyya, a Muslim woman in her 90s, was widowed thirty years ago and today lives on her own in a dilapidated shanty only a few steps from the apartment building where Hanna lives. Hanna is a Jewish Moroccan woman in her 70s who has been widowed for twenty years. Despite the class differences between Safiyya and Hanna, which are metaphorically embodied in the buildings they inhabit—a ramshackle hut on the one hand and a tidy apartment building on the other—the two elderly women have found a common ground that they use to nourish their symbiotic friendship. Aside from living in geographic and functional proximity to each other, both women came from strict patriarchal families (Safiyya's husband used to forbid her to leave the house, and Hanna's husband was jealous and violent), and both gained considerable personal freedom after their husbands' deaths; both speak Arabic and share a common cultural background; and both are going through the experience of aging. Although Hanna, aided by her welfare-funded housekeeper, shows concern for Safiyya, whose means are more limited, by supplying the food for their daily rendezvous, Safiyya keeps Hanna company and makes this pleasant morning routine possible.

The political and social reality in Jaffa that brought Safiyya and Hanna together constitutes an unexpected "contact zone" of contrived coexistence,[6] a social medium that both separates and relates the city's Jewish and Arab inhabitants. In this book we focus on this ambivalent encounter between strangers through the analysis of life stories recorded by twelve of Jaffa's elderly residents—Arab and Jewish, male and female, rich and poor. Between the dreamt-of vision that Gabi 'Abed projects and the lived-in pragmatism that binds Safiyya Dabbah to Hanna Swissa is a space of friendship and alienation in the shadow of nationalism.

In the agonistic landscape of Palestine/Israel, no place has been more continuously inflected by the tension between intimate proximity and visceral violence than binational milieus, such as the city of Jaffa. The dangerous liaisons of urban cohabitation between Jews and Palestinians set the scene for a personal and political encounter that allows individuals to challenge dominant notions of nationalism.

Against the backdrop of a century-long conflict between the Jewish and the Palestinian national movements, the everyday experience of lived space and neighborly relations in the politically and culturally contested urban setting of ethnically mixed cities reenacts both connectivity and hostility.[7] Although most scholars conceptualize both Palestinian and Jewish national collective identities as separate and antagonistic projects—indeed as independent ideologies of autochthony defined only by the negation and exclusion of the other—we throw into relief instead the relations of mutual determination between these communities, relations that are often rendered invisible in nationalism studies.[8] Even though the notions of nation and person in Israel/Palestine have been reduced to collective narratives of conflict, revenge, survival, and redemption, we propose to view the political through the personal to reveal the correlation between life trajectories and the construction of cultural identities.

The protagonists of this ethnography unravel the violence of coexistence by reflecting on a century of life in Jaffa. From their perspective of generational marginality, they radically grapple with notions of both Palestinian and Jewish nationalism. Individual figures rather than abstract sociological categories voice personal strategies of engagement with nation, narration, age, and ethnic violence. Echoing the medieval adage "City air makes free," Jews and Palestinians slip through the shackles of hegemonic memory and find ways to liberate themselves from the tyranny of territorial nationalism. The stories they tell about themselves reveal a perspective that has often been silenced by both Jews and Palestinians. The narrators thus operate as allegorical types along an itinerary of dissipating frames of hegemonic national identities. Thematically, they bear the scars of a deep sense of betrayal by political leaders, the local community, the state, and the grand narratives they represent.

Jaffa as a Binational City

As Palestine's major port, pre-1948 Jaffa was a cosmopolitan Arab metropolis.[9] It was also the gateway through which Zionist settlers entered the country.[10] In fact, until the early 1920s Jaffa was the capital of the Zionist national community and, at the same time, a symbol of the birth of Palestinian modernity. In 1909 Jaffa begat Tel Aviv, and in 1948—like the sorcerer's apprentice—this Jewish suburb of Jaffa turned its ancient mother city into the dilapidated "District 7," with no independent municipal status to speak of. After a period of martial law, during which the Palestinian residents were confined to a ghetto (in 'Ajami), in 1950 Jaffa was annexed to Tel Aviv, transforming its Arab community into a national minority in a Jewish city. Out of a pre-1948 population of 70,000 Arabs, only 3,900 remained. Because of the calamity that befell the Palestinians in the wake of the 1948 war—commonly coined the Nakba (catastrophe)—Arab Jaffa lost its entire intellectual elite, middle class, and political leadership. Tens of thousands of Jewish immigrants quickly poured into the emptied city, but soon enough the more prosperous of them left Jaffa, which remained home to a working-class population with a 30 percent Arab minority. Nowadays Jaffa is home to a heterogeneous population from various backgrounds and social classes: a Palestinian community numbering 20,000; a Jewish population of 40,000 that includes a growing number of wealthy gentrifiers; and hundreds of migrant laborers and Palestinian collaborators who have been relocated from the Occupied Territories for security reasons. The ambivalence and complexity associated with Jaffa and its residents ever since its annexation to Tel Aviv gave rise to numerous political and sociocultural dilemmas, which we address in this book.

The relationship between Zionist settlers and the Arab indigenous population was already charged under late Ottoman rule (1517–1917) and even more so during the colonial British rule (1917–1948).[11] The early twentieth century was a time of land purchases, dispossession of peasant populations, and struggles over territory, but it was also a time of cooperation in business ventures, class-based coalitions, mixed residential areas, and municipal partnerships.[12] Before 1948 Tel Aviv and Jaffa were major foci for the molding of the Zionist and Palestinian national collectives, which evolved alongside each other in a series of intertwined processes.[13] Despite emanating from blatantly unequal starting points, the national and local identities shaped one another through relationships of contradiction, confrontation, and mimicry.[14]

Jaffa's history has produced a fragmentary geographic and social space, creating Jewish spaces within Arab places and Palestinian spaces within Israeli ones. Unlike nationally homogeneous cities such as Bat Yam or divided cities such as Jerusalem, Jaffa's social boundaries (between Arabs and Jews and between rich and poor) are not commensurate with its spatial boundaries (between neighborhoods). The city's demographic structure is a product of the haphazard events and the consequences of the 1948 war. The mixed city with its Arab minority remained an underplanned and incomplete spatial fact. Lacking any clear social center, each interest group in Jaffa crystallized its own ideology and political outlook around local issues and particular identities, without explicitly addressing the sociopolitical whole.

In public discourse it is hardly surprising that the term *mixed city* triggers resistance and intense emotions. It is both intriguing and enticing, for it holds promise and contention alike. Some scholars and activists reject the notion of urban mix, because they view urban space as predominantly divided along lines of various politics of identity.[15] The term *mixed city* is nevertheless used by both Jews and Arabs, conservative and critical residents, activists, NGOs, and state institutions.

Three main sociological groups can be currently identified in Jaffa: the Palestinian community; the (relatively) long-standing Jewish population; and the growing group of new Jewish residents, the outcome of a rapid gentrification process that began in the 1990s. Each group promotes a political-cultural project of localism as it attempts to justify its claims in relation to the other groups and in relation to municipal and state authorities.

Jaffa's Palestinians: Identity Bereft of Community

The communal organizing principle of Jaffa's Palestinian residents crystallized out of a profound sense of discrimination and a demand for equality combined with a reformulation of an indigenous Palestinian identity. This identity framework has proved to be stronger than the sectarian and political schisms between Muslims and Christians or between religious and secular groups. Indeed, even the many Palestinians who migrated to Jaffa from other parts of the country after 1948 frequently perceive and present themselves as Jaffaites (*abna' al-balad*), and their descendants tend to remain in the city. Their absorption is both economically and culturally feasible because the city offers opportunities that are lacking in Arab villages and because Jaffa's image is one of an open city.

In Palestinian discourse, Jaffa, the Mother of the Stranger, is an urban hub for labor migrants and travelers from all over the region.[16] This ideology of indigenous belonging is imbued with a nostalgic taint of a glorious past. Notwithstanding a deeply divided social and political structure, this discourse of belonging allows the Arab minority to present a united front of social solidarity. A Jaffa Palestinian intellectual summed it up as follows: "Jaffa is an identity bereft of a community."

Three key terms constitute Jaffa's Palestinian image: Bride of the Sea (*'arus al-bahar*), which locates it in a Mediterranean setting; Bride of Palestine (*'arus falastin*), which links Jaffa to the national liberation movement; and Mother of the Stranger (*umm al-gharib*), which portrays Jaffa as a vibrant urban center that welcomes every foreigner. In 1948, however, the Nakba deprived Palestinian Jaffa of its urban centrality. Following this colossal trauma, the meaning of *umm al-gharib* was turned upside down, such that it now signifies Jaffa's plight and alienation within Israeli space and state; Jaffa's Palestinian population is unable to prevent armed collaborators from entering or to halt the process of gentrification (read "Judaization"). An elderly Jaffaite remarked, "Jaffa is the Mother of the Stranger. . . . It welcomes him [the Jewish stranger] and feeds him, while it neglects its own sons and leaves them to starve."[17]

In local Palestinian discourse Jaffa is perceived as a peripheral space; it is excluded from Jewish centers of power, from the Palestinian national project in the Occupied Territories, and from the decision-making circles of the Palestinian minority in Israel.[18] To the Arab residents this pronounced marginality is apparent in their status on the national level as second-class citizens and at the municipal level as an urban ethnic minority. Hence the concept of "double minority" is widely used by the city's political activists to describe their predicament.

The Long-Standing Jewish Community:
Dismembered Identity, Remembered Community

Jaffa's longtime Jewish residents arrived in the city as it was licking the wounds of the Nakba. In the 1949 *Jaffa Guide* issued for this immigrant population, the postwar city is likened to an "empty shell" that needs to be filled with substance.

> Massive immigration (*'aliyah*) brought about the creation in Jaffa of a Jewish settlement (*yishuv*) of 50,000 or more—the largest urban community created by the current ingathering of the exiles. This new-old Jewish city is like a sealed book—not only for most Israelis living elsewhere but also for those living nearby. Jaffa has already become an Israeli city but not yet a Hebrew city. . . . This is not the normal process of building a new city. Here, the empty shells—the houses themselves—were ready-made. What was left to be done was to breathe life into this ghost town. . . . Materially and externally, Hebrew Jaffa is nothing but the heritage of Arab Jaffa prior to May 1948.[19]

The Jewish immigrants succeeded in establishing a vibrant community of petty traders and artisans, even though they were subjected to harsh material conditions and came from a position of inferiority in relation to Tel Aviv, whose leaders were reluctant to annex Jaffa. And they maintained utilitarian neighborly relations with the remaining Arabs. At the height of its prosperity in the 1950s and 1960s, the Jewish community numbered 40,000 inhabitants. The largest and most prosperous ethnic group was the Bulgarian community, to such an extent that Jaffa was nicknamed Little Bulgaria.[20] Yet because the Jewish residents enjoyed social and spatial mobility, beginning in the 1960s Jaffa gradually became a transit city, a stop on the way to new housing projects in neighboring towns. Most second- and third-generation residents did not remain in Jaffa. This led to the gradual disintegration of Jewish community life and a perceived loss of control in relation to growing Palestinian influence. An aged Bulgarian resident thus expressed her frustration: "Jaffa was once a Bulgarian city, but what the Jews took by force, the Arabs now take by money."

Apart from their self-definition in relation to the Arab inhabitants, the Jewish immigrants also differentiate themselves in terms of social class and ethnicity from the prosperous and mainly Ashkenazic Jews who began moving into Jaffa in the 1990s. These gentrifiers are seen as "north-siders" (*tzfonim*), that is, representatives of the alienated upper class from northern Tel Aviv.[21]

The New Jewish Residents: A Community in Search of Identity

Largely made up of bourgeois bohemians, the new Jewish resident population segment is politically driven by a liberal ideology of coexistence and, at the urban level, by romantic nostalgia for authentic Mediterranean neighborliness. Many of these newcomers are artists and professionals, and they stand out in the Jaffa landscape in terms of their Ashkenazic origin, higher class status, and hipster lifestyle. They are well organized as a social community and interest group, with significant clout in town hall, but they are engaged in a complex quest for a local identity that would merge the Tel Aviv bourgeoisie with the alleged authenticity of Jaffa.

In this book we enlist the testimonies of the Palestinian and long-standing Jewish groups; they are the products of the post-1948 jointly generated urban space. Our principal line of inquiry focuses on the subjects' attitudes toward community, city, nation, and state, in particular, their ambivalence toward the space in which they live. As a sociological perspective on alterity, Jaffa enables us to articulate the dilemmas generated by life in the mixed city in dialectical terms of belonging and alienation without reducing Jaffa to the stereotypes of a colonial city or a liberal space of (wishful) coexistence.

The tribulations of diversity and adversity in Jaffa paradoxically facilitate the emergence of a nascent form of a social world where steadfast categories of nationhood, community, gender, and age are revisited and reshuffled. This communicative experience renders the mixed city an enabling milieu for alternative imagined and actual communities.

Jaffa is a city of strangers, for good or ill. Its unique profile is predicated on the mitigating effect of cultural and functional proximity between rival social types and disparate trajectories. Ordinary citizens, under conditions of contrived coexistence and enabled by the pragmatics of utilitarian transactions with the state and their neighbors, rewrite their place in the national order of things and reformulate hegemonic scripts of nationalist subjectivity.

From this relational perspective, the mixed urban space can be seen as an enabling environment that produces social dispositions and cultural imaginaries that would otherwise be impossible in mononational cities or villages by virtue of ethnic monitoring and spatial segregation.

Methodological Nationalism Revisited

Much of nationalism studies is trapped in a vicious circle that condemns its scholars to uncritically reproduce their own categories of analysis. This self-sustaining perspective, often dubbed methodological nationalism, replicates the logic of normative nationalism, thus rendering the concept of collective identity infertile and defunct.[22] Methodological nationalism notoriously privileges primordial consciousness over the dynamic of situations and interactions. By default, it obfuscates practices and ideas that defy the hegemonic homogeneity of the imagined community. More than a choice of unit of analysis, methodological nationalism dovetails a predisposition that regards all nonnational things as marginal and epiphenomenal. For ethnographers of nationalism it is the foremost risk of anachronism, essentialism, and reification.

The historiography of relations between Jews and Arabs in Palestine provides a clear example of methodological nationalism. The functionalist school founded by S. N. Eisenstadt portrays Jews and Arabs according to the dual society model; the Jewish and Palestinian societies are presented as two disparate entities and as separate movements that have failed to maintain reciprocal relations.[23] Relational historian Zachary Lockman blames this paradigm for a fundamental misconception.

> The Arab and Jewish communities in Palestine are represented as primordial, self-contained, and largely monolithic entities. By extension communal identities are regarded as natural rather than as constructed. . . . This approach has rendered their mutually constitutive impact virtually invisible, tended to downplay intracommunal divisions, and focused attention on episodes of violent conflict, implicitly assumed to be the sole normal or even possible form of interaction.[24]

Methodological nationalism shackles social agents to preset binary historical roles, thereby dismissing any pattern that fails to conform to the nationalist logic that generates them. A similar bias informs both Palestinian and Jewish critics,[25] whose writings presuppose a perfect correspondence between the collective narrative and the personal story and between the national and the local spheres. According to this perspective, social relationships are dictated by a single cultural axiom that postulates a primary nationalist bedrock from which both politics and lived experiences sprout.

Because methodological nationalism equates societies in general with nation-state societies and views states and their national ideologies as the cornerstones of social-scientific analysis, the concept has become the ruling paradigm in urban studies as well. This methodological stance is a deep-rooted epistemological position that cuts across the spectrum of both Palestinian and Israeli political viewpoints and operates by fixating social agents as independent oppositional actors (settlers versus natives, colonizers versus colonized). Under its spell, urban scholars have conceptualized social relations and cityscapes in mixed towns in dualistic terms, namely, as historical anomalies or as segregated ghettos.[26]

The standard narrative of this approach is premised on a functionalist convergence of variables, which results in systemic geopolitical effects. Thus, for neoconservative geographer Arnon Soffer, Israel's wealth, combined with structural demographic disadvantages in relation to the growing Palestinian population, will eventually result in Israel's annihilation unless drastic measures are taken to ensure a Jewish majority and to "decrease" (read "transfer") the Palestinian population between the Jordan River and the Mediterranean Sea.[27] Conversely, the critical theory of ethnocracy postulates a systemic effort by the Israeli state toward ethnic discrimination, domination, and subordination of its Palestinian citizens, and this effort hinges on the territorial segregation of the two populations.[28] By conceptualizing nationalism as a top-down and state-centric process, both theories turn a blind eye to the unresolved tensions among the constitutive elements of the urban sociospatial order (ethnonationalism, capitalist logic, and modern governance) and to the quotidian relations between majority and minority groups in Israel.

Methodological nationalism, however, is not merely a distinct scholarly position. It transcends disciplinary boundaries and encompasses the whole gamut of the culture of memory regarding the historical antecedents of communal identity. The agents of the new politics of memory generally justify their methodological nationalism and its ensuing strategic essentialism[29] by asserting that a remedial measure is called for to enable the Palestinians to make their voice heard and thus sustain a sense of identity in the face of the dominant, oppressive Zionist narrative.[30] Thus, despite the intention to reach postnational reconciliation, criticism of Jewish nationalism freezes alternative memory as an antithesis of Zionism and maintains the nationalist discourse it seeks to undermine. Indeed, despite being couched in postcolonial terms, promoting the new discourse reproduces the old politics of memory. This nationalist gaze on mixed cities turns neighbors living cheek by jowl into people who are culturally and politically alienated foes. Jews and Arabs are constructed as ultimate Others, too distant to share the same symbolic space of trust, interests, and values. The common space is torn apart by two distinct timelines; in one, the Palestinian is tossed out of history and unwillingly drawn into a national myth, whereas in the other, the Zionist takes up a position within a hegemonic history that is conducting a convoluted dialogue with its foundational myths.

Indeed, there can be no national movement or resistance to nationalism without a collective memory, and there can be no collective memory without a unifying narrative. Thus, throughout the evolution of both the Zionist and the Palestinian national movements, stories have been assiduously crafted about the historical bonds between the people and the land that justify the mutually exclusive existence of these movements. These self-contained, metonymic links are inherent to the project of modern nationalism. They rest on symbolic violence that represents an unyielding attempt to establish an identity and a history within territorial boundaries while stressing "the impossible unity of the nation as a symbolic force."[31] Elites use the modernist linear narrative to carve out a story of origin, which, as Homi Bhabha maintains, should be exposed as a compulsive project destined to fail because of its inherent ambivalence. This instability emerges from a growing awareness that, "despite the certainty with which historians speak of the 'origins' of nation as a sign of the 'modernity' of society, the cultural temporality of the nation inscribes a much more transitional social reality."[32]

How, then, do everyday social situations throw this ambivalence of nationalism into greater relief? We grapple with this key question in this book. The perspective of subaltern studies offers a useful critique of nationalism as a product of bourgeois-patriarchal metanarratives that trickle down from power centers to imagined publics and personal demeanor.[33] In stark contradiction, the stories presented in this book spring from below, from the everyday lives of real people, namely, the residents who maintain a troubled relationship with the imagined communities to which they are assumed to belong. Personal narratives are entrenched in the local context of each storyteller within the broader nationalism-saturated environment. All the narrators have managed to free themselves of nationalism's tethers to some extent, each in their own way but not always to their advantage. How, then, does the notion of nationalism operate in tales of everyday life and in different social contexts? The circumstances under which the personal story of life in Jaffa contends with hegemonic representations of identity unravel a bargain with nationalism, which either affirms or renounces it.[34] Can the "awkward encounter" between the foes whom Mahmoud Darwish writes about generate a novel insight into the understanding of nationalism?

Evolving modes of nationalism display an autobiographical drama that reveals the intricate and fraught relationships between the personal and the political. In the process the individual voice liberates itself from the clutches of methodological nationalism, reveals the symbolic violence inherent to it, and thereby highlights the identity-sustaining strategies that serve to reinforce or repudiate it. The city of Jaffa facilitates (and at times imposes) an encounter between Palestinians and Jews: They live as diachronic and synchronic neighbors[35] and do not meet solely within the formal spheres of work, study, police checkpoints, and political gatherings.

Furthermore, the elderly provide a vantage point predicated on their assumed marginality, which frees them from the constraints of normative cultural performance. Thus, unlike Gabi 'Abed's play, which offers a monolithic story in which nationalism dominates all, the twelve protagonists in this book are immersed in the business of living, which involves ongoing and spontaneous production of discourse rather than pilgrimage to public sites of memory.

At first glance, Palestinian and Jewish elderly people in Jaffa inhabit two parallel and incommensurable existential planes. The Jews' national story unfolds from Diaspora to immigration (aliyah) and from Holocaust to nation building, whereas the Palestinian collective story is one of traumatic passage

from the golden "days of the Arabs" (*ayyam al-'Arab*) to the national defeat of
the Nakba in 1948. Their ensuing civil exclusion and economic marginaliza-
tion is represented as resistance (*muqawama*) and steadfastness (*sumud*).

On the one hand, these collective narratives tell a success story of
settlement, progress, and return (*shivat tzion*); but on the other hand, they illustrate a story of dispersion (*shatat*), decline, and struggle. This is the official
narrative, which has been produced and reproduced by the social institutions
in charge of maintaining the national collective memory. Indeed, on this
collective level the main relationship between the Israeli memory and the
Palestinian memory is that of negation and mutual exclusion.[36] This frame of
reference creates a one-sided paradigm of liberation versus victimhood that
nourishes the biographical narrative, which in itself can either adopt it, reject
it, or alter it to suit its own needs.

Notwithstanding collective representations of the nation, a close exami-
nation of personal life stories unravels a whole universe of contradictions.
Some of Jaffa's Arab residents reject major chunks of the Palestinian national
narrative, and some Jewish residents do not see their own trajectories as the
metonymic celebration of the "predatory" nationalist project.[37] Often, they
personally identify with the predicament of the Palestinians. The result is a
fascinating set of multilayered personal histories that differentially reposi-
tion citizens in relation to the state and the nation. The discrepancy between
the top-down collective memory and local biographical memories reveals a
lifeworld of tensions and tribulations. These tensions give voice to private experiences that have been systematically censored by the hegemonic national
register.[38]

We present our argument for dismantling the dichotomous totality of
nationalist categories through an analytical scrutiny of three main themes
that present themselves in the recorded life stories: (1) nation and community, (2) gender and family, and (3) liminality and old age. Rooted in specific
religious, ethnic, and gender- and class-based positions, the interviewees de-
lineate the binational relational field in Jaffa, exposing it as a stratified web
of cultural meanings and informal social relations. In revisiting the collective
doxa of both Palestinian and Jewish national essentialisms, these narrators
invoke the twilight zone surrounding the margins of the collective self as a
much wider and muddier quagmire than we may have been led to believe.

These ambivalent stories, which are constantly in dialogue with the national narration, illustrate that the Israeli and the Palestinian narratives do not consist of a proverbially single nationalist, antinationalist, or postnationalist narrative but are a mosaic of memories and reminiscences. Thus, rather than act as a monolithic script of self and Other, aligned along imagined communities and myths of redemption, these narratives interweave political violence (uprooting, immigration, and imprisonment) with an experience of social proximity and cultural intimacy. Disabling a flat image of the Other, the critical narration of the nation enables residents to redefine contrived coexistence and escape the mythscape.[39]

Metanationalism and the Biographical Illusion

The human being is a storyteller, or *Homo narrans.*[40] Indeed, as Victor Turner notes, "Culture in general—specific cultures, and the fabric of meaning that constitute any single human existence—is the 'story' we tell about ourselves."[41] The tale "certifies the fact of being and gives sense at the same time."[42] Facing the existential themes of life and death, national pride and defeat, continuity and finality, the life stories of Palestinian and Jewish elderly people in Jaffa tease meaning and identity out of their memories and experiences.

The documentation of life stories in Israel/Palestine poses a challenge that is both theoretical and methodological. The conundrum is best put in negative terms: How can we analyze personal narratives of Jews and Palestinians, who are steeped in economic and political power relations, without overlooking the complexity that at times dismantles the same power relations? In the following discussion we draw on the insight that both apolitical narratives and politicizing tactics are the product of identity politics; this insight applies to the hegemonic nationalist discourse and subordinate discourses alike. Instead of rejecting the validity of these narratives or, conversely, accepting them at face value,[43] we position them inside the Jaffa force field to decipher the tension between the personal and the political.[44]

Reflexively treating these narratives as stories "is not to reduce them to fictions made up out of whole cloth and therefore false."[45] Thus, rather than treating them as a "Rashomon tale, a multi-stranded set of equally plausible claims," we "recoup the inconsistencies of these narratives, to explore how subaltern inflections entered these stories . . . tangled by multiple meanings that could not be easily read."[46] We address these concerns by resorting to an analytical approach that can be characterized as metanationalist. Like metaphysics (which can be defined as second-order thinking about the phenomenal world), metanationalism is a second-order reflexive unpacking of national narratives through and of speech.[47] This inquiry necessitates a systematic mapping of the life stories and their embedded representation of collective memories. As a response to the critique of methodological nationalism, metanationalism is first and foremost a call for ethnographic sensibility as a means for dealing with this bias. Conceptualizing the elderly Palestinians as a minority "trapped between nation and state"[48] prevents their stories from being subordinated to a stance that reduces them to either stories of resistance or fanciful tales of coexistence.

An additional challenge concerns the tendency of the life story narrative genre to superimpose coherence where there is none.[49] The aged person's life story is often presented as an evolving internal myth whose elements unfold sequentially to create unity and purpose.[50] The myth—from the Greek word *mythos*, meaning "word and story"—is arguably a coherent framework constructed by the narrator to arm her- or himself with a *telos*—destination and meaning. However, as a mode of symbolic interaction, one's identity is forged by the story one tells oneself and one's significant others in the ethnographic present. Often this story is told, especially in a situation of a life story interview, as an orderly and meaningful chain of events. Pierre Bourdieu terms this tendency "the biographical illusion" and calls it into question as a trajectory within social spaces: "To produce a life history or to consider life as history, that is, as a coherent narrative of a significant and directed sequence of events, is perhaps to conform to a rhetorical illusion, to the common representation of existence that a whole literary tradition has always and still continues to reinforce."[51]

The discontinuity that defines Palestinian experience and the drama of Jewish immigration renders such "coherent narratives" barely sustainable. Thus, like the difficulty in maintaining a cohesive collective community discourse in times of enduring crisis, it is difficult to maintain the biographical illusion in the generational context of old age. The analytical challenge is therefore to follow the dynamics of narration in a mixed cultural environment and to capture its significations at the crossroads of gender, ethnicity, age, and nationality. If the epistemological status of the life story is that of a nonreferential "text,"[52] then we take it as present-bound reflections on the past and read it against the context of its production. In telling the story of their lives to themselves and to the interviewer, the protagonists navigate between different frames of reference and identity—rewriting in the process the relationships between self and Other.

The category and the experience of aging are of crucial importance in understanding the mutual constitution of biographic reminiscence, collective memory, and life history as mediated by the narrators' experiential interpretations of nationalism and the state. The limbo position of the elderly enables them to raise criticisms that do not surface in earlier stages of the life cycle.[53] In contrast to middle-age adults, the elderly—Jews and Arabs alike—are situated on the margins of society and on the edge of their life careers and therefore are less reluctant to reflect out loud on the complex facets of their personal and political condition and the "tyranny" of the younger majority that excludes them. Their invisibility marginalizes them to a point beyond normative culture, from which they can observe life in an unconventional, often evocative stoic manner.[54]

Apart from the freedom from conformity it affords, the "unbearable lightness of retirement"[55] brings with it departure from rigid and predetermined timelines. Senior citizens' perception of time does not necessarily correspond to the mythical-historical time of the collective narrative but rather generates a present-progressive story of survival and everyday tasks and chores. Because they do not idealize or adhere to the collective rituals of nationalism, their stories are filled with calamity, dissociation, betrayal, and cantankerous criticism. This social critique finds its way into their life stories and their poetically reflexive insights into the passing of time and the experience of old age. Following Theodor Adorno, Edward Said called this cognitive orientation "late style."[56] Said, however, applied his insights to renowned creative figures in Western culture, whereas our subjects testify to this style's presence among ordinary folk as well.

In addition to the presumed national divide (Arabs and Jews), the gender dimension places women and men on opposite sides.[57] The tales related by most of the men start with nostalgic recollections of the Palestinian heyday before the Nakba or the bustling period of Jewish community building in Jaffa after 1948, and they end in personal loss and communal atrophy. The women's stories, on the other hand, frequently begin with a critical portrayal of adolescence under the patriarchal yoke and culminate in their present liberation, which owes much to state support. The transition of Palestinian women from an inferior status of poverty in a patriarchal society to the official status of citizens eligible for social benefits independent of their men, alongside their experience as a subordinate minority in a mixed city over a period of seventy years, has engendered in most of them a complex perception of the Jewish Other. The tales of Mizrahi Jewish widows from Syria and Morocco echo a similar transition from life under patriarchy and communal isolation to personal autonomy supported by state institutions.

The unexpected structural similarity of the Jewish and Palestinian women's stories, which contrasts with the shared pessimism of the men's accounts, suggests that these life stories should be read also or primarily in terms of gender rather than exclusively through the lens of ethnicity or nationalism. These seemingly paradoxical narratives facilitated by Jaffa are the historical product of an ambivalent subject position,[58] such as that of elderly Palestinians who are also citizens of the state that occupied their villages and towns and brought about their national ruin. The stories reflect and effect intimate yet tense relationships between the generation of Palestinian survivors and the generation of Jewish immigrants who lived side by side, quite often in the same building or even the same apartment.

The existential position of our elderly interviewees determines the manner in which their stories are manufactured as memory. Memory thus operates not as a set reservoir of experience from which the narrators draw the validity of their version but rather as the direct product of the ethnographic continuous present and of the contingent interaction between interviewer and interviewee. The narrators generate memory as they engage in the act of remembering while talking about the experience of remembering. The narration of reminiscing is a speech act. It locks the narrator into a historical trajectory as an indigenous auto-ethnographer. In the absence of a unifying metanarrative and common frame of reference, memory in Jaffa—as a cultural-political category of practice—is dismembered into memories and recollections that maintain the narrative act.

Thus, without resorting to the technical apparatus of semiotic and linguistic anthropology,[59] we study the narratives as a product of both the historical urban context and the interaction between researcher and interviewee. To do so, we use an open interview that confronts the narrators with their own identity categories. Our interview approach can be characterized as "participant conversation" (in addition to the canonical participant observation), which enables us to unveil the story as a "situated narrative."[60] From a pragmatic perspective, the narrators reveal their own strategies of engagement with the national order through their presentation of self. The life story of the mixed city's elderly residents reads like a performance of nationalism in both senses of the term: as a re-presentation of the discourse of nationalism and as a speech act.

By drawing on the multifaceted phenomena found at the crossroads of gender, ethnicity, age, and nationalism, we investigate the epistemology of the mixed city as an enabling community. Our aim is to offer a fresh assessment of this community's narrative products, which represent and generate social fragmentation, spatial division, and cultural alienation. This apparent curse is converted into a tangible blessing, because these discontinuities and deficiencies of identity are turned into existential resources of survival.

Sunset, Dusk, Nightfall

This book is indeed an ethnography of a concrete and yet symbolic urban encounter between the researchers, the interviewees, and the city in the shadow of the nation. Relying on our previous acquaintance with the city's inhabitants, we chose to interview articulate and critical individuals cast in Jaffa's image. In Smadar Lavie's terminology, these are allegorical types who tell personal stories that reflect and deflect the public context from which they emerge.[61] The allegorical type is neither an abstract ideal type that purports to represent the collective nor a unique and exceptional type in its immediate social environment. Each allegorical type manifests a coping strategy—one among many—with the events of the past and personal choices. Whereas the poetic attributes of these stories are frequently dramatic, their primary force lies in the prevalent discourse that criticizes and interprets the locale and the epoch.

The stories' allegorical nature came into sharper focus after we had collected the material between 2003 and 2006. As we proceeded to sort through it, we discovered that it not only facilitated a different perspective on the elements of nationalism in our subjects' identity but that it also covered the range of theoretical possibilities in the study of nationalism. To illustrate this range, we have arranged the stories according to their growing distance from the elements of the classical model of territorial nationalism. The complete collection generates a relational overarching scheme that we propose as an alternative to methodological nationalism.

The narrated life stories do not support the description of nationalism as an ideology that mobilizes individuals by way of sentiment, belief, and uncompromising identification with the collective body.[62] Nor do they support an institutional system, that is, a legal or territorial generative order.[63] Rather, nationalism emerges as an acted narrative that mediates between temporal trajectories and spatial positionings, thereby revealing a gamut of social interpretations, manipulations, and cultural choices. A variety of strategies of self-positioning thus unfold within the dynamic matrix of intentions and possibilities embedded in representations of nationalism. Each storyteller embodies a phase on the continuum between adherence to the classic discourse of nationalism and its unreserved repudiation. In between these poles lies a plethora of intermediate stages. Among these are withdrawal from the utopian territorial-political foundation that supports classical nationalism with subsequent movement toward a system that embraces intimate ethnic or religious community (i.e., individuals do not think in terms of national collectives but in smaller scale terms, such as their own ethnic group);[64] renunciation of the foundational patriarchal hegemony[65] by turning inward to the family, which has always served as a key metaphor for nationalism;[66] and, finally, a position of existence, per se, that is devoid of design, essence, or purpose and is disconnected from any nationalist framing.

Rather than an imagined community[67] or an invented tradition,[68] nationalism defines a possible type of order, but one that does not determine any definite and absolute identity. The dependent variable in our study is a structural one: the relations between the narrators' identity components. In each narrative strategy these constituents become a part of a distinct layout, from which each narrator's perception of nationalism and identity is drawn. According to this conception, a narrative is a dramatic sequence structure of statements about oneself and the world, and one's national identity or its renunciation is an outcome of this sequence structure.

Old age as an existential category facilitates this range of critical outlooks. In the local context, even though the storytellers' heyday paints their lives in the glaring light of nationalist presence—the Nakba for most Palestinians and immigration for most Jews—old age dims it and presages its fading into sunset, dusk, and ultimately nightfall—three metaphors used here for the receding presence of hegemonic nationalism in our interviewees' stories.

In Part I, "Sunset," we trace the contours of nationalism through the eyes of three male pillars of the community who grapple painfully with the trauma of betrayal and failure meted out by their community. The idealized notion of the nation is driven by the power of the imagined community. Circumstances, however, often subvert such imagination. When this happens, how do private citizens uphold their faith in the utopian nation when reality punches them in the face? Both the imagining subject and the imagined object are likely to be transformed in the process. We thus expect that these storytellers, whose imagination has been fired by the imagery of the ideal national community, will adjust their narratives to the changed circumstances, to the disparity between desire and reality.

The three stories are adduced to demonstrate the coping strategies of aging men who nevertheless insist on clinging to the hegemonic image of nationalism and are compelled to take issue with it and hence reluctantly to adjust their way of life to the change forced on them. In our conversations with these three men, we sought to comprehend the nature and function of their concept of nation and to ponder their strategies of self-presentation and the shades of interpretation to which they resort. Whereas most of their kith and kin abandoned both the image of the national community and the community of its faithful supporters, these three still retain their mythic national imagination. They are thus suspended in an existential state of dissonance between imagination and reality, between past and present, between who they want to be and who they are. Unwilling or unable to adjust their conceptions of nationalism and identity to the present, they are trapped between faithfulness to the traditional image of the nation and the reality of its crisis. The physical and symbolic paths that shape their current identities pass through landmarks where they are able to retain something of the image of

what *should have* become of the national community and of them as a part
of it, and other sites where national yearnings are no longer relevant. In a
city devoid of community leadership, the guardians of the national ethos are
left in a quandary. These male narrators live in a twilight zone in which the
remnants of nationalism continue to glimmer in the impending darkness of
extinction.

In Part II, "Dusk," we attend to a body of narratives used in identity
building that revolve around the axis of gender. Whereas the men portrayed
in Part I are engaged in justifying their identity as collective time erodes
around them, the women whose stories are presented in Part II live in the
continuous present and often willingly step outside collective time; they tend
to focus on the domestic and the local domains, observing the public sphere
critically from within the confines of their home.

In the constructed narrative spectrum that we propose, the women occupy an intermediate position of power and autonomy: between the big place
of collective myths and political affairs and the small place of quotidian life in
a nonimagined community.[69] Safely ensconced in their private domain, they
actively shape time and control the meaning of space, thereby also playing a
transformative role that emasculates the collective. Contrary to the men in
Part I, who are constantly at loggerheads with the myth, these women live
in historical time and in the family present, sometimes releasing themselves
from the imagined national community. The dusk of nationalism is thus a
strategy of functional partitioning that enables them at times to separate
the private from the public realm and the personal from the political. These
women's accounts are redolent with peace and empathy, which are perhaps
sustained by this compartmentalization and optimist agency.

In Part III, "Nightfall," we mark the total meltdown of nationalism's frame
of reference. We present three storytellers who position themselves in a disjointed and fragmented timeframe, foreshadowed by the already constricting
temporality of the women portrayed in Part II. Yet the temporality of these
men, like the contours of their life stories, is neither collective nor communal.
This part marks the utmost stage of the national order's dissolution as a master narrative. The stories presented here are personal tales that are unrelated to
any nationalist metaplot and, in the most extreme case, that lack any plot or
structural narrative whatsoever.

Part III points to a distinct existential sphere of possibilities that plays out in the shadow of the national order. The storytellers who embody the decline of nationalism do not resist it but simply suspend its solidifying power; they juggle a variety of alternative identities that are embedded in their individual worlds of meaning. Here, too, the sociological categories of class, ethnicity, and gender are vital to understanding the biographical and contingent context, both within and beyond the conversation setting. In this instance, however, masculinity serves to express a patronizing patriarchal identity rather than a communal metaphor, class mobility is no more than an individual achievement, and the ethnic group serves as an idiom of cultural intimacy that resists translation into identity politics terms. Either free or bereft of history and myth, the three men celebrate or lament their own existence without taking politicians to task for their misdeeds or wistfully wishing for historical justice. This position entails no ideological moral but is a part of an organic urban, cultural, and gendered fabric that unapologetically refuses to be harnessed to the nationalist wagon.

The stories in Part III suggest a trampled subjectivity devoid of the nationalist agency that shapes reality by providing meaning and mission. The shrinking existential space inhabited by those lost in the obscurity of collective memory underpins a narrated experiential sphere that transcends the modern subject. Inside the fissure that emerges between the personal and the public spheres, and at the crossroads of nationality and ethnicity, East and West, memory dissolves into decontextualized fragments. The plot thus decomposes into anecdotes, identity becomes a carnival, and the story turns into a fable. In dismembering collective memory, this incoherent story turns into a maze of nebulous memories. The very act of bearing witness becomes unbearable.

We close the discussion of nationalism's narrative configurations in the Conclusion. Having commenced with the territorial form of nationalism that requires a well-defined political subject, our journey ends with the dissolution of the modern subject, the absence of which precludes any narrative sequence and completely erodes any remnant of identity. We revisit theories of nationalism, conceptualizing nationalism as a social resource that loses viability in old age. The ethos of nationalism becomes more flexible and adapts itself to the reality of the narrators' lives but nevertheless remains a burden or a symbol at the end of the day. In their old age the interviewees unburden their mythic appendage. The stories offer a fresh theoretical and political perspective on the presence of nationalism in everyday life, anchored in existential, symbolic, and material relations of exchange. Faced with a profound sense of disillusionment, bereavement, and despair, those who were once trapped in the iron cage of nationalism are no longer imprisoned.

SUNSET

(CHAPTER 1)

BESIEGED NATIONALISM

Fakhri Jday and the Decline of the Elites

Under siege, time turns into a place
that has petrified into its own eternity.
Under siege, a place turns into time
that has missed its term.

Mahmoud Darwish, "State of Siege"

Day in and day out, Fakhri Jday leaves his home and walks to the pharmacy
that his father built in the early twentieth century. There, he serves customers
from all sections of Jaffaite society, and he is their undisputed medical authority. Yet a dark shadow looms over his daily bourgeois routine of regular working hours, an afternoon siesta, and the reading of Arabic and English daily
newspapers. Born in 1926, Jday is the sole scion of the old Palestinian elite,
and he proudly fulfills the role of *samed*, a Palestinian steadfastly rooted in
the land. The central theme of his story is encapsulated in his motto, "Power
cannot suppress free will." This motto reflects his refusal to surrender to the
prevalent trend toward "Israelization" among Israeli Palestinians in the face
of demands that they accept the yoke of citizenship and kowtow to the state.
His story is one of prolonged struggle, which made him a living symbol for
the Arabs of Jaffa.

Jday is the starting point of the twilight of nationalism because he is
emblematic of the hegemonic ensnarement of nationalism: uncompromising insistence on his national identity and a clear-sighted depiction of the
national tragedy, agents of betrayal, and ultimate loss of direction. We interviewed him in his luxurious home, which affords a view of a private orchard.
The orchard, by its very existence and its anachronistic, heavily contoured,
and foreboding design, defies the passing of time, the disappearance of the
old elite, and Jday's splendid isolation.[1]

Hicham Chabaita

Fakhri Jday is a tragic hero. In Jaffa he is perceived as a national symbol, a residue of a former social class, and a one-man urban pedestal. He portrays himself as having lived under protracted siege ever since 1948, "in a time that has missed its term," as Mahmoud Darwish writes. For thirty years Jday was the only academic in Jaffa, and his national identity became the focal point of his public life. He was crowned the spiritual father of the generation of educated Palestinians who emerged in the 1970s and was one of the founders of the nationalist al-Ard movement[2] and later the Association of Jaffa's Arabs.[3] He is regarded as the community's most eloquent and assertive nationalist spokesperson, and, as such, he is frequently interviewed by the international press and regularly writes articles for the local Jaffa newspaper.

And yet, during our interview, Jday articulates a critical and bitter narrative quite different from the nationalist pan-Arab discourse we had expected. He levels severe criticism against both the state and the Arab bourgeoisie and national and local politicians. As seen in this chapter, the dominant theme in the narrative of the community's icon is one of estrangement and loss of direction. Jaffa's last aristocrat mourns the loss of the Palestinian city and its erstwhile flourishing bourgeoisie and culture. His story simultane-

ously voices the community's official and "authentic" discourse and the cracks
in it that cannot be repaired.

I Would Stroll Around the Streets and Weep for Jaffa

Jday's life is locked in a permanent bind between being an essentially conservative and law-abiding bourgeois citizen and being an Arab nationalist
who offers a radical critique of Israeli society as well as his own. This apparent paradox leads him to adopt a principled standpoint and to reject any
pragmatic measure that would require him to forgo his demand to restore
his stolen land and national values. At the same time, however, he leads the
normative life of a citizen who pays taxes to the state responsible for the ruin
of his people. It is this tension that turns Jday's story into a tragic account of
alienation and frustration, of a losing battle against a fate dictated by overwhelming and insurmountable forces. Jday's story, however, is completely
devoid of any tone of victimhood or self-pity. His disillusionment and sense
of betrayal are manifest in a bitter narrative that lashes out in all directions.
Like old Samed 'abd al-Baqi al-Maslub in Gabi 'Abed's show, Jday begins his
tale by describing Jaffa's heyday before the Israeli occupation, underscoring
Jaffa's key role in the Palestinian national project.

BEFORE 1948 Jaffa was the foremost city in all Palestine in every respect.
At the national level, most public figures who defended the Palestinian cause hailed from Jaffa. I know them because they were my father's
attorneys. My father owned a pharmacy on Bustros [currently Razi'el]
Street, in partnership with Dr. Fuad al-Dajani, near the Clock Tower, and
on February 24, 1924, my father opened the pharmacy here in 'Ajami. In
1945 I traveled to Beirut to study pharmacy. From my class in Jaffa, four
or five went to [study in] Cairo, four or five to Baghdad, but the majority [went] to Beirut. They studied at the Lebanese university [al-Jami'a
al-Wataniya] or at the American or French university. I studied at the
French university. I graduated in 1950 and returned to Jaffa on October 15
of that year. I returned at a time when the Family Reunion Law was still
in force. I was the last one to come back, and then they closed [the country to returnees]. My father, mother, and brother were here. There was
still martial law in Jaffa.

Because Jday was not in Jaffa during the 1948 war, the transition back to the city was abrupt, and the disparity between the Jaffa he remembered from his youth and the Jaffa he found upon his return was sharp and painful. Jaffa's mythical construction as the Bride of Palestine forms the leitmotif of his life story; in comparison, contemporary Jaffa as experienced today is nothing but a forlorn and miserable mirror image.

The reality to which the young pharmacist returned in 1950 was sobering, if not shattering: a ghost town populated by a depleted community. And at home he was confronted with the family dilemma of whether he should remain in the "abandoned city" (*al-madina al-mahjura*). Most of the city's wealthy families had been forced to leave during the war, and many chose to emigrate after it ended, but the Jday family decided to stay on the insistence of Fakhri's sister and ailing mother. Upon his return, Jday's father put him in charge of the family pharmacy, which he has been diligently managing to this day.

> I STILL HAD a vivid mental image of Jaffa built up and full of people, and when I arrived only 3,200 people remained. I would stroll around the streets and weep for Jaffa. Everybody left, all the people you knew, families, friends. Why had I come? What kind of life was that? When I arrived, I found my mother ill. They told me, "Where will you go and leave us behind?" My father considered leaving, but my mother and sister wouldn't have it. They told him, "Go if you want to. We're staying."

Young Fakhri and his father considered leaving but nevertheless stayed at the mother's side. Jday never ceases to ponder that choice in the course of his narrative, particularly in the context of chance meetings with friends from his time in Beirut and with his brothers, who settled in London and the United States. Images of bygone Jaffa constantly haunt his dreams. These memories generate painful reflections, giving him reason to question whether his personal sacrifice was justified. His life as a nationalist middle-class student in the city of his youth in no way resembles his life today. Jday laments the loss as he compares his life to that of his brothers.

> HAD I KNOWN it would come to this, I would have left long ago. What am I doing here? I have friends who studied with me at Beirut University who now come to visit; Dr. al-Siri's brother came and said to me, "Fakhri,

what are you doing? What is this garbage dump you're sitting in?" He said, "Look, I live in Chicago. I have four children. The boys study medicine, surgeons, and the girls are pharmacists. And I work six months of the year and for six months I travel the world." We stayed with Dr. Abdallah Khoury, director of the French hospital in Jerusalem. In Beirut we had lived in the same room at the university. He too said to me, "What are you doing in Jaffa? Come and live here with us! Is there even a respectable club you can go to?" Before the Intifada we would go to Ramallah and Jerusalem to visit friends and talk to people. Not like the asses here! There's no hope here.

Sometimes I sit here and I start thinking about the way the families used to be in those days. Where have they all gone? I sometimes dream of them at night. I used to live a certain kind of life, and now it's a different life, as if one were living in paradise and the other on a garbage heap. Even when my brother had come back from America . . . He had left Jaffa in 1945 and went to study political economy, and then the war broke out and he stayed there and married there. He didn't come here until 1979. When he saw Jaffa like this, he remonstrated with me: "How can you live in this dump?" Like that, he said, "dump." He told me, "Sell up and come to us." He intended to stay for a year, but he ran off after just three months.

We Owned 2,384 Dunams of Land, Which Were Requisitioned

Having described the family's dilemma, Jday elaborates on the judicial apparatus that led to the expropriation of the family's land. Whereas many families were forced out of their homes and into the fenced "ghetto," the Jday family was able to remain in their home in 'Ajami. Yet the fact that they continued to live there only blackened the shadow of absence and ultimately heightened Jday's present sense of living in a futile time of limbo. "The cruelest thing that Israel did," Jday confessed during the interview, "was to leave Arabs in Jaffa after 1948."

NO ONE WAS LEFT after '48. You would stroll around the city and feel as if it were abandoned. Those who lived a little farther away were moved to 'Ajami, where they set up a fence. I arrived in October 1950, and they took down the fence in June I think. The purpose of martial law was to take the land. How were they to steal the land? They passed a law. You know, in Israel they can pass a law every 24 hours. Israel is a world leader in legislation. Any minor official can pass a law. They know how to steal land; every day there's a new law. They tell you, "Okay, it's your land," and then they come up with a law: "If someone doesn't cultivate his land for a month, it's confiscated." "OK, but I want to cultivate it. Give me a permit." "That's forbidden, military rule. If you set foot here, we'll shoot you." So how am I supposed to cultivate it? They canceled martial law in Jaffa earlier than in other parts of the country, because they had completed the job; they took whatever they wished. Anyone who had land, they requisitioned it.

Jday did not spotlight his personal victimhood but rather stressed his attempts to oppose the regime by taking responsibility for the outcomes of his own decisions.

BARAKAT had two citrus groves. He sold them and left; after all, they couldn't stay and rebuild Jaffa because of martial law. Would they have allowed them to do so? The entire country was requisitioned. We owned 2,384 dunams [238.4 hectares] of land in Bat Yam which were requisitioned. In '53 my father went there and saw that they were building there. They told him: "confiscated." We had all the maps and the title deeds [*kushan*]. We appealed in court and it reached the HCJ [High Court of Justice], and it authorized the requisition. In 1939 the Jewish National Fund offered us a million Palestine pounds, at a time when in all of Palestine no one had half a million. My father refused to sell. Today it would be worth over a billion dollars. Where the [War] Monument stands today [in the center of Bat Yam], that's our land.

Jday utterly repudiates the legitimacy of the state's attempts to legalize the expropriation of his land, which, adding insult to injury, is now the home of a major war memorial in the neighboring Jewish city of Bat Yam. Having eventually lost all hope that the court would restore the land to its rightful owner, Jday contrasts the HCJ's official seal with the heritage of Gamal 'Abd al-Nasser, who during the 1950s and 1960s was regarded as the one who could liberate the Palestinians from Zionist occupation.

THEY CONFISCATED EVERYTHING from others in Jaffa as well. From Amin Andraus [one of the pre-1948 community's leaders and a signatory to the city's terms of surrender] they took the citrus grove and gave him a few pennies in return, and when he appealed to the court, they gave him 4,000 Israeli liras. He told them, "I don't want them. You can throw them down the toilet. When Abu-Khaled comes, he'll give me back my land." The HCJ judge asked his attorney, "Who is this Abu-Khaled?" He told him, "Abu-Khaled is Gamal 'Abd al-Nasser." It's recorded in the court minutes.

Although one might associate Jday with the sociological group that Rabinowitz and Abu-Baker (2005) call "the generation of survivors," Jday refuses to defer.[4] His story uses every opportunity to confront the establishment. Just the same, we consider him the harbinger of the stand-tall generation of young Palestinians who followed him. Perhaps this provides an indication that, despite what appears to be an intergenerational split, Palestinian national identity was alive already in the Nakba generation.[5] The state's control mechanisms, however, prevented it from manifesting and making itself readily available to ethnographic observation.

Divide and Rule

Jday's proud national identity constitutes another arena of struggle against the state and the Zionist project. Even though the Palestinians have indeed suffered a crushing defeat, a high-horse nationalist identity has allowed some of them to stake out an uncompromising ideological position that delineates the boundaries of the collective and the Other. To Jday the story is an opportunity for signification that sustains his self-esteem.

IN THE PAST, had you asked someone, "What are you?" he would have replied, "A Palestinian." No one would have replied otherwise. Were you to ask, "Where are you from?"—From Jaffa. But what are you?—Palestinian. That's the most important thing, for the Palestinian was the most respected person in the entire Arab world. No one would say they were British. No one with any self-respect would have said this, or they would have thrown them out of town. Everyone hated the English. Also at the time of the Turks. I'm from Syria [al-Sham], I'm from Palestine. My father studied in Istanbul and served as a pharmacist in the Turkish army but would never identify himself as a Turk. Nowadays in Jaffa it's the same story all over again. One finds in Jaffa scoundrels who say, "I'm a Christian," "I'm a Muslim." Whoever would have spoken like this back then? We never heard such things. It is only at the time of Israel that people began to say, I'm Christian, or Muslim, or Druze or Circassian or Bedouin. And who knows what the government would come up with in the future. Divide and rule. Before he died, Father used to say, "If anyone comes into our house and says I'm a Muslim or a Christian, throw him out."

One by one, Jday rejects all the possible self-representations available to him over the years as manifestations of sectarian hypocrisy and an anti-Arab policy of divide and rule. There is only one identity he is willing to contemplate.

Why Is This Allowed to Jews but Prohibited to Arabs?

With his forthright and unequivocal identity, Jday portrays the relations between Jews and Arabs as a dire political struggle totally devoid of romanticism. Although he has many Jewish customers and acquaintances, he refuses to turn a blind eye to the battle for the homeland and to paint these neighborly relations in a lighter hue, or to even suspend his engagement with the conflict if only for a moment.

RELATIONS between Jews and Arabs before '48 were normal. There were Jews with me at school, because the grand [Sephardic] families of Tel Aviv would send their children to the French school [Collège des Frères]. They didn't send them to school in Tel Aviv. The police commander, Chelouche, was a graduate of the French school. Until the war began, we used to go to the movies in Tel Aviv. And then people fled and the conquerors came. This is my home after all. You come and take it and say, "This is mine"? Of course there will be hatred. You take my land and my house, and I should still love you? How can I love you? Do the Jews love Germany? Why is it allowed to Jews but prohibited to Arabs? It's the same thing!

Jday's story constitutes an unashamedly nationalist-political subject and winds a history around an essential kernel of authenticity. Every attempt

made during the interview to present the conflict in a more optimistic light
was met with insistence on the superiority of Arab culture and the hypocrisy
of the Israeli left. Jday regards any suggestion that could be construed as a
challenge to this hierarchy of values and an attempt to alleviate the Jews'
burden of historical responsibility as "licking the boots." Throughout, he explicitly maintains the coherence of his self-perception: "I have not changed
over the years. My political objectives remain the same; my worldview has
not changed. My understanding of the world and of who constitutes a
stranger [*ajnabi*] has not changed."

> IN BEIRUT I once had a conversation with a monk who was the principal
> of the French school in Beirut, the best school there. He fell ill with can-
> cer and was admitted to the hospital where I did my internship. We would
> sit and talk politics. He hated the English and the Americans. We were
> on the same wavelength. He said, "Look here, Fakhri, I want to tell you
> something you should keep in your mind and your heart and never forget.
> I've been a monk for fifty years now, and there are three things that you
> Arabs don't understand. First of all, never respect a stranger unless he
> respects you first. I'm a Frenchman and a stranger, but I tell you the truth.
> Every foreign priest, welcome him from a distance, and in the other hand
> hold a stick." He then told me, "The second thing, never believe a stranger.
> When he stands before the Arab, he will lie, even if he's straight with you."
> Not all of them, perhaps there are ten good ones, a hundred. "The third
> thing," he said to me, "has to do with Arab honor. That should be between
> one Arab and another, not between the Arab and a stranger. They ridicule
> you. The stranger exploits this with you." The foreign priests—take the
> patriarch in Jerusalem, for example—that's foreign imperialism. When
> the archbishop came, they said to me, "Fakhri, don't you want to go and
> welcome him?" I said, "I won't go to welcome him. He should come to
> bless me and to introduce himself, and then I'll return his blessing." If you
> come and steal my land, why should I love you? For your pretty eyes? I
> once told visitors from the Abraham Foundation, "You want coexistence.
> Where is this coexistence? You come here to mock the people."

This presentation of self rests on belief in the Arabs' prerogative and is
couched in terms of hospitality that is met with ingratitude on the part of

the perfidious stranger who benefits from it yet opposes the landlord, his benefactor. Because the Jew has broken the rules of hospitality, he has lost the right to share the Palestinian's home.

A Dog Doesn't Bite His Brother

Jday's national identity sets the course of his narrative. At the same time, it is imbued with a professional class identity. The continuity spanning three generations in the family pharmacy provides a solid functional foundation for his identity that he has no intention of forgoing: "I am 76 years old. I shall work as long as I live. Until my son arrives—he is currently doing his internship in Liverpool, at the Royal Pharmaceutical Society—I shall go on working until the day I collapse."

From the security of the pharmacy, Jday observes the disintegrating Arab community and the racism of his Jewish clientele with frustration. His worldview is embedded in a hierarchical class structure that he associates with the halcyon days before 1948.

> THERE ARE CLASSES in every city of the world. I was a Freemason. There were classes in Jaffa; there's no such thing as a classless society. Even in Russia at the time of Stalin, there were classes. Anyone who says otherwise is a liar, he mocks himself.

Jday's analysis highlights his attachment to his professional identity. Notwithstanding his acceptance of the vitality of the class system, he believes that the lack of Arab solidarity at a time of trial marks the failure of communality: "The Jew doesn't bite his brother, but the Arab does so because of his lack of awareness. The Jew knows how to bite, as he uses his brains." Jday compensates for his disillusionment with the community that bites itself by retreating to his pharmacy, which he has fashioned into an independent nationalist enclave.

I Close the Pharmacy at 7 and Don't Want to Hear What's Going On in Jaffa

In the first thirty years after his return to Jaffa, Jday invested considerable energy in reorganizing its civil society. Yet despite these efforts, the social ruins that he had found on his return were not rebuilt, and to this day Jday faces an impasse. He does not mince words when criticizing his brethren, the members of Jaffa's Palestinian community. Whereas state authorities, in particular, the Israel Security Agency (ISA), so he asserts, have made it their business to split the community and separate Christians from Muslims, Jaffa's emerging middle class is obsessed with greed. Jday considers this a moral failure, hypocrisy, and materialistic self-interest, and in recent years he has reacted with condescending social withdrawal grounded in an ideological position that is totally impervious to the zeitgeist and historical circumstances.

NOWADAYS there are no classes in Jaffa, an upper and middle class existed only before '48. Nowadays the majority is shit—excuse the expression—and there are very few good people. That's why there's no room for improvement. In the past I founded al-Rabita [Association of Jaffa's Arabs] in order to create an educated class, and thank God, today there is an educated class and there are academics. But I'm afraid that between 90 and 95 percent of them want only money. "Acting for the community? That's not for me." Those of the new generation have no say in the city, because there is no active framework that can impose itself on the entire society. I was head of al-Rabita for five years, we created a respectable society that had some influence. When the parties began to lay their hands on al-Rabita, particularly the Communist Party, I felt that I didn't want to quarrel with them, and I told them, "Guys, I came in peace and I'm leaving in friendship. Goodbye and au-revoir."

Having thus entrenched himself, Jday has of late found himself under attack by his fellow nationals. Several years ago some local Arabs attempted to rob his pharmacy. During the course of the robbery, the thugs shot at him but miraculously missed. The attempted robbery embittered Jday, destroying his faith in his invulnerable stature in the community and prompting him to withdraw even further into his private domain.

THAT'S TODAY'S SOCIETY, and because of this I've kept my distance from everything. Now there's nothing. I close the pharmacy at 7 and don't want to hear what's going on in Jaffa, because there's nothing that makes me happy. There are no longer people who love one another. They all hate one another. They all want to steal from one another. I've given up.

And yet, despite his decision to disengage from the public sphere, Jday has turned the pharmacy into a site of political confrontation and debate. Across the counter, he aims his barbs at party politics and confronts journalists, ISA (Israel Security Agency) officers, and customers. He describes his uncompromising position with undisguised glee.

> I PERSONALLY HATE all the parties. Each party is dirtier than the next. There isn't one sincere party. At the time of the elections for Barak, "the man of peace," people from Israeli TV came to the pharmacy, and I was sitting with a Jewish guy, one of those they call artists in the Old City, and discussing politics. And right then the TV people came in and said, "We've come because of the elections." I told them, "So what? The elections are not for me." I told them, "Go to the dignitaries of Jaffa [*wujaha al-balad*]. Don't come to me. Who can I vote for? If 'Azmi Bishara were still a candidate, I'd vote for him." I told them, "Over the past fifty-two years there were only two Arab members of parliament who were decent people: Muhammad Mi'ari and 'Azmi Bishara. All the rest—to the trash.

Although it is not only journalists who get to hear Jday's truths, he makes a point of giving them in particular a dressing-down that serves to bolster an implacable view of Arab dignity while exposing the hypocrisy of Jewish Israeli society.

> MANY JOURNALISTS COME HERE, and I give each of them an earful. They tell me, "We sit down with everyone. Of all these people, no one talks to us like you do." I said, "I have never learned how to be spineless. I have my self-respect."

Jaffa Hasn't Changed Since October 2000

Although Fakhri Jday levels his criticism squarely at the Zionist project as responsible for the Palestinians' dispossession, his narrative likewise embodies tension and ambivalence with regard to the Arab nationalist discourse. He depicts the political situation as the product of unequal negotiations between Jaffa's Arabs and Israeli institutions, such as the ISA, or the Communist Party, for that matter. The outcome of this process and struggle was

that the national movement in Jaffa transmuted from a broad social movement into a narrow local interest group that is doomed to fail.

I WAS ONE OF THOSE who founded al-Ard. It encompassed the entire
country. Ninety percent of Israel's Arabs supported the al-Ard movement. And those who opposed us more than the ISA were the Communist Party, because we took over the entire street from them. And they
didn't even allow an Arab MP to speak Arabic at their meetings. They
are the most imperialist. The State and [Prime Minister] Levi Eshkol
decreed it an illegal movement in 1965. We established al-Rabita in 1979,
and between '65 and '79 we didn't form a political movement because it
was prohibited. Anyone who founded a political movement was imprisoned for ten years and fined 10,000 liras.

Later, when I founded al-Rabita with Justice Farid Wajdi al-Tabari and
we used to meet in my house, Jaffa's dignitaries went and complained to the
ISA, saying, "Fakhri is trying to revive the al-Ard movement." Someone
[from the ISA] came to me. I told him, "If I wanted to revive it, I wouldn't
be afraid to do so, but I won't revive it, because that's over and done with."
They brought me the letters they had written, and I know who wrote them,
in order to set us against one another. I told them, "What do I care? These
are all your garbage, bootlickers." They said to me, "All right, we'll allow you
this. Open al-Rabita. We know you're sincere and speak your mind." At
the time I used to write political articles in the foreign press, in the *Guardian*, the *Herald Tribune*, and the *Sunday Times*. And then the ISA people
returned and said, "If you don't write in the foreign papers, we'll stay away
from you. Write as much as you like here—we don't care. But abroad—no."
They said, "We'll make a gentlemen's agreement with you." I said, "I accept the agreement, although you're not gentlemen." They allowed us to set
up al-Rabita because they knew we weren't interested in political affairs.
And we publicized this principle in our first manifesto: no political parties
and no ethnic parties. We focused on the good of Jaffa's Arab society. We
campaigned for schools, for housing. We have been demanding a school
for fifty years now, and have they opened one? And will they open one in
another hundred years or two hundred years? If Sharon decides tomorrow
to throw out all the Arabs of Israel and the West Bank, who can stop him?
Is there anyone in the world who can prevent this?

Contrary to the official narrative, which celebrates the events of October 2000 and the subsequent al-Aqsa Intifada as a symbol of national struggle—a story that Jday himself reiterates in his press articles and his public appearances—Jday speaks of them not as historic events that have transformed power relations and political structures[6] but rather as a transient phenomenon that has melted away because of the narrow material interests of the city's shopkeepers. He contrasts Jaffa's current lack of political initiative with the political activity undertaken by the al-Ard movement in the 1950s.

AT THE TIME of the Intifada, in Jaffa some of the people were fired up and took action. But Jaffa hasn't changed since then. Everything has returned to the way it was. Here, regretfully, what people find important is money. They would come to me to moan, "They went on demonstrations and closed the streets. The Jews stopped coming." They all began to moan. There is not one of them who owns a store who didn't moan. About what? About the Jews not coming here for a month? A journalist came to me, [and] I told him, "Whoever comes to buy, welcome. Whoever doesn't want to come, I'll throw an old shoe at him and at his father." He said, "I've never heard such an answer."

All the Arab Rulers Are Dogs

Jday's story ends on a nostalgic note as he reminisces about the time of his studies at Beirut University in the 1940s. This period of personal growth, "awareness," and "dignity" is likewise the point in his story where Jday chooses to unveil the perfidy of kings 'Abdallah, Feisal, and Hussein and to contrast them with the hero of pan-Arab nationalism, Gamal 'Abd al-Nasser.

I REMEMBER, when I was still in Beirut, when the people left, there was this man George Beiruti, a member of Jaffa's municipal council. I met him in Beirut on his way to Amman. He went to King 'Abdallah and asked him, "Why didn't you come? Why didn't you send the army? We were waiting for you." 'Abdallah replied, "Now you're asking me? When you had blues and reds, you didn't know me." The blues and reds were the colors of the banknotes. It is well known that King 'Abdallah was a thief and a swindler. He would wander around the stores in Jerusalem and take what he wanted. That was the best time of my life. The best time is always the time of university studies. There one meets students from all over the world, and they all respect you. There were Iraqi students at the time who cursed King Feisal's acolytes. There were students who had substance and awareness. That was the most wonderful time. Afterward, over the past fifty years, there was the time of al-Ard and when 'Abd al-Nasser was in power. Those were the days of glory. What 'Abd al-Nasser did, from gulf to gulf, one should kiss his shoes. In all respects, he gave them dignity and astounded all European countries. Not like today. Kings Hussein and 'Abdallah run off to the airport like children to welcome Powell.[7] All the Arab rulers are dogs.

Nationalism's Lieux de Mémoire

Elias Khoury's *Bab al-Shams* (Gate of the Sun)[8] relates the story of the Palestinian refugees in Lebanon through the figure of the elderly Umm Hassan, a midwife from al-Kweikat village in the Galilee, and her adopted son, Younis. Upon returning from one of her forays to the village of her birth, Umm Hassan brings back the branch of an orange tree and offers it to the narrator.

> I DON'T UNDERSTAND, SON. Your village is deserted. The roads have disappeared, and the houses aren't demolished but are collapsing and almost in ruins. I don't know why houses go like that when their people abandon them. An abandoned house is like an abandoned woman; it hunches over itself as though it were falling down. There's no sign of life in your village.[9]

When the narrator picked an orange so he could "taste Palestine," Umm Hassan cried out, "No! It's not for eating, it's Palestine." The narrator felt ashamed and hung the branch on the wall. When he told his interlocutor what had happened, the latter scolded him: "You should have eaten the oranges." "But Umm Hassan stopped me and said they were from the homeland." "Umm Hassan's senile," replied his companion. "You should have eaten the oranges. You should have eaten the oranges, because the homeland is something we have to consume, not let consume us. We have to devour the oranges of Palestine and we have to devour Palestine and Galilee."[10]

The narrator then wished to bury the orange tree branch with awe and reverence, as if it were a holy relic. His companion reacted dismissively and cast the branch away: "Outrageous! What are these old women's superstitions? Before hanging a scrap of the homeland up on the wall, it'd be better to knock the wall down and leave. We have to eat every last orange in the world and not be afraid, because the homeland isn't oranges. The home-land is us."[11]

It appears that in his old age Jday is not party to this dilemma. Throughout the interview, he relates his unresolved relationship with the place called homeland and with the choice it demands: Is it something sacred, or should one perhaps swallow it and make it part of everyday life? Jday's choice is clearcut: He chooses to sanctify the orange branch, Palestine, *Yafa*, and, in doing so, turn his back on present-day Jaffa. The outcome of his choice is that his principal frame of reference is constituted by the memory of the place that used to be and the identity embedded therein, both of which no longer exist and will never return to what they were.

In his work on the realms of memory (*lieux de mémoire*), Pierre Nora defines cultural sites that under certain circumstances become detached from the course of history and take on a life of their own in the sphere of collective memory.[12]

THESE *LIEUX DE MÉMOIRE* are fundamentally remains, the ultimate embodiments of a memorial consciousness that has barely survived in a historical age that calls out for memory because it has abandoned it. . . .

The remnants of experience still lived in the warmth of tradition, in the silence of custom, in the repetition of the ancestral, have been displaced under the pressure of a fundamentally historical sensibility. Self-consciousness emerges under the sign of that which has already happened, as the fulfillment of something always already begun. We speak so much of memory because there is so little of it left.

Our interest in *lieux de mémoire* where memory crystallizes and secretes itself has occurred at a particular historical moment, a turning point where consciousness of a break with the past is bound up with the sense that memory has been torn—but torn in such a way as to pose the problem of the embodiment of memory in certain sites where a sense of historical continuity persists. There are *lieux de mémoire*, sites of memory, because there are no longer *milieux de memoire*, real environments of memory.

Contrary to historical objects, however, *lieux de mémoire* have no referent in reality; or, rather, they are their own referent: pure, exclusively self-referential signs. . . . The *lieux* we speak of, then, are mixed, hybrid, mutant, bound intimately with life and death, with time and eternity; enveloped in a Mobius strip of the collective and the individual, the sacred and the profane, the immutable and the mobile. . . . The most fundamental purpose of the *lieu de mémoire* is to stop time, to block the work of forgetting, to establish a state of things, to immortalize death, to materialize the immaterial.[13]

Memory marks a location devoid of a concrete signifier. Emotional and political commitment to a place detached from historical time cannot accommodate pragmatic compromise, and Jday therefore lives with a sense of detachment and loss. Under siege, as Darwish writes, "a place turns into time that has missed its term." For Jday, the meaningful place is no longer the city in which he lives but the *notion* of the city that exists on a parallel plane, in a different time. This is the big place of national pride, which transcends the small place of quotidian life.[14] The big place constitutes a mythical sphere that occupies only stories and books. Both conceptual clusters (big place and eternal time) underpin the nationalist ideology to which Jday is committed, and both create a unified front versus the pragmatic perception of life in the small place. To Jday and other exiles of his generation and class who constitute the Palestinian Diaspora, with whom he maintains close ties, surrendering to the small place is to resign oneself to a life as a submissive and marginal minority. To them, it is pusillanimous to submerge into a world of symbolic and palpable impotence; it is tantamount to treason.

Nevertheless, Jday has found a way to sustain his national pride and class distinction without cutting himself off altogether from the urban milieu, despite his repeated declarations to the effect that he "has despaired." From his pharmacy outpost, the daily and uncompromising skirmishing with Jaffa's political scene and with its Jewish and Arab protagonists constitutes Jday's Sisyphean struggle. The pharmacy does indeed serve as Jday's external vantage point from which he observes and confronts the big place and the small place. From the squalid and neglected sidewalk of contemporary Jaffa, Jday ascends to what remains of the city's sanctity, the cosmopolitan metropolis that was once and lives on in the orange branch. From this mediating sanctuary Jday is able to safely quarrel with Jews and Arabs, to espouse impassioned ideologies, and to debate current affairs with his clients.[15] The professional and generational continuity within which he resides grants him a measure of confidence in his Jaffaite heritage and explains the anxiety and disillusionment he felt in the wake of the criminal invasion of the last refuge of his identity. His profound faith in romantic nationalism consigns him to a tragic life of rejection of the present place and time and sanctification of the past. Jday cherishes the pharmacy as an outpost on the last battlefront, as though it were beyond time and place. He is thus the self-appointed last guardian of the seal of lost nationalism and faded authenticity.

(CHAPTER 2)

WORN-OUT NATIONALISM

Rabbi Avraham Bachar and the Community's Betrayal

I have nevertheless reached the age where life,
for everyone, is accepted defeat.

Marguerite Yourcenar, *Memoirs of Hadrian*

Rabbi Avraham Bachar is Fakhri Jday's alter ego. His story is the mirror image of that of his Palestinian fellow city dweller, as they both look back at a community that has let them down. Rabbi Bachar was born in 1913 in Edirne, Turkey, and served as the Jaffa Bulgarian community's rabbi until his death in 2004. Trained in circumcision and ritual slaughter, he immigrated to Israel in 1948 with his wife and two children. His wife became renowned as Israel's first female cantor and died a year before him.

In its heyday, Jaffa's Bulgarian Jewish community numbered in the tens of thousands, but it later shrank considerably and now only a few thousand remain, mostly elderly. The Sinai Synagogue over which Rabbi Bachar presided, despite opposition from the Israeli rabbinic establishment, now stands forlorn on Jerusalem Boulevard. Impoverished and acrimonious, Rabbi Bachar spent his final years at the Bulgarian old age home in Rishon LeZion, where the interview was conducted.[1]

Because Rabbi Bachar had served as the congregation's rabbi since 1948, his story is woven into the collective narrative of immigration and nation building, although this context emerges precisely at the junctures where he expresses his disappointment with the community and country. Despite Rabbi Bachar and Jday's attempts to present a resolutely nationalistic position, the main theme in both of their narratives is that of estrangement and defeat, bereavement and failure. Whereas the Palestinian bemoans the disap-

Hicham Chabaita

pearance of the Palestinian city and its secular nationalistic bourgeoisie, the Jew laments the loss of community life and the dwindling future generation.

Methodologically, in this chapter we focus on another authentic and official representative of Jaffa's communities with a view to demonstrating how they mediate the national narrative and interpret it from within the fields of location, class, and ethnic group. Notwithstanding the obvious differences in their social standings and narrative standpoints, Fakhri Jday and Avraham Bachar similarly narrate their stories from the authoritative position of community representatives. As mentioned in Chapter 1, this position actually constitutes them as dethroned strangers in their own city: Jday has been deprived of his family's class and political privilege, whereas Bachar is too poor to grow old with dignity. Ninety years old at the time of the interview, Rabbi Bachar voices frustration with the community to which he has contributed so much. Unlike Jday, who is a man of property, Bachar has only a small apartment on the crowded and noisy Jerusalem Boulevard and the synagogue for which he cannot find a suitable buyer. Bachar lives in a small room in a senior citizens home in return for providing religious services. From this room the rabbi feels the pain of the dwindling community that he had worked so hard to establish over many years. Ironically, despite being clearly positioned on opposite sides of the national divide, Jday's and Bachar's sons have attended the French school on Yefet Street. And like Jday, who aims his critical barbs at both the (Israeli and Arab) regimes and the Jaffa community, Bachar's frustration is vented both at the ungrateful community and the rabbinic establishment that has never recognized him.

God Helped Us Generously

During the 1950s and 1960s Jaffa was home to a wide variety of Jewish immigrant populations. The Bulgarians managed to establish a sustainable communal identity, whereas the other communities were small and disorganized. In his book *From Sofia to Jaffa: The Jews of Bulgaria and Israel*, Guy Haskell traces the annals of Bulgarian Jewry from the Ottoman period to the mass migration to Jaffa.[2] According to Haskell, "Jaffa was the only place Jewish Bulgaria could survive, albeit ephemerally."[3] Within a brief period (1948–1949), 45,000 Bulgarian Jews settled in Jaffa.

> WITHIN TWO YEARS of the opening of the gates of immigration, the focus of life moved from Sofia to Jaffa. Bulgarian became the language of the streets, and shop signs in Bulgarian appeared almost overnight. Bulgarian branches of the major political parties were set up and a newspaper, *Far* (Lighthouse), was published daily in Bulgarian. The Tsadikov Choir was reestablished, and a library of books brought from the old country was founded. Restaurants serving Bulgarian food appeared, and coffee shops and clubs for conversation and games opened along Shderot Jerusalem, the main street of Bulgarian Jaffa.[4]

As described in *Madrikh Yafo* (The Jaffa Guide; 1949), the city's veteran Jewish residents arrived in Jaffa in the midst of attempts to Judaize the ghost town. Rabbi Bachar begins his story against this backdrop, which, like Jday's preface, is painted in glowing hues. The elation generated by mass immigration and the return to Zion overshadowed the physical and economic hardships and helped Rabbi Bachar "get along" as he engaged in a series of occupations before opening the synagogue.

> I ARRIVED IN '48, on July 30, from Bulgaria to Haifa, together with the great immigration. All of them, one after the other, 50,000 people came. I came by ship—1,600 people in truly appalling conditions. We were in

a transit camp for seventy days. In the meantime Jaffa was liberated, the
Arabs fled, and they transferred us from there to Jaffa. They gave us an
apartment at the port, in the ruins—don't ask. But we were happy: We
knew we had reached safety. After two or three months they gave us an
apartment in Jaffa on Nuzhah Street [today's Jerusalem Boulevard], and
we got by. I opened a fish-smoking business at the port. I spotted a dump
and entered. Without money, with nothing. Later on I saw that this was
going nowhere. I cleaned cesspools; I cleaned streets, roofs, everything.
Finally we bought a store for 22,000 liras and we built a synagogue there.
I smuggled three Torah scrolls from Bulgaria. One is ancient, 400 years
old; I still have it. Can you imagine that God helped us generously? The
whole synagogue was full, 400 people.

My Great Mistake

Under harsh material conditions and from a position of inferiority relative to
Tel Aviv, whose municipality was loath to annex Jaffa, the new immigrants
succeeded in establishing a vibrant community of petty traders and artisans.
This pulsating civil society was a manifestation of the social capital of the
emergent Bulgarian community. Yet as Bachar sees it, the spirit of generosity
is also what led to his own downfall.

> COMMUNITY ORGANIZATIONS sprung up in Jaffa. Each of them asked me
> to participate. I was an honorary member of all and would perform memo-
> rial services, weddings, all free of charge. This politics eventually led to my
> ruin. Fifty years ago I thought I was Baron Rothschild without a penny in
> my pocket: funerals for free, circumcisions for free. I was an altruist, an ide-
> alist. That was my greatest mistake in life. Because of that idealism, today I
> can't get into the senior citizens home. I work here as a rabbi, but I don't live
> here. I stay here temporarily because my son has traveled to America to ar-
> range his social security and he'll return. And one more thing, a disaster. My
> daughter died three years ago. It destroyed our family. But my private life is
> not so important. I was number one in all the associations. Jaffa flourished.

Bachar blames his poverty on his naïveté, on the community that abandoned him, and on the rabbinic establishment that refused to recognize him.

He regards his precarious status in the senior citizens home as the result of a series of betrayals and the ingratitude of national authorities and the Bulgarian immigrants.

I AM NOT RECOGNIZED by the rabbinate. Why is that? Because I'm un-Orthodox. I drive on the Sabbath, go to watch football on the Sabbath, and that was unacceptable to the rabbis, who didn't support me. For fifty years I didn't receive a penny from the Chief Rabbinate, the Ministry of Religious Services, or the municipalities; I was ostracized, even though I was the best cantor and rabbi. In Jaffa and everywhere else they would call me to perform circumcisions. With my own hands I have performed over 2,000 circumcisions here. There isn't a mohel in the world who has performed 2,000 circumcisions. Ritual slaughter, funerals, weddings, divorce, the lot—I did it, and for free. That's my great mistake.

There wasn't a day that I didn't work for the Bulgarian immigration. And today I have no place in the seniors home, I can't sell the house because I have a son, and the Welfare Ministry wants the house from me. I have my own synagogue. I want to sell it—they offer me forty, fifty thousand dollars, and it's worth a hundred and twenty, a hundred and thirty thousand dollars.

I have grown old, I am 89, nearly 90, but I'm disappointed. The Bulgarian immigration should have taken me under its wing and arranged a seniors home for me, without payment.

Despite his forlorn hope to receive support from the authorities, Bachar's frame of reference is not the State of Israel or the Jewish nation but rather "the Bulgarian people" who have abandoned him in his old age. It is this betrayal by the community that forces him to consider selling his life's endeavor, thereby converting faith into capital. In this respect Rabbi Bachar's status is quite the opposite of Fakhri Jday's, who, despite the collapse of his community, is not compelled to sell the pharmacy in order to support himself. His pharmacist son ensures the family's professional continuity. Bachar has none of that—he is the first and last rabbi of Jaffa's dying Bulgarian community: "I have learned a few things in my life, and have been disappointed by many things. Today it's not the same Jaffa. You should know that we are in constant decline."

The Football Rabbi

Apart from the synagogue that was his life project, Rabbi Bachar is renowned
as one of the founders and supporters of the Maccabi Jaffa soccer club.[5] He
also volunteered his religious services to its players, in his own un-Orthodox way. "When I broke the glass at my wedding," relates former star player
Moshe Onana, he cried out 'Goal!'"[6] This blurring of categories that appeared
perfectly natural to Rabbi Bachar testifies to a conception built on local religious symbolism,[7] which blends the sacred and the mundane in a way that
revives a form of local civil religion.[8] Yet unlike the state-promoted symbols
that constitute the Zionist civil religion (such as the prayer shawl that turned
into a flag), Rabbi Bachar operates in the state's backyard, among immigrants
located on the margins of the metropolis. Despite the humorous and playful
undertones of this hybrid combination of religion and soccer, it has become
a major component of post-1948 Jewish Jaffa's urban identity[9] and, to a certain extent, of the entire Bulgarian community in Israel. Moreover, it has
nationalist undertones, as evidenced by the fact that the only reference to the
concept of patriotism in Bachar's testimony is in the context of soccer.

> I WAS A GREAT PATRIOT of the State of Israel. I founded Maccabi Jaffa
> together with four others, and what destroyed us was the thieving chair-
> man who arrived. People used to come to the stadium like an overflow-
> ing fountain. Anyone who managed a draw against Maccabi Jaffa would
> throw a party. We founded the team without money. Everyone donated
> a little. We bought jerseys. And so people began to come gradually, and
> we flourished. We had well-known talents. They worked for peanuts; they
> didn't ask for money. Patriots, until a thief arrived, destroyed the team,
> and all was lost.

All This Didn't Line My Pockets

Despite the gloom that pervades Rabbi Bachar's narrative, his autobiography
is an impressive tale of personal survival and social mobility against all odds.
His father, who owned a butcher shop in Edirne, was killed when Avraham
was only 5 years old. Later, Avramiko, as he was known as a boy, was sent
to an orphanage in Bulgaria, where he studied Hebrew and Judaism. Upon

returning to Turkey in 1927, he continued his rabbinic studies and was also trained in circumcision and ritual slaughter.

I WAS 8 when they put me in an orphanage in Plovdiv, Bulgaria's second largest city. At the orphanage we had a teacher who taught us the Bible. That was a great innovation in Bulgaria [i.e., in Bulgaria's secular Jewish community]—teaching the Bible to children. I studied and began training as a cantor, and by the age of 16 and a half I was already the chief cantor in the town of Roshchook [Ruse] in a small synagogue. Six months later they transferred me to the large synagogue. They began to compete over me between the towns; they all wanted me as their chief cantor. I would go here on one festivity and there on another, and all that too was for free. And so I studied until I came to this country. I never stopped studying. But all this didn't line my pockets. I was too naïve. I thought to myself: Now is the time to work for the people.

Despite his esteemed status among the Bulgarians of Jaffa, the only person who helped Bachar in his time of need was an outsider, Max Hirsch, a Bulgarian Jew who emigrated to Brazil after Bachar had rescued him from the Nazis. Even though Hirsch married a Christian woman and enriched himself by smuggling pornographic movies, Rabbi Bachar bears no grudge against him and speaks of him with forgiveness and gratitude.

THERE IS THIS MAN from Brazil, Max Hirsch. I inscribed his name in illuminated letters on a plaque in the synagogue, "Charity saves from death," and he sent me a ticket to Brazil. He brought me to Brazil, to São Paulo. I meant to stay for five days; six months I spent there. He paid the hotel for me, the only Jew who ever helped me. I rescued him at the last minute from shooting and death. He and another two smugglers crossed the Bulgarian border, and they caught them in Romania. The Nazis accused them of espionage and ordered them to be summarily shot. And on the night before they were about to kill them, I heard that there were three lads from Bulgaria [in trouble]. I immediately took a truck from Bulgaria to Dobriche. I asked, "Who are the Bulgarians here?" They told me, "Forget it. Tomorrow they'll shoot them." I said, "Let me talk to them. I'm a rabbi." Their commander studied with me eighteen years be-

fore in Bulgaria. I asked him, "Why are you killing them?" He said, "They
are spies." I told him, "You are wrong. This one plays cards for money; he
has no money. The second is a drunkard; the third works with prostitutes.
Give them to me. I'll send them to Israel." And in the middle of the
night he handed them over to me, and I sent them to Brazil. Max didn't
forget that. He said, "You can live with me for fifty years at my expense."
Max Hirsch, what a guy. He married a Brazilian Christian from a large
mafia [family], and they didn't let him come to Israel. He became a genuine mafioso. Thirty years ago he would smuggle pornographic movies in
Brazil. He alone helped me.

Bachar's story about his relations with Hirsch reveals two aspects of his
identity perception. The first is his survival by virtue of his personal relationship with a person of dubious moral standing who did not belong to his
community in Jaffa, and the second is his casual reference to the events of
World War II in the context of initiative, daring, and resourcefulness rather
than through the lens of the Holocaust and national heroism. Both these
aspects cast shame on those who failed him, who neglected to repay the rabbi
for his good deeds and loyalty to the Bulgarian community.

Bulgaria, not Israel, Was the Land of Milk and Honey

In Bulgaria the young Bachar became renowned as the hero of the flood in the
town of Vidin in 1942. In his book *The Land of Israel: The Melting Pot*, Yitzhak-
Moshe Emanuel relates how Bachar, on horseback, "with his own two hands
rescued 718 men and women. As a gesture of gratitude and appreciation, he was
awarded a badge of excellence from King Boris, and a salary of 100 thousand
Lev."[10] The Jewish community's singular status as a distinct and united community loyal to King Boris, emerges from Bachar's nostalgic reminiscences.

WE SUFFERED a great deal from the Communists, from the Fascists, from
the villagers, from the rural party. They were all against us, but the people
were with us. Then we found out that the king had refused to give an
army to fight against Russia and refused to hand over the Jews, who are
the most loyal to the state. When they killed the king, we all left straight
to Israel. Bulgaria was emptied during the course of four months.

The Bulgarian Jews are not devout, but they observe the traditions. They obey the rabbi; they respect the rabbi, but not for the Bible. The rabbi is a special person of high stature who interprets the Bible, but no more than that. They used to eat nonkosher food. They would all travel on the Sabbath—they would go to football matches, to the beach. None of that stopped them being good Jews. Every Bulgarian Jew was valued and welcomed by the Bulgarian people. When the Bulgarian minister of trade came here thirty years ago, they asked him, "What can we do here for the Bulgarians? Allow us to express the tremendous gratitude for your having rescued us." He said, "Give me back the Jews, only for five years will be enough, and we shall immediately flourish." Because Bulgaria has declined a great deal. What can I tell you, the situation there is dire. Bulgaria, and not Israel, was said to be the Land of Milk and Honey.

Characterizing the Bulgarians as traditional Jews who respect the rabbi as a communal authority and not "for the Bible" is typical of the Ottoman cultural heritage. Under Ottoman rule, minorities were granted communal autonomy and encouraged to integrate socioeconomically, so long as they did not interfere in matters of state. Sensitive to the people's wishes, Bachar realized that it was impossible to impose the authority of state-sponsored Jewish Orthodoxy on the Bulgarians in Jaffa. Thus, when the community crowned him their authority on Jewish law, he ruled that it was permitted to watch the matches of Maccabi Jaffa on the Sabbath, but he continued to demand that religion play a major role in community life. Yet Bachar feels that he has failed in his attempt to bridge the sacred and the mundane, and he expresses remorse.

I DIDN'T SUCCEED in organizing religious life here. Because I'm free, I allowed them to travel on the Sabbath, I allowed them to turn on the light on Sabbath, to watch sport on television on Sabbath eve. That spoiled them, and I'm to blame. I had no choice. I had to be like that so that they would accept me and to allow them to maintain respect between me and them.

Bachar identifies this failure as an unresolvable communal crisis. In a way, he admits that the aspiration to maintain a religious atmosphere in Jaffa was

doomed to fail, beginning with the loss of religious tradition and ending with
the disintegration of the entire Jewish community. In his eyes, the normative
and demographic crises are closely intertwined.

> ALL THE SYNAGOGUES in Jaffa, including those of the Moroccans, the
> Libyans, the Turks, they all lack a minyan [a quorum of ten men required
> to hold a prayer service]. They pay people 20, 30 shekels per day to come
> to the synagogue. People gradually leave. I tell you, in ten years' time
> religiosity and faith will decline to zero. The youth is terribly lost. Go on
> a bus once and see for yourself. Not one youngster will offer a seat to an
> elderly person. Once they used to call an old man "father."

Jaffa Has No Future

Rabbi Bachar associates the decline of the Bulgarian community with the
bleak future of Jewish presence in Jaffa. Of the 40,000 Bulgarians living in
Jaffa in the 1960s, "barely 3,000 remain." The loss of control over the urban
sphere is signified by the dwindling prevalence of Hebrew and Bulgarian
compared to the spread of Russian and Arabic.

> WE WERE the bosses of Jaffa. Jaffa the Bulgarian city, that's how they
> called it. We used to love the city, care for the city; we built housing proj-
> ects in the city. Families grew, over fifty-three years. Nowadays they're all
> leaving. They are gradually all moving out because there's no livelihood
> in Jaffa.
> Jaffa has no future. There is no future for Bulgarians, for Jewry, for Jaffa.
> Coexistence with the Arabs will come about only once there's an Arab
> state and there are good relations with it. We are no longer a force in Jaffa.
> You now hear Arabic and Russian more than Bulgarian and more than
> Hebrew.

Despite the reference to the presence of Jewish immigrants from the former Soviet Union as symbolizing the loss of control over the area, it is clearly
the growth of the Arab population in what used to be Bulgarian areas that
annoys Rabbi Bachar, along with the increasingly tense relations between
Jewish and Arab neighbors. True to the general gist of his story, which depicts a transition from dizzying heights to abject depths, he also describes

this aspect of life in Jaffa in terms of progressive decline, albeit not without some ambivalence toward the Arab Other.

> RELATIONS between Jews and Arabs in Jaffa were always good. Relations between the Bulgarians and the Christians were excellent. I'm telling you, we sent our children to the French school rather than to a Jewish school. We established Maccabi Jaffa, and Arabs joined the team. We lived as brothers. Now masses of Arabs have begun coming into Jaffa, and each house sold in Jaffa is bought by Arabs. They do it deliberately, so one day they'll say, "This is our city again." It's politics: Jaffa, Haifa, Lydda, Ramla—they are waiting for the day when they will have a state and they will ask for it all. Yet it is only we who are to blame, not the Arabs. We took their lands from them, we took everything, so they want to return. We are okay with our Arabs. It is peaceful nowadays, but it's burning underneath. They are waiting for an opportunity, and we won't give it to them for sure. But they come and buy houses. In '48 we won the war. Where should they have put us? We came here and looked for a house, and we moved into what the government gave us. The Arabs ran away, left the food in the oven and fled. And we entered their houses and found everything ready. Later they started saying, "My father was here"; thirty, forty years later, "I want this room, if possible." Like that, very slowly, like snakes they entered, and that doesn't allow us to believe that things will turn out well here.

Rabbi Bachar labors to create a terminology of proximity and distance through categories of time and space: Whereas "our Arabs"—namely, the nearby and familiar neighbors—do not pose a threat, the notion of the Palestinian return and the influx of Arab residents "like snakes" overshadows the future of coexistence. This is a world of suspended time, as the city awaits the inevitable flood that will overwhelm its Jewish inhabitants in a future that will not include Rabbi Bachar. As though parallel to the gradual historical decline, Bachar's references to the inevitable ethnic conflict grow bleaker in tone as the interview progresses.

> IT CAN'T BE STOPPED. Yet if we don't stop it, we'll regret it. Why? Because they are gradually, very calculatingly, introducing another Arab,

another six children, eight children, nine children, and are growing ever more.

There were never truly good relations. It was convenient, but in their hearts they hated us very much. We took their houses, we took their lands, we took everything from them. I do not anticipate coexistence between Arabs and Jews.

Although fear and mistrust of the Other are far from rare in Israeli Jewish public discourse, note the recurring emphasis on those who bear responsibility for the Palestinian tragedy: "It is only we who are to blame, not the Arabs. We took their lands . . . so they want to return."

To whom exactly is Rabbi Bachar referring? Does the first-person *we* refer to Israeli society, to the state, the Bulgarian immigrants, or all combined? We can assume that Bachar is grappling here with his own past as an immigrant who in July 1948 took up residence in the house of a Palestinian refugee. This implied attempt at confronting the past manifests an admittedly marginal, de facto recognition of the Palestinian tragedy on the part of inhabitants of mixed cities, a recognition that has failed to elicit much public and scholarly interest. Such recognition is typical of a periphery whose residents' awareness does not constitute a conventional source of information for the arbiters of taste and the articulators of historiography who occupy the hegemonic centers of power. The concept of diachronic neighbors, a term coined by Yfaat Weiss, appropriately describes the invisible presence of a city's Palestinian past.[11] In his narrative Rabbi Bachar expresses the anxieties of Jaffa's veteran Jewish inhabitants of losing control over the area and paradoxically reflects the anxieties that emerge from the Arab community with regard to the city's Judaization. Despite the asymmetric power relations, it appears that both local communities feel threatened by the return of myth and history. This mutual antagonism enables both communities to function as unaccountable strangers (because there is no one to hear their account) without undermining their status as victims of forces beyond their control. Thus, despite the political commitment to a Jewish majority in Jaffa that emerges from Bachar's narrative, he allows the Palestinian presence to infiltrate the discourse just as it infiltrates the former Bulgarian neighborhoods, and this is what singles him out among other representatives of Jewish communities in mixed cities.[12]

I No Longer Hope for a Future for Myself

The calamity that Rabbi Bachar articulates revolves around an absence of communality, of social status, of vitality. Having failed to lead the community in his old age, he retreats into the confines of the senior citizens home from which he looks back at a life that began with a national utopia, proceeded through the dystopia of public failure and community betrayal, and ended with the heterotopia of crisis and deviance located beyond mythical and social time. He depicts the period of old age as one of incapacity, impotence, and yearning.

IT'S GOOD that we have senior citizens homes, it's very good. That's good, but it's all only for the money. Money makes the world go round. In Bulgaria very few used to think about senior citizens homes. Old people were connected, respected. At home they would be taken care of. Old people came first. In Bulgaria there were morals. In Bulgaria there was happiness. People would eat bread and olives but would respect the family. They wouldn't sit at the table before the head of family had sat down.

I'm now 90 years old, what should I think? I married at the age of 23, and thank God, a faithful, good wife, bore me two children, a son and a daughter. One passed away, died of cancer, and since then my family has been destroyed. Nothing is important to me any longer. My son didn't make it in America. He returned home to his father with nothing. He is 60 years old already; he can't work here.

Fifteen years ago, we celebrated our golden wedding anniversary. We wanted to throw a grand party and invite 2,000 guests. But I told my wife, "Forget it. I'll buy a ticket for a round-the-world trip." We traveled the world for nine months. Today we are here, in the senior citizens home. We thought we could go as we please. Then old age crept up and decided things for us. "Many are the plans in a person's heart, but it is the Lord's purpose that prevails."

Rabbi Bachar senses that his time has passed, and he presents himself as a living dead person who is unable to rid himself of the remnants of life and the remains of his past. He is likewise unable to join his ancestors in a manner befitting his elevated standing. In limbo, he is en route from one intermediate environment (Jaffa, the immigrants' transit city) to another (the institution in which he will pass away).[13] Whereas his wife continues to live in the present and leads a fully functional life, he pines for the past. His longing is manifested in glorification of the past and fond reminiscences of the grandiose voyage around the world. Yet the existential reality of the senior citizens home foils his plans, and thus, in his parting words, he finds himself lodged in a romantic-nostalgic territory that resembles what Samed 'abd al-Baqi al-Maslub portrays in Gabi 'Abed's show.

> NOWADAYS I AM SICKLY, I have no energy. There are 600 people here in the home: 300 crazy people, and another 300 who should be in an asylum. So they are always quarreling and swearing. There is egoism here among the Jews; it has erupted like at the time of Pilate. The Second Temple was destroyed by gratuitous hatred, and here the Jews hate and slander.
>
> I was always very strong. Today I'm not the same. I'm finished now. I have resigned to my end. How long will I live? A year, two years, perhaps three, who knows? Perhaps ten days. My wife deludes herself and thinks she still has ten or fifteen years to live. She's fallen in love with the old folks' home. I pine for Jaffa very much.

The three paths down the precipice—the personal, the communal, and the national—led Bachar to the nursing home from which he can observe his life with subdued resignation, leaving no place for redemption of any kind. Unlike Jday's pharmacy, Bachar's milieu does not enable him to cling to a lived reality, and a nostalgic narrative is his only refuge.

A Transit City from Cultural to Political Nationalism

Research on the immigration of Bulgaria's Jews concludes that Israel's melting pot ideology proved successful. Although the Bulgarian Jews migrated to Jaffa for a variety of economic, ideological, and social reasons, Haskell asserts that the immigrants adopted a Zionist culture aligned with that of Israel's native Jews.

> THE TOTAL ZIONIZATION of the Jews of Bulgaria was the result of the development of an original, native philosophy which predated the emergence of Zionist ideology in the rest of Europe. Zionism became indis-

tinguishable from Judaism; it became part of the way of life, tradition, worldview, and culture of the Jews of Bulgaria.[14]

From this perspective the collective desire to be absorbed into Israeli society (an option largely denied to Mizrahi communities who also settled in Jaffa) explains to some extent the community's nostalgia and the fading of their distinctive Bulgarian ethnic identity. Contrary to Haskell, we maintain that the spectacle of patriotism on the part of the Bulgarians of Jaffa is not a manifestation of political nationalism but rather an example of what can be termed cultural nationalism, or "cultural intimacy" in Michael Herzfeld's terms:[15] a framework of belonging and proximity that stems from the tension between inner communal consciousness and collective political representation and that provides members of the community with their "assurance for common sociality."[16]

The city serves here as a platform for the articulation of personal and communal identities that have not necessarily passed through the press of ideological politicization and state indoctrination. In a manner reminiscent of Ahad Ha'am's Spiritual Zionism,[17] Jaffa's Bulgarian Jews did not regard themselves as the territorial envoys of the political Zionist project, nor did they seek to dispossess Jaffa's Arab inhabitants. In fact, they maintained neighborly relations with the city's Palestinians, largely unhindered by political tensions. According to the story woven by Bachar, the reciprocal relations between the national-cultural arena and political reality, which made for tolerance and practical modus vivendi, were the fruit of hundreds of years of living under the Muslim Ottoman regime and of a long history of coexistence with the Christian majority in Bulgaria. One example is the Likud Party branch on Jerusalem Boulevard, which Bulgarian pensioners frequent to play cards, without regarding it as a political party branch but rather as a members' club. In a similar vein, the patriotism that Rabbi Bachar attributes to Maccabi Jaffa serves to assert communal cohesion, mutual responsibility, and a spirit of volunteerism rather than a national-political identity.[18] During a football match we recently attended in 2016, the only flag raised by Maccabi Jaffa was the Bulgarian flag, not the Israeli one.

In *Jews and Arabs in a Mixed Neighborhood of Jaffa*, Orly Hadas and Amiram Gonen report "a calm atmosphere" and "neighborly relations devoid of disputes."[19] They furthermore note that close social relationships failed to materialize, despite the neighbors' similar socioeconomic characteristics, and they report consistent social asymmetries between Jews and Arabs. According to their study, more Arabs than Jews tend to maintain contact with neighbors of the other nationality, whereas a greater proportion of Jews express a positive attitude toward life in a mixed neighborhood. A large majority of the Jews wish to be the dominant majority in the mixed neighborhood, yet only one-fifth of them consider the presence of Arab residents in the neighborhood a drawback. Hadas and Gonen conclude that, so long as the Jewish residents constitute a majority, most are prepared to accept this state of affairs and will not leave Jaffa. The status quo is widely perceived as temporary and unstable, however, because the number of Arab residents in the mixed neighborhoods is seen as likely to increase, and the Jewish residents, like Rabbi Bachar, are apprehensive about this.

Since the late 1990s Jaffa has become a city in flux. Given the waves of gentrification and the rise in real estate values in the city,[20] it appears that members of the veteran Jewish population are located on the margins of the development project and are unlikely to derive tangible benefits from it.[21] Although they are not ostensibly excluded from the hegemonic political project, they populate a declining urban space that has been abandoned by a large part of the founder generation and its descendants. As Hadas and Gonen demonstrate, when these Jews lose their demographic dominance, they will leave the city.

"Jaffa once belonged to the Bulgarians," declared Paulina, another old-time member of the Bulgarian community, "but what the Jews took by war, the Arabs are taking with money." Jaffa, or at least the Jerusalem Boulevard area where Paulina used to live, preserved a mere iota of its Bulgarian character over the years and gradually became a mixed quarter, which is currently populated equally by Arabs and Jews. Lily Avraham, who is quoted in Haskell's book, moved to Bat Yam, but she makes a point of visiting Jaffa once a week: "I get Bulgarian atmosphere in Jaffa. I do my shopping in Jaffa, they have Bulgarian cheese so I go to Jaffa, hear some gossip, and with that I finish with my Bulgarian-ness."[22] Haskell likewise quotes Chepo Pasi, a Jaffaite Bulgarian who describes the town's dwindling community life.

I THINK that here it's not an ideological matter. Life in Jaffa isn't fulfilling for the young people, and they feel as if they are in a kind of ghetto. In actuality Jaffa served as a kind of transit camp. . . . The young people left, after they got settled, had a trade, and left for Holon, Bat Yam, the surrounding areas. The older people remained, either because they didn't have the opportunity to find apartments in other areas, or because there is a concentration of retired people, who have all kinds of clubs and organizations, who share a common language and common experiences.[23]

Nowadays most Bulgarians reside in the cities adjacent to Jaffa, having moved there in the 1960s and the 1970s when permanent housing became available to them. Few community organizations are still active, but as Haskell concludes, "Bulgarian Jaffa has become the waiting room for the Rishon LeZion old age home."[24]

Seen through Rabbi Bachar's personal story, the local history of the Bulgarians in Jaffa offers a singular test case for an unsuccessful attempt to establish an ethnic community in the former Palestinian city. Like the Bulgarians, most immigrant populations never considered Jaffa as more than a transit city or camp. Once it had lost the majority of the second generation, the demographic profile of the veteran Jewish population of Jaffa remained divided and aging. Despite Jaffa's construction as the emotional object of communal nostalgia, the migration of the city's middle class has left it with an indigent Jewish population unable to sustain a local identity or stable community.

The concept of community in Bulgarian Jaffa is conspicuous by its absence. In certain contexts, such as Project Renewal,[25] the concept of community was indeed proclaimed and bureaucratically enforced and became a prevalent rhetorical practice, but at the same time an explicit discourse arose that questioned its relevance. In other contexts, too, the term *community* crops up spontaneously as an ordering social concept,[26] yet Rabbi Bachar fails to mention it even once. In its stead he anachronistically refers to the "Bulgarian immigration," which reflects a lack of alignment between the term used in the 1950s and the contemporary phenomenon, thereby illustrating the temporary and fragile nature of the way of life that Rabbi Bachar still pines for.

Jaffa's Bulgarian community is thus a signified without a signifier, a network of signified phenomena that expresses social capital and mutual responsibility but refers to an ethnic group and a public that no longer exist. In Rabbi Bachar's narrative this public does not make up a political community but rather a congregation of worshippers and a crowd of supporters, a group of like-minded people who express a yearning for a primary state of *communitas*[27] and that falls apart because of "egoism," "gratuitous hatred," and the betrayal of the nonimagined community.

Because Jaffa is a transit city, the tension between communal and individual existence that pervades it loosens the shackles of the national myth, enabling one to recognize the Other and maintain a basic level of human relationships within and between communities without having to account for oneself in grand historical or normative terms. As it disintegrates, the mixed city turns into a sphere that converts, disrupts, and creates unruly identities. In the stories of both Avraham Bachar and Fakhri Jday, the period of waiting—for the inevitable expiry of the Bulgarian community and the dissolution of the Palestinian community, respectively, and for their own imminent death—is what fires up Jday's sparks of nationalism and turns Bachar into a broken man. Nevertheless, both men manifest bereavement and collective failure. Jday is immersed in sanctifying the nation, the land, and the rights of its indigenous inhabitants. Because the myth of return and national revival has failed to materialize and remains a pipe dream, he has withdrawn from Jaffaite society. In Rabbi Bachar's story the sovereign nation is axiomatic and Zionism is an established fact; it does not require a pioneering spirit, a mobilizing territorial element, and makes do with a local form of patriotism. The bond with the place, the essence of nationalism, is not couched in political terms but rather in microcultural, communal, and civilian terms.

As the sun sets on the "Bulgarian immigration," Rabbi Bachar's nationalism unravels to become an inanimate object. He is left in a quandary: Whereas his soul yearns for Jaffa, his body is trapped within the walls of the nursing home in Rishon LeZion. At the end of the day, he is compelled to sever himself even from the place to which he has devoted his entire life and where many still remember him with a deep sense of gratitude and indebtedness.

CHAPTER 3

SURVIVING NATIONALISM

Isma'il abu-Shehade and Testimony amid the Ruins

Jaffa was one big orchard.[1]

Abu-Shehade in the film *Palestine Street*

The rest—yes, that's me! The papers haven't ignored me. How can
you claim not to have heard of me? I truly am remarkable. For no
paper with wide coverage, having sources, resources, advertisements,
celebrity writers, and a reputation, can ignore me. Those like me are
everywhere—towns, villages, bars, everywhere. I am "the rest." I am
remarkable indeed!

Emile Habiby, *The Secret Life of Saeed: The Pessoptimist*

Isma'il abu-Shehade (Abu-Subhi) was born in 1927 in the village of Tel
al-Rish on the outskirts of Jaffa. He resided there with his family until 1948,
when, like many internally displaced Palestinians, the family was forced to
move to the city.[2] Abu-Subhi's story touches on the essence of testimony—
be it a private personal document or a public commemoration—that sub-
stantiates claims to national identity and the rights that derive from it.
The leitmotif of his story—"Those who hear are unlike those who see"[3]—
establishes him as an eyewitness through the course of his entire life, which
is intertwined with the history of the city and branches out from it with a
form and substance of its own. Accordingly, Abu-Subhi is willing and able to
bear both private and public witness and to alternate between the two modes
as conditions and circumstances require. As such, Abu-Subhi observes the
destructiveness of national movements and the social feuds in which Jaffa is
entangled as an omniscient and unbiased narrator; at the same time he criticizes and deconstructs the ostensibly naïve tale by weaving shadowy stories

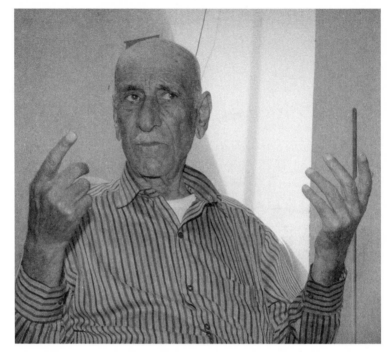

replete with implications and insinuations. This Janus-faced standpoint stems not from the narrator's subversive interpretation or from a desire to stamp his personal imprint on history but from the social position in which he finds himself, which is not of his choosing and against his own interest. This position lends his story-testimony both private and public modes of interpretation.

Abu-Subhi's tale proposes an attitude of survivor nationalism, which rests on the built-in tension between private and public modes. It recounts the escapades of a man of great resourcefulness, a pump technician and a fisherman by trade who moved to Jaffa after 1948 from his adjacent village. This is not a stirring tale of heroism, nor is it a narrative of tenacious *sumud* (steadfastness); rather, it is a portrayal of an exchange relationship between an individual and discriminatory state authorities and a review of the quotidian routine of the common man who perceives himself to be a random victim.

The relationship with Israel's security services was forced upon Abu-Subhi early on in his life. In return for his release from the detention in which he found himself when the hostilities ended in 1948, he was obliged to operate pumps for Jaffa's newly founded military government, a skill he had learned in Jaffa's orchards in his youth. Subsequently, to make a living, Abu-Subhi chose to continue working "with the Jews," portraying these relationships with an air of acceptance, eschewing demonization or idealization. By relegating the collective narrative to the background of his story and focusing on his own survival, Abu-Subhi stakes out a position that goes further than Rabbi Bachar's (Chapter 2). His strategy of identity suggests a transition from communal identity politics to a politics of existence, which distances itself somewhat more from the run-of-the-mill concept of nationalism and gradually disengages from the imagined community. From the distinct class position of someone who does not partake in the bourgeois project, Abu-Subhi traces the map of the homeland Falastin in national-spatial terms. Yet this map reflects his own cultural space, which was created from his own personal perspective, and it is not necessarily congruent with the publicly perceived national political sphere.

In his depiction of the city's social way of life and history, Abu-Subhi acts as an authentic spokesman of Jaffa, as someone who belongs to one of the twenty "original" families that, so he maintains, are the only ones empowered to truly represent it. Although this indigenous localism forms part of the national narrative, it assigns the right to the place to a handful of people, thereby undermining the axiomatic structuring of the city's identity as unquestionably Palestinian. Jaffa's boundaries are thus traced as a reflection of organic indigenous social boundaries rather than as a mythscape that reflects the complexion of the nation.[4] Consequently, Abu-Subhi does not bear witness to an archetypal national way of life but rather claims primordial local authenticity unmediated by extraneous mythical-ideological justifications. The roots of his testimony are planted in a foundational experience, which, despite its blatant nationalist overtones, Abu-Subhi presents as a personal trauma rather than evidence of collective wrongdoing.

When I Saw Them, I Fainted

On January 4, 1948, about a month after the Irgun (Etzel) first attacked Jaffa, and about four months before the city's fall, the marketplace was thrown into turmoil. A vehicle packed with explosives was blown up by the Stern

Gang (Lehi), leaving twenty-eight local Arabs dead and dozens wounded.[5]
The Turkish government building (Saraya), which was alleged to house the
offices of the Palestinian national headquarters of the campaign against Tel
Aviv and the liaison with the forces of Haj Amin al-Huseyni, collapsed on its
occupants. Fifty-four years later, Abu-Subhi relates what happened that day
and insists that the building housed an orphanage. His detailed description
illustrates how vividly the horror is etched on his memory.

> I TOOK PART in a film once, at the Saraya in front of the police station,
> with young people like you, also Jews. There are good Jews . . . And I
> refused to speak until I received a permit from Jaffa's police chief. They
> maintained that the Saraya was the base for the Jaffa defense organiza-
> tion, and I told them, "No, that's not true. It was an orphanage." On
> Sundays, the Christian brethren didn't work, and only children under the
> age of 14 remained there, from the age of 7 to 14. The place was destroyed.
> Not everyone died; some were injured. A vehicle drove up, parked next to
> the Saraya, and exploded. When the building collapsed, we heard people
> screaming. I saw boys and girls with broken legs and the bone exposed.
> When I saw them, I fainted. I was a young man, younger than you. When
> you see something like that for the first time, it knocks you down. There
> were dozens of children inside.

The dread and the trauma were clearly discernible in Abu-Subhi's voice,
in a way that matches the historical account of the attack. In the annals of the
city the event is mentioned in the same breath as the Deir Yassin massacre of
April 1948 as one of the key factors that drove Jaffa's frightened inhabitants
into exile.[6] Yet Abu-Subhi does not recount the events as directly as Fakhri
Jday does in describing Mandatory Jaffa (Chapter 1); rather, he interweaves
two supposedly separate plots as he describes a documentary film in which
he played a part, his historical debate with the filmmakers, and his conversation with the police chief.

The fact that a police permit was deemed necessary over half a century
after martial law was lifted from Jaffa testifies to the depths to which a regime of surveillance was stamped onto the consciousness of Abu-Subhi's
generation.[7] Thus it would seem as though Abu-Subhi, according to his own
testimony, fits the bill of the subservient generation that surrendered uncondi-

tionally to Israeli rule,[8] a subject of an authoritarian regime rather than a free citizen in a democratic state.[9] Nevertheless, his awareness of the interpretive choice that he applies to the memory of the event in his debate with the film-makers indicates his control over testimony as a form of representation.

Furthermore, Abu-Subhi summons testimony as a means of commemoration charting a definitive version of history: defusing the nationalist element of the Saraya incident and replacing it with a humanitarian disaster—a trauma involving the destruction of an orphanage—thus displacing localized private memories from the particular Palestinian sphere to the universal human realm. The vicissitudes of Abu-Subhi's life and his involvement with both Jews and Arabs demonstrate that the exigencies of navigating relationships with both sides prevails over the dictates of prescribed collective memory.

How Can I Work with You?

Unlike Jday and Rabbi Bachar, Abu-Subhi does not begin by depicting Jaffa's heyday, because, as a manual laborer from a peasant family, he was not a member of the flourishing urban bourgeoisie and because his defining experience was the trauma of war rather than the nostalgic imagined community. His experience of the terrorist attack is not a heroic tale; rather, it endures to this day as the passive and frightened testimony of a young man ill-equipped to cope with the horror unfolding before his eyes.

Like Saeed abu al-Nahs ("the unfortunate")—the pessoptimist in Emile Habiby's surreal novel,[10] an ironic undertone is woven into Abu-Subhi's story that betrays an alternative story seething beneath the explicit narrative. Having survived war in the city, Abu-Subhi describes how he was imprisoned together with most of the city's young men and how his release was made conditional on his agreement to help the military government train people to draw water from the wells in the abandoned orchards around the city to ensure a regular supply of water to Israeli Defense Forces troops. Following his initial reservations ("How can I work with you?"), Abu-Subhi resigned himself to the necessity of collaboration and learned to regard this purely as a job. Although this decision may have stemmed from the need to survive, it established exchange relations between Abu-Subhi and "the Jews" that were maintained throughout his life.

SOME PEOPLE stayed in Jaffa. When the Jews entered in '48, they issued a mere 396 identity cards. They produced cards for the adults on the spot. When the army entered the city, they detained all the youngsters. At that time, when my father was still alive, we lived in an orchard. He would come to the prison each day and bring me two pita breads and a few tomatoes. One of the guards approached me once and asked, "Abu-Shehade, are you going to eat all this on your own? That's a lot." He took one pita for himself and his companion and left me the other. The guard was hungry; he had nothing to eat.

A guy called Moshe asked me once, "Why are you detained? I will release you, but only if you'll work with us for a while." I asked him, "How can I work with you?" He said, "Just draw water." Eventually he got me out of jail, and he'd come each day to pick me up with a jeep and take me to the orchards to operate the engine, and I would draw water, and they would take the water container with them. The soldiers had no water, and my job was simply to operate the pump engine. They gave me bread and a can of sardines. After a month they brought someone and told me, "Teach him," and took me to a different orchard. I trained some five people, and after that they no longer needed me and sent me home. But they didn't detain me again. I returned to the orchard where we had lived. We worked for Hassan Barakat. The orchard survived until '57. After that they uprooted the orchards and built houses instead.

Abu-Subhi relates the story of his arrest and release in a matter-of-fact tone and with ironic distance, as though it were someone else's adventure rather than the outcome of a collective calamity and an act of coercion that involved danger. He does not regard his willingness to collaborate as a shameful act but rather as a minor incident that enabled him to return to the orchards, which dominated life in Jaffa and where he felt at home. As Abu-Subhi declared when interviewed for al-Jazeera's documentary *Palestine Street*, "Jaffa was just one big orchard." It was neither a major Palestinian urban center nor a relic of the promised land to be hung on the wall. It was just fruitful soil that yielded edible oranges. Even though the orchards were indeed Abu-Subhi's family's source of vitality and livelihood, in contrast to the centrality of agricultural crops in general and Jaffa oranges in particular to both the Zionist and the Palestinian ethos, for Abu-Subhi they were an object of irrigation and labor.[11] Before the war, members of Abu-Subhi's family worked as tenant farmers in the orchard owned by Hassan Barakat, one of the city's richest men. Acceptance of the class hierarchy, which is presented as an immutable natural state, likewise emerges in Abu-Subhi's description of everyday life under the British Mandate and even in his description of the Jewish National Fund's purchase of the land, which he labels simply "land profiteering" (*samsara*), namely, an economic exchange rather than a political act that would have dire national repercussions.

> THE ENGLISH RULE was good and fair. The English didn't take one inch of Arab soil. But they burdened the Arabs with taxes. Many sank into debt. And you know, if you have land and you owe money, and then the time comes to pay taxes, if someone owns a cow, they take it. The landowners felt the pressure, and that's how people began to sell plots of land. What's the use of land if you are in debt? Anyone unable to pay taxes sold land. Take the Keren Kayemet [Jewish National Fund], for example. Some people said, "I don't want to sell to the Jews," but some said, "Why not sell to the Jews?" Someone would come and buy land and then transfer it to Keren Kayemet. That was land profiteering.

Everyone Spoke Arabic, and So Everyone Lived in Peace

As we did with all the other storytellers in this book, we asked Abu-Subhi to compare the present situation to the pre-1948 period. His story reveals a daily routine that stresses the similarity between the two rival populations: "Before '48 you wouldn't hear the word Jew or Arab." The village's collective way of life and mutual dependence left no place for ideological struggles. Quotidian life was dictated primarily by the rural and religious calendars. The religious calendar sustained religious distinctions and even justified communal differences, yet it relegated national and political affairs to the margins of the social world. As indicated by Rabbi Bachar's depiction of the life of the Bulgarian community, here too we are made aware of the Ottoman heritage that anchors communal identity in a distinctive ethnic sphere and celebrates the ethos of respect between the ethnoreligious groups.[12]

BEFORE '48 you wouldn't hear the word Jew or Arab. There was nothing of the kind. We would work together. During the Ramadan fast, the Jew would take his young son to the large market in Jaffa and would not allow him to eat because during Ramadan people fast. He wouldn't even buy his son a cookie. There was respect. Do you want to hear about respect? We are originally residents of Tel al-Rish village, which is nowadays called Tel Giborim. My grandfather owned a large orchard known as Karm al-Madfa'.[13] Beyond the hill lived seven Jewish families. On the last day of Passover, my father would say, "Today our neighbors can eat [leavened] bread, and they have no bread." We used to bake bread at home—we would make fifty, sixty pitas a day. My mother would give me five, ten pitas: "Go to the home of Abu-Ya'akov and give the Jewish neighbors bread." We didn't know then who was Ashkenazi and who was Mizrahi. They were all *khawajat* [a term of respect for non-Arabs].

On the outskirts of Jaffa, daily life was dictated to a large extent by one's socioeconomic status. The exchange relations within this system transcended national differences and generated a complex picture of geographic boundaries that could be crossed also by the indigent villagers. According to this map, Syria was the economic center that "supplied goods to Palestine," whereas Beirut was the recreational center. Abu-Subhi's nostalgic and enthusiastic description informs us that before the urbanization forced on the residents of Jaffa's periphery after 1948, their agricultural way of life revolved around the seasons. The common denominators between Jews and Arabs were their similar class position, the mutual respect shown to cultural attributes, and the Arabic language: "Our neighbors spoke Arabic. Everyone spoke Arabic, and so everyone lived in peace."

WE ATE according to the season. That is, all summer long we ate tomatoes, but in wintertime who could find tomatoes? There were none. All summer we would eat cucumbers, but in wintertime who could find cucumbers? There were no greenhouses back then. Nowadays it's amazing. In the middle of winter you can find grapes. All in all not too many fruits grew in Palestine, because Syria supplied Palestine with produce. Palestine couldn't compete with Syria in fruits. In Syria they have apples, peaches, apricots, almonds—all the fruits of the Syrian region (*al-Sham*).

Culturally, the open borders facilitated encounters that could not take place in Jaffa (with women from Beirut and Tel Aviv, for example), and economically, Jaffa's cosmopolitan nature turned it into a regional center of employment. In line with the predominantly mundane tone of his story, Abu-Subhi chooses to depict Jaffa as the Mother of the Stranger, a place where a migrant worker could enter the labor market, rather than as the nationalist imagery of Jaffa as the Bride of the Sea or the Bride of Palestine, as does al-Maslub in Gabi 'Abed's performance. Through the reporting of his own history, Abu-Subhi positions himself as a narrator of culture, and his narrative focuses on popular culture, religious customs, and folklore. In contrast to Fakhri Jday, Abu-Subhi's narrative style and content reveal a transition from political to cultural matters.

IN THE DAYS of the English [*ayyam al-Ingliz*] I would travel to Lebanon and I visited Egypt by taxi. Beirut is not far. Four or five of us would travel to Beirut and back by taxi. It was more fun hanging out in Beirut than in Jaffa, but residents of Beirut would come to Jaffa to make a living. Jaffa was a center of employment to which workers would come from Syria and from Egypt. There were perhaps a hundred thousand people living in Jaffa. That's why they called it Mother of the Stranger. The stranger was not humiliated—the stranger would come to do menial jobs. In Beirut we would go dancing—what is there to do in Beirut after all? It's full of bars. That's what Beirut was like! On the beach we would see the girls with provocative clothing, as one sees also today. You could see today's swimsuits in Beirut fifty, seventy years ago. But people didn't dress that way in Jaffa. In Jaffa the women were covered, modest. I remember that Fakhri Jday's mother wore a veil. The Christians also covered themselves and didn't go around exposed. There was no idle talk.

I Lived with Them

Abu-Subhi's circuitous path through life led him from Tel al-Rish to Kibbutz Nir 'Am and from there to work in the British army camps. As a young boy he joined his father, who set out for the area "between Ashqelon and Gaza" to plant an orchard. For a while the family lived in Kibbutz Nir 'Am, founded in 1943.[14]

OUR FINANCIAL SITUATION was good. Our father made a decent living, and he could therefore afford to enroll us in school. In Palestine there were many who couldn't read and write. There was much illiteracy in the villages. I studied in a rickety wooden hut with another thirty-five pupils. We sat on the sand. There were no floor tiles like today, not even a mat! If someone didn't want his son to sit on the sand, he would bring him a mat. We didn't learn English, just Arabic, arithmetic, and the Quran. We had to complete the entire Quran [*min surat al-fatiha l-al-baqara*] in four years, reading, writing, and interpretation. A child was sent to school at the age of 5 or 6. I completed the *kuttab* [first four years] and studied a further two years at school [*al-'umaria*]. Then they transferred us, because my father was working between Ashqelon and Gaza in an orchard that belonged to a certain Hammudi al-Kashef, where Kibbutz Nir 'Am stands today. We bought a house in the kibbutz. There were five girls and fifteen boys in the kibbutz. That was the entire kibbutz. I lived with them.

The political significance of a Palestinian family living in a relatively isolated Zionist outpost was lost on everyone, and the young Abu-Subhi took it for granted. In his words, "I was 15. I was unaware. I didn't understand what was happening." Similar to his description of shared life at Tel al-Rish, he recalls this period as a pleasant time that was cut short by World War II. According to Abu-Subhi, in Mandatory Palestine spatial boundaries were interpreted in social terms embedded in daily life rather than as symbolic definers of national categories.

I LIVED in the kibbutz, and to this day I remember the girl's names. They were slightly older than I. If I were to go to the kibbutz today and ask where is so-and-so, I may find some of them, old women. I would like to go, but I'd like someone to come with me. We were good friends. Sometimes their bread would run out, and we would bake and bring them. There was this poor guy they called the *mukhtar* [Arabic for village chief], whose name was Griton, an old man. I knew the girls—Tsipora, Pnina, and Esther—I remember them all. When the trees grew, World War II broke out, and instead of my father handing the orchard over to the owner, the owner fled. Many people from Palestine abandoned the orchards and left.

Abu-Subhi's narrative is based on the cultural Arabization of Jewish life in Mandatory Palestine. Just as he relates how an Ashkenazi *mukhtar* headed the kibbutz, so does he repeatedly stress Arab cultural dominance and the major role Jaffa played in relation to burgeoning Tel Aviv. Both Palestinians and Jews, maintains Abu-Subhi, are victims of the "intrigues" of British colonialism. And yet the fat salaries that His Majesty's army paid tempted him to work for them.

AT THAT TIME people spoke Arabic, not Hebrew. The Jew was obliged to speak Arabic. At the time of the English there was no problem to come and go from Tel Aviv to Jaffa. They had no market, so they would come to buy in Jaffa. Tel Aviv was merely a neighborhood of tin shacks [*tanak*]. The shooting from Jaffa on Tel Aviv began only in '36. I was 10 years old then. But the shots were fired not only at the Jews but also at the English. The Englishman was an "agitator" [he uses the Hebrew word *sakhsekhan*], shooting two Jews there and two Arabs here. The Jews shot at them from here, and the Arabs from there. The English are to blame for the entanglement. But in '36 there was a revolt that lasted two years [*sic*], and in '39 World War II broke out.

People were excited about the war [*miltahin*]. During World War II both Tel Aviv and Jaffa were bombed. There were Germans in Tel Aviv. Wagner owned the largest engine factory, next to Chelouche Street. The ships bombarded Tel Aviv, and it was prohibited to turn on the light at night. During World War II all of Palestine became full of army camps and English soldiers. And we worked in the camps. I operated water pumps. And the English would pay handsomely because of the labor shortage. But if anyone tells you there was famine, that is not so. There was never a famine in Palestine. In the land of Palestine there were orchards, oranges, and vineyards.

Because of his farming background, Abu-Subhi feels obliged to speak for those who work the land and who are responsible for supplying food to the rest of the populace. He perceives the famine that allegedly prevailed in Palestine as a personal failure and is quick to reject the notion as a mere rumor. The period between World War II and 1948 is portrayed as one of economic prosperity and commercial cooperation that benefited both Arabs and Jews.

AFTER THE WAR the markets opened up. Palestine lived in greater prosperity by virtue of the oranges. Jaffa oranges were most of the export.
Jaffa Orange, the oranges of Palestine, were world famous. To this day
Israel exports oranges named Jaffa Orange, even though there isn't even
one orange left in Jaffa. My father used to sell and export oranges. He
had a Jewish partner, Abu-Ya'akov was his name. I think he was an Ashkenazi, because his name was Yoav Zuckerman. But they spoke Arabic to
each other, better than we do. My father would bring oranges from our
orchard, and he from his. Business was booming. We didn't know what
an Ashkenazi was, only a Jew. Only later did we distinguish between a
Sephardi and an Ashkenazi. At the time we knew that this was a Muslim
and that was a Jew, and that was that.

To Abu-Subhi, the indistinct ethnic categories were part and parcel of a
life of genuine partnership. He began to note the politicization of these categories only after the establishment of the state of Israel. At this point in the
conversation Abu-Subhi's grandson Isma'il intervenes. He is a postgradu-
ate student at Tel Aviv University and also studies at the Islamic College at
Umm al-Fahm. Isma'il quotes from Edward Said's memoir *Out of Place*[15]
to reinforce his grandfather's assertion that there was no racial separation
(*tafriqa 'irqiya*) before 1948 and that Jaffa was truly pluralistic: "This was a
multicultural and multireligious society, a mosaic of minorities." Concluding
the discussion, Abu-Subhi declared, "We didn't know what racism was. Ask
any Jew and he'll tell you the same."[16]
A member of the stand-tall generation thus recruits the memories of
his survivor grandfather to create a shared basis from which to comprehend
the origins of the Palestinian condition. Even though the grandfather does
not appear willing to use the nationalist discourse as set forth in Edward
Said's autobiography and as suggested by his grandson, he does not deny the
calamity of his people. His story takes a turn toward national memory as he
depicts the events of the Nakba. Yet here again Abu-Subhi's firsthand account addresses primarily the brutality of the occupation, the harm it brings
upon people, and the transformation it generated in the demographic structure of the Palestinian people, rather than its significance for Palestinian
national identity. On the contrary, the afflictions of the Arab population are

presented as a catastrophic consequence of the national dispute, for which all sides bear responsibility.[17]

Those Years, I Don't Want to Remember Them

At this point Abu-Subhi abandons the reconciliatory note that has characterized his narrative thus far as he begins to describe the 1948 war: "The occupation of Jaffa was barbaric." The war resulted in the forced urbanization of those who remained in the rural outskirts of Jaffa, the expropriation of their lands, and their herding into the 'Ajami enclosure called the ghetto by both Arabs and Jews.

> AFTER '48 came the occupation and martial law. There was a "ghetto" in Jaffa, a fenced-in area in 'Ajami that was totally enclosed by a barbed-wire fence, gates, guards, and dogs. We lived here in the heart of the ghetto, and Hassan Barakat and Amin Andraus were in the same boat as I. In order to pass through the gate, we had to get a permit. I've kept the permit to this day. You could go [about a mile] out to Sabil abu-Nabut [in Abu Kabir] and that's it, no further. With the permit I could go out; no one questioned you. I dressed up, combed my hair, and took a bus to Tiberias. Anyone who went down to the sea at Jaffa was shot, and that's how it was up to '56, when they took down the fence.

Abu-Subhi links his sad fate to that of the remaining Jaffa elite. His tale of the way the city was drained of its Arabs coupled with the rapid influx of new immigrants from Bulgaria and Romania is a blend of human tragedy and dispassionate observation of the surrealistic way of life that generated anomalies such as "to this day you can find elderly Arabs who speak Romanian." Yet even among the ruins of the community, so Abu-Subhi testifies, pragmatic necessity dominated interpersonal communication.

> JAFFA EMPTIED OUT. When the Jewish immigrants began to arrive, they put them up with those who had three or four rooms. They vacated two rooms and gave them to the immigrants. But what did they do? After all, the Jews are hard-hearted ['atlin], as you know. What did they do? When they built the housing projects for the Jews, they vacated them from the

houses and demolished them. That is, they took from you two rooms, and
when those who lived there left, they tore down the roof.

We had ID cards, but we remained fenced in until '56. To this day
you can find elderly people who speak Romanian, those in whose homes
Romanians and Bulgarians lived. They lived together for five, six years,
until they learned to speak like them. Those who came spoke neither
Arabic nor Hebrew. They spoke Romanian and Bulgarian. One had to
communicate with them in the language they understood. Those years,
I don't want to remember them, because they were the six most screwed
up [a'ras] years of my life. There are people who to this day come from
Ramallah and Jerusalem to ask about the history of the capture of Jaffa—
you begin to weep.

We Are in a Prison, Locked In

The cosmopolitan lifestyle and fluid ethnic boundaries are a thing of the past.
When the interview took place, immediately after the outbreak of the al-Aqsa
Intifada, the Arabs of Jaffa were under siege and had a hard time making a
living. Alongside the implicit allegation that the Arabs of Jaffa were paying
the price for the nationalist struggle as the innocent victims of Ariel Sharon's
provocation, Abu-Subhi declared defiantly that "one cannot get rid neither of
the Jews nor of the Arabs."

THERE IS A PROVERB that says "The spark ignites evil" [al-shar min al-
sharara]. What is the spark? Just like when you strike a stone with another stone, a spark emerges, so did Sharon ignite a spark. Here in Jaffa
I was done for as far as work was concerned. One's livelihood was cut off
in an unreasonable manner. You perhaps do not notice how all work has
ground to a standstill. Not one store has remained open, and there isn't a
business that does well. Before the Intifada there were between forty and
forty-five laborers who worked right next to here, and nowadays each
works as best he can. There was a small company here that had forty employees, and today one remains. There used to be forty grocery stores and
ten remain! Where have they all gone?

Before the intifada I used to go to Qalqilia and Tulkarem—the vegetables are cheaper there, the meat is cheaper and fresher and tastier.

[Nowadays] we are in a prison, locked in. A week ago I visited Jerusalem and I was scared. I didn't feel "secure" [in Hebrew]. Previously, I would wander around at ease; they didn't throw stones or shoot at you. One can't get rid of the Jews nor of the Arabs. I have a friend called Eliyahu from Netanya, who would take his wife and children to lunch in Tulkarem. He would eat half a kilo of grilled meat and salad and hummus for 50 shekels rather than have his wife cook at home.

The dominant theme that runs through the narrative is that of normality, of mundane and desirable modus vivendi. The dual aspects of insecurity—the physical and the economic—mark, in Abu-Subhi's eyes, the state of emergency and the siege that he was subjected to as part of the political community after the events of October 2000. As his story unfolds, Abu-Subhi uses an economic metaphor to describe flawed social relations ("Nowadays the life of the Israeli Arab is worth a shekel"), but by virtue of this depressing economic predicament, he manages to summon up his personal experience to express a cautiously optimistic sentiment regarding the prospects for reconciliation.

NOWADAYS the life of the Israeli Arab is worth a shekel, a shekel and a half. Everyone knows, and even the government knows, that if there is peace here in Israel, it will be "paradise" [he uses the Hebrew word]. Jaffa had the worst of it! As soon as they entered, they began to demolish houses and to level sites. Manshiya is gone, and in the '80s they stopped the demolition. Everything you see here was built recently. They dumped all the rubble of Jaffa into the sea, and then they woke up and said, "Why should we destroy? We shall renovate." But today, if you wish to buy a house in Jaffa, an Arab or a Jewish one, a house such as mine, for example, would cost 300,000 dollars. Is there anyone in Jaffa who has 300,000 dollars? Nobody!

I bought the house here in '56. At the time we lived in an orchard and they told us, "You have to leave. We intend to build." We left. I bought here for 2,000 liras. But there wasn't a house here. There was only this room. I built the rest myself. In order to save 2,000 liras, I worked in Tiberias for four years. I lived in an orchard, and I moved to Tiberias to work on a project involving water [pumping] engines. The project cost me 10,000, 15,000 liras, and I made 500 liras from it. I wasn't a laborer, I was a "technical contractor."

According to Abu-Subhi, examples of destruction and construction are
mixed together and even emanate from one another in a form of creative
destruction[18] and thus offer hope for a future that is not the outcome of ideological and political restructuring but of the vitality of the urge for survival
that drives universal humanity.

The Wretched Came and Lived in the Finest Houses

Abu-Subhi continues by offering a detailed and almost detached historical
reconstruction of the events of his life, which he casually traces without seeking to establish justice or adopt a moral standpoint. The turmoil that resulted
from amassing displaced Palestinians from the villages into Jaffa paradoxically generated a new social and spatial order that enabled destitute refugees
to live in spacious homes that had been reserved for the exiled members of
the old Palestinian elite.

> IT WAS a difficult time even for those who worked in those days. It wasn't
> just hard; the houses were empty in Jaffa. No one lived in them. There
> were those who entered furnished houses. These were people whom they
> brought from beyond the city, outside of Jaffa. They concentrated all the
> Arabs from afar who lived here and there—"Come to Jaffa, take a house
> for yourself and live there"—in order to enclose the people within a fence.
> People assembled from afar. Those who came from outside took the nice
> houses. Those who were well-to-do remained in their home, and then five
> years later they told them to leave. There were many Egyptians, Syrians.
> The wretched came and lived in the nicest houses. But we were not angry.
> Why should we be angry? After all, it isn't mine; let them take the houses.
> I resided in my home. The people of the city remained in their homes.

The mixing of the population and the housing of refugees forced upon
the city by the orders of the military government, which sought to control the
Palestinian "minority" within a constricted space,[19] turned things topsy-turvy
in Jaffa. In historical hindsight, the unintended consequences of this policy
paradoxically planted the seeds of 'Ajami's Palestinian political community,
but in Abu-Subhi's view the housing policy mainly disrupted the city's demographic makeup and threatened Jaffa's indigenous "original" character. His

narrative at this point is (also) a mixture—of Arabic and Hebrew (in quotation marks).

> NINETY PERCENT OF JAFFA IS STRANGERS. Now, with this Intifada, they brought in 320 families from the [refugee] camps, collaborators. Ask him where he is from, he will say Jaffa. In his ID card "the address" is Jaffa, and he has never seen Jaffa. In the "original" Jaffa there are no more than twenty families. Three hundred and ninety-six ID cards. Those who are from Jaffa take care of it. I may curse my father, but I won't curse Jaffa. You didn't know Jaffa. She was beautiful, she was beautiful. Once, just imagine, there were 120,000 people living here.

A relative who joined the conversation added:

> IT WOULD HAVE BEEN BETTER had she not been beautiful; then no one would have coveted her, and she would have been left for her owners. Because she was beautiful, everyone wanted her. Later, after '56, people from the villages began to arrive. They came, they worked, and they lived in Jaffa. One could buy a house for a thousand liras, for 2,000 liras. And it was not impossible to get hold of a thousand liras. He would find a sealed house [blocked up with bricks by the authorities] and "invade."

The strangers' presence symbolizes the demise of "authentic" urbanism, but the rearguard battle over Jaffa's threatened identity led Abu-Subhi to recount, on the one hand, the names of the original families and, on the other, to decompose Jaffa as a spatial national category into separate quasi-urban neighborhoods that had nothing in common. As he concludes his description, Abu-Subhi even finds himself questioning *his own* Jaffaite credentials.

> BUT JAFFA IS DEAD. Look, opposite us is a hospital. There used to be an English hospital, and nowadays it's called the Scottish House. There were five big hospitals in Jaffa. Fu'ad al-Dajani inherited from his father a house and an orchard. He sold part of the orchard and built a hospital. Wolfson Hospital is built in sakanet al-Darwish; they took land from the Qasas and Abu-Qa'ud families. The Hamad family is from Sheikh Munis, Kabob is a long-standing Jaffa family, Mashhrawi from Jaffa, Abu-Ramadan, Sukkar, Zaqaq, Dik—all of them Jaffa. Shaqr is not from

Jaffa and not even Palestinian—Egyptian Copts who joined the Orthodox Church. Gabi al-'Abed is from Bethlehem, not from Jaffa. His father
worked in Jaffa and remained.

ALL OF JAFFA was neighborhoods [*sakanat*, quasi-urban neighborhoods].
'Ajami was *sakanet* al-Ajami. All of this is Jaffa. But the real Jaffa was old
Jaffa. We were called *birawi*, because we lived in the orchards beyond Jaffa.
[Now facing Mussa abu-Ramadan:] If you ask someone like your father
or like my father, he'll tell you, "We are not from Jaffa; we are from sakanet
al-Darwish." People left old Jaffa. In old Jaffa there were whorehouses, un-
clean houses. A son of 'Ajami will tell you, "I'm not from Jaffa—I'm from
'Ajami, I'm from Nuzhah [nowadays Jerusalem Boulevard]." All kinds of
types of people lived in old Jaffa—good people, bad people, all sorts.

The distinction Abu-Subhi makes between the city's original core, the
Old City of Jaffa, and its assortment of unworthy multitudes deprives the ex-
isting population of any cultural and consequently national claim to embody
the authentic spirit of Jaffa. Abu-Subhi himself is aware of his marginality
in the circles of Jaffaism, but because even those who reside in the heart of
the city are denied genuine Jaffaite identity, hardly any representatives of in-
disputable Jaffaite residency remain. The disconnection between the urban
sphere and its random inhabitants turns the inhabitants into objects worthy
of compassion and assistance but not identification or respect.

My Father Ran To and Fro and Told Everyone, "Don't Leave!"

Having dismantled Jaffa into its constituent parts, Abu-Subhi proceeds to
trace the family history that has brought him to his present position. The
narrative begins with World War I, under the Ottoman regime.

WHEN MY FATHER WAS STILL ALIVE—in 1965 he was 96 years old—
the Turks recruited him and his father who [subsequently] died in the
1914 war. They forced them to join—they had to! In those days only one
out of 10,000 could read, and my father was knowledgeable and learned.
He would pick up a book and read. They took him to Turkey, where he
worked as a telegram scribe. They made him an officer. But when the war
broke out, people left Jaffa [*hajarat al-nas*]. The English reached the Suez

Canal, and the people were afraid of the English and fled. The families left—my grandmother and my young uncles left. From Jaffa they moved to villages, within Palestine; they moved inland.

My father heard that the English were approaching Jaffa and deserted. He and another five soldiers from Palestine conspired to leave Turkey and return to Jaffa via Syria. The women and the children and the girls were afraid of the English, but the adult men, like you, knew that there was no difference between Turkish and English imperialism. They wanted their families. "We want the family. How can we not come?" They returned on foot—it took them six months.

The father's tales of adventure are spiced with an existential and political moral that counters the reflex that drove people to flee the city at time of war. Abu-Subhi thereby constitutes his father as a witness, implying that, had the people heeded his words, the state of the community in general would have been different. Moreover, the example provided by the father's insistence on remaining in the city casts doubt on the link between forced refugeehood and nationalism, which underpins the Palestine national movement. Abu-Subhi refrains from interpreting events, but in his view his family's tenacious clinging to the land under foreign occupation is preferable to an imaginary nationalism that relinquishes its grip on the soil and is left with an unrealizable idea and symbol—a proverbial orange branch. This attitude toward refugeehood and the Palestinian Diaspora is alluded to in the following story.

> HE USED TO SAY, "I have seen how people flee, humiliated and dying of hunger. Fleeing is humiliation [*bahdala*]." He ran to and fro about the city and told everyone, "Don't leave! I have seen what it means to flee. Let no one leave. In the name of God, stay on your land!" That was in '48 and he [turning to Mussa abu-Ramadan] was the one who influenced your grandfather Abu-Ramadan to stay, and he also influenced several others. "Don't leave. Fleeing leads to humiliation."

Following this passing yet highly significant digression from the thread of the plot, Abu-Subhi continues to relate how his father met his future wife in 1916. He works the personal event into the annals of the changing colonial regime in the Middle East and links it to irresistible imperial forces.

HE RETURNED on his own. His mother originally came from a village named Qaiqub. He hid in the orchards and reached Tel al-Rish. Hussein [Abu-Subhi's father] hid in the vineyard for fear that the Turkish soldiers would notice him. Had they found him, they would have shot him on the spot, a summary execution. My grandmother would send him food. With whom? With Khadija, her daughter. Hussein eyed her; she found favor with him, and they got married in the vineyard. Her mother is wise, someone who wants to wed her daughter. That was in the year 1916–1917, during the war. Less than three months after they were married the English entered. But after the wedding he sent his mother and his sisters back home, to Qaiqub, between Beit Lid and Hadera [Khudayrah]. His father died, and he began to tend a plot of land we had in Jaffa. He tended it all his life.

And then the English entered, and they didn't harass the Arabs: "You are an Arab. You are a son of the land. Remain in place." They naturally expelled the Turks, and the English came. But the English didn't come alone; there were English and French. France took Syria and Lebanon, and the English took Palestine and Jordan and Iraq. They divided it up between them, like a fallen cow, and each grabs a knife and takes a part.

Nationalism is dwarfed and even rendered absurd when faced with these world powers, and the only anchor of stability that is left to the individual is his blood relations and the land, in the local kinship sense. This is a nonnational and in a certain sense a subnational commitment, whose interpersonal implications in a tangible face-to-face community are stronger than the implied identification with the imagined community. In this sense, one's immediate identification with the local social network does not correspond with the abstract concept of nation.

Those Who Hear Are Unlike Those Who See

The loss experienced by all Palestinians did not pass over the Abu-Shehades, despite their spirit of entrepreneurship and their ability to extricate themselves from trouble. Abu-Subhi assiduously presents himself as a survivor, and he relates the family tragedy through the figure of his father, whose heart was broken by the injustice done to him by the devious and perfidious state through its emissaries in the High Court of Justice (HCJ).

MY FATHER would bring laborers to work for him. At the time of martial law, in order to issue a permit, they asked, "Whom do you work for?" "For Abu-Shehade." And my father would come and sign, "This is my laborer," and they gave him a permit. There was a certain man named Nissim Antebe from the security service [Israel Security Agency], who came and told my father, "I see you have twenty laborers, but you have signed for a hundred. Where are they?" They were working at other locations and he had signed for them. My father said to him, "Let them live, and to hell with the money." Anyone who came and wished to work, he told them, "Work for me," but they didn't work. But they slept in his orchard.

He had my uncle's orchard and Hassan Barakat's orchard. Where the ORT school is today was an orchard for which he received as compensation a plot of land in Sakhneh and a plot of land where Bezeq stands today. He received this as compensation for the land next to our house. That's my father's land. They told him, "Take a few dunams in the heart of Jaffa," but they didn't register it, and when they came to take the land from him, he petitioned the HCJ, and the court ruled that the land was his and that was that. In court he began to leap with joy and say, "Long live justice!" But the justice minister said, "It's not yours. Expropriation" [Hebrew word]. That's the crazy law in Israel. They offered to compensate him to the tune of 70 liras per dunam. What is 70 liras per dunam? A dunam is worth 2,000, 3,000 liras. "They gave me 70 liras . . ." He sat and wept, and when they came to uproot the trees in the orchard, he continued to weep until he died. He died while still weeping.

Abu-Subhi contends with the national frame of reference and with collective history through the mediation of his personal memories. Yet the History, with a capital H (al-ta'rikh) that he perceives primarily as a series of tragedies and defeats is better forgotten.

I DON'T LIKE to remember history. I want to forget it. People say to me, "Abu-Subhi, write it down!" I tell them, "I don't want to write." But others write. To this day people come to me from Ramallah and Jerusalem and write. They sit with me for two, three hours and exhaust me. But those who hear are unlike those who see: "War is only that which you experienced and tasted, and not through dubious hearsay" [this is a quote

from the classical poet Zuhayr bin Abi Sulma]. And I have tasted it. My
generation is now finished; all are dead. How much longer will we live?
How long does anyone actually want to live? The entire young generation
will perhaps learn from books.

Abu-Subhi is prepared to talk about the events of his life but refuses to
record them in writing. His firsthand testimony is truly known only to him
and cannot be genuinely comprehended by another. And when the generation of witnesses has passed from this world, only books will remain, only
"dubious hearsay."

A Witness Without Testimony

Abu-Subhi's refusal to document what he has observed differentiates the
speaker who remembers from the speaker who bears witness. He remembers
the past from the position of a bystander who reports in a matter-of-fact
manner, in response to the listener's prompting. He is aware that his story
has little to do with establishing a collective memory or with shaping the
identity and image of those he mentions, so his words do not constitute testimony that has the power to mold memory. This rather stoic awareness of the
futility of shared memory in Abu-Subhi's world is related to the trauma of
war and the workings of evil.

Two fields of reference clash here. The first is that of the individual's impotence in the face of forces that cannot be vanquished, comprehended, or
negotiated with, such as world powers, wars, and terrorism; the other is the
need and capacity to survive in defiance of these titanic political and human
forces through resourcefulness unhindered by moral compunctions. The individual's powerlessness entails meek acceptance of one's fate, whereas the
capacity to survive encourages resistance and survival at all cost. Although
they appear to be mutually exclusive, this is in fact not so, because Abu-
Subhi makes a distinction between futile opposition to that which is beyond
his power and the daily efforts of survival. Because only the daily efforts
are likely to be effective, Abu-Subhi lives in a timeframe of contemporary
improvisation that cannot bear the memory of testimony, because the past
not only fails to explain and justify the transient present but even stands
in its way. The unbearable burden of memory obstructs the effective trans-

formation of identities that informs Abu-Subhi's capacity for survival. He himself is aware of this, and between the lines of his reports we can read the occasional hint to his opinions about wrongdoing, justice, and guilt, which do not coalesce into a coherent and binding moral code. The suspended time that Abu-Subhi inhabits leaves no room for permanent eternal mythic time. It makes total demands on the traumatized survivor's resources and vitality and thus cannot encompass victims and victimizers, because addressing these is liable to detract from the cunning, ingenuity, and Odyssean agility that are necessary to observe reality dispassionately and accurately without illusions.

Yet Abu-Subhi is no nihilist. He makes veiled references to belonging and identity. This connects him and his family to the concrete, tangible land and to their origins. This soil is saturated with the blood of its sons, but this blood is genuine, in that it is neither metaphoric nor symbolic and cannot therefore serve as a foundation for the emergence of a mythical national consciousness. Through his prompted memories, Abu-Subhi evokes a prenationalist or rather postnationalist outlook that views the link between blood and soil in terms of a literal indigenousness that is apathetic toward the symbolic sphere of collective identity. The rights of the indigenous Jaffaites, according to this perception, are not subject to question or negotiation because they are anchored in the soil that spawned them.

Although Abu-Subhi laments the blood that has been shed, he does not mourn the dead. He places himself in the role of undertaker of his deceased relatives and acquaintances but does not enshroud them in a symbolic mantle of sacrifice and heroism. The bloodbath that he witnessed turns him into a dead man who unwillingly lifts his hand from the grave to write unwanted memoirs. The soil of Jaffa will continue to exist and bring forth orchards, impervious to the origin of the blood that it absorbs and to those who tend it. Contrary to Fakhri Jday (Chapter 1)—the walking dead, the bedrock of nationalism,[20] who is consumed by the fires of nationalism he continues to nourish—Abu-Subhi's entire world is confined to his life on the soil of Jaffa.

The visceral rhetoric of blood is used as a metaphor to symbolize victimization and sacrifice. Thus Abu-Subhi stands both beyond history and beyond myth: beyond history because the course of events that he experienced is denied by the Zionists responsible for it, and beyond myth because Abu-Subhi fails to comply with the Palestinian national interpretative and identity-forming framework and can thus find no rhyme or reason in his own story. Between the rock of misrepresentation of history and the hard place of imagined myth, the capacity of testimony to serve as a meaningful text is totally eroded. It has no audience worthy of hearing about the experiences forced upon this storyteller, who remains uncommitted to any political apocalyptic or utopian agenda. The infeasibility of testimony that eludes the symbolic categories that would grant it the quality of a mobilizing signifier turns the words of this witness into an obscure text that can be expressed but not deciphered, because just like the notion of Jaffa itself, it falls short of political signification.

The predicament of the witness devoid of testimony is reminiscent of Shoshana Felman and Dori Laub's[21] assertion regarding the crisis of testimony among Holocaust survivors. Their testimony exposes them to unprocessed trauma that dogs them and reverberates in posttraumatic shockwaves throughout their lives. The disparity between the impression made by the traumatic experience on one's consciousness and the impression of the present prevents memory from working through the testimony, and, in the words of Dominick LaCapra, "The individual returns to there and is present here at one and the same time, and is also able to distinguish between the two."[22] Abu-Subhi is indeed caught betwixt and between: His repudiation of history and of myth prevents him from connecting past to present, which he regards as a prerequisite to be able to bear witness.

⌢

Fakhri Jday, Rabbi Bachar, and Abu-Subhi depict a fractured nationalist standpoint that is constantly eroding, contrary to its exponents' will. From within the collapsing edifice, the narrators are obliged to take up a position between uncompromising declarations that constitute political nationalism and a reality that disrupts the image of the mythical national community. This is also the point at which differences emerge between the national narratives: Whereas Jday's comfortable financial means enable him to cast off the community that he scorns, to barricade himself in a bourgeois and professional ivory tower, and to defend the ideological principles of proud pan-Arabism from there, Rabbi Bachar's vulnerability and material distress force him into a more conciliatory position, which is susceptible to both material and symbolic negotiation. Rabbi Bachar's frame of reference is no longer that of the state, blood and soil, but rather the local community. This narrowing of the frame of reference marks a broadening of the fissure in classical nationalism and his disillusionment with it in the face of the stinging experience of betrayal by the community. Compared with these two men, Abu-Subhi appears more like someone who has dodged the draft into the ranks of the utopian or apocalyptic national project, because he refuses to work through his memories to the point of coherent testimony. The compromises he has made and the trenchant interpretation he offers of the ways of nationalist politics indicate a moral awareness and a critical position that combine to form a romantic perception of local indigenousness. His avoidance of the national subject, thrown into relief by the flexible use of the foundations of his identity, enables him to focus above all on day-to-day survival without relinquishing his position as an observing witness. In this manner he manages both to recreate his own memory of the city he loves and to preserve something of the cultural conception of nationalism that he seeks to pass on to the succeeding generations of his Jaffaite descendants.

PART II

DUSK

(CHAPTER 4)

CIRCUMVENTING NATIONALISM

The Hakim Sisters and the Cosmopolitan Experience

I have never coveted a master's property,
And I have ended up by coveting his servant's servant.[1]
A stanza in a poem often quoted by the sisters' father

Wasim Hakim, a car importer and one of the city's notables, was born in 1898 and died in Jaffa in 1972. In his capacity as a member of the National Emergency Committee, he represented Jaffa's inhabitants in the surrender negotiations in 1948 and thus left behind him a highly controversial legacy. His three daughters—Nadia (a retired deputy consul at the British Embassy), Fadia (a retired teacher at the Tabitha Scottish School in Jaffa), and Ranin (a retired purser at the Scottish School)—live together in a fenced villa that looks out onto the sea, al-Kazakhana Muslim Cemetery, and the recently constructed Peres Peace Center. The sisters share a gender-related story of a class that has withered away from the public sphere but continues to flourish within the domestic sphere. The wall that surrounds their splendid residence marks a symbolic boundary that incorporates them into a cosmopolitan bourgeois culture, one that is not couched in ethnic terms but from which they derive their identity.[2]

The three Hakim sisters are scions of one of the founders of Jaffa's political nationalism. Their ongoing need to contend with their father's legacy dictates the course of their narrative—and life. Ranin, Fadia, and Nadia worked for British-affiliated institutions. The family annals are replete with dramatic episodes of enrichment and loss, war and reconciliation, orphanage, departure, border smuggling, and family reunion. Although the patriarchal head of the family overshadows every sentence, from their position atop the hill the sisters succeed in converting the spirit of the place and the city into a pristine cosmopolitan culture that both straddles boundaries and is "indigenous" (*asliyya*). Their home becomes a bastion, a refuge from the spirit of the times. Yet at the same time it constitutes an *axis mundi*, a starting point for a history of the nation that embraces their childhood and is narrated in a combination of Arabic, Hebrew, and English. The stanza that the sisters suggested as an epigraph for this chapter was always on their father's lips and illustrates their loss but also the vibrancy of a life that continues unabated. According to them, "The poem says that even when you have lost everything and may even end up coveting a servant, don't forget that happiness comes from within, or from the home you grew up in and which fashioned your identity."

We Were Here but Not Here

As the conversation begins, Nadia describes a new year's party to which she was invited. It was held on the twenty-fifth story of a hotel, in the apartment of the British deputy consul. "The place is amazing," said Nadia. "I peered down and felt giddy owing to the great height. We are accustomed to seeing Jaffa from Tel Aviv, but from above it's different. Looking at it from afar, I once again discovered how beautiful is my hometown." The unusual vantage point offers a fresh outlook, both physical and narrative. From the top of the tower that extends beyond the immediate horizon of events, the familiar vista appears different and enables the sisters to recall the upheavals visited upon them by the 1948 war.

> NADIA: In truth, our story begins with the Nakba, because it has impacted our lives since then and to this day. We often say, "Gone with the wind": In the blink of an eye, in one day, everything changed. My father was a successful car importer. He had many friends, and they were all conscientious people who didn't seek only profit. Jaffa and the way it was progressing was important to them. When we left for Jordan in '48—and that's another story—we tried to smuggle across the border and return, but then they discovered us and turned us back. When we finally came back to Jaffa in 1950, we returned to the [Scottish] School. It was the same school, the same structure, but the people had changed. There were Jews from Iraq, Romania,

and Bulgaria. . . . I remember, on the first day we held hands and
gazed about us.

FADIA: We were the only Arab family in the school. We had been there
before the war, but when we returned, all the families were new immigrants from Iraq, Bulgaria, and Romania. We are still friendly with
them to this day. Ovadia Sofer attended the school and graduated. He
was the Israeli ambassador to France. He belonged to that generation.

The elevated perspective serves the sisters as an Archimedean point from
which the familiar yet different panorama is revealed to them, giving rise to
their interpretations of the place, the people who inhabit it, and the actions
they took or could have taken in post-1948 Jaffa.

NADIA: We were here but not here. We all worked most of the time. We
don't speak Arabic outside the home. Outside it's just English or Hebrew, and it's the same with Ranin and Fadia. Many don't know me,
because I go to work at the English embassy, return home, and it's as
if the house is an utterly different city. There is not much mixing with
people. I meet them at weddings, christenings, and at funerals. The people of Jaffa, some of them are not the original Jaffa residents [*ahl Yafa
al-asliyyin*]. Each war transforms the demography of the place.

RANIN: When we were looking for work, they always wanted to know
if we had done military service. That's why we don't work at Jewish
places but rather in private places. I remember that when I was young,
I wanted to be a flight attendant. They asked me, "Did you serve in
the military?" I said no. They pushed the file aside, and I never heard
from them again, and there were many like me.

Upon returning to surroundings that had become foreign to them, the
sisters distanced themselves from the place. As a result of the disruption in
the continuity of community and class in Jaffa and of the limited employment options available, the Hakim family found itself in a liminal position
that prompted them toward the British way of life, to which—much unlike
Abu-Subhi (Chapter 3)—they felt some cultural affinity. This orientation was
manifested in their limited use of Arabic in public and in the narrowing of
their local social networks. They weave a tale of personal history, yet the col-

lective national narrative is clearly vital to understanding the upheavals that the family endured. Lacking a contemporary frame of meaning, the sisters turn to the family's past, to the events that led their father to build his home opposite the Muslim cemetery in 1930.

> RANIN: Nowadays everything has changed. For example, this neighbor-hood was called Jabaliya. They demolished many houses, and only now they are building. This street, for example—I remember that fa-ther built it. There was nothing there. Here was 60th Street, previ-ously called al-Jabaliya. Much has changed since them. There were other buildings here. When my father built the house, they told him, "Don't build there. It is all cemeteries." He said to them, "These are the best neighbors." Subsequently, others began to buy land. The Mansour family built next to your aunt.[3] The Beit Nurit Hospital, an old age home, that was the Mansour family home.

As they dwell on the theme of change, the sisters change their focus from the contemporary urban environment to their pre-1948 neighbors. Be-cause the neighborhood's residents are not part of the Hakim sisters' horizon of relevance,[4] they recount the story of a visit by the Mansour family, their neighbors who left in 1948 and never returned. Yet this memory is clouded and faded.

> NADIA: When Jana and her father, Hassan Mansour, came to us for the first time, in 1997, we sat outside. We are accustomed to people who come, ring the bell, and search for their house. We know them by name only; we don't remember them. The bell rang, and someone asked, "Is this the house of Wasim Hakim?" I said yes. He said, "I am Hassan Mansour." Jana brought them to see where they used to live. They came here, and we sat and exchanged memories. We remem-bered the name but not the person. Hassan Mansour is retired and has time on his hands. He recorded his entire life story and what Jaffa was like, how they left, and how we used to live. We didn't know that at the time. He is older, more aware, and remembered more.

The sisters do not readily invoke collective memory. Keeping their hold on both memory and oblivion allows them to continue leading a peaceful domestic life, whereas the historical memory facilitated from the twenty-fifth story city apartment—where the horizon is clear and nothing obstructs the view—preserves freedom of movement, freedom to construct an identity in between the small and the big place, at once here and not here, now and then.

Father Protected the City

Having portrayed what befell the neighbors who used to be part of their environment, the sisters proceed to trace the figure of their heroic and authoritative father, who took care of his daughters following the death of his wife. Upon the outbreak of hostilities in 1948, Wasim Hakim sent his daughters to Jordan to weather the storm, but he remained in the city "to defend it" (*yihmiha*). Citing contemporary documents, the sisters laud their father's struggle to save the city from total destruction and preserve its status as an open city.[5]

> NADIA: We left before my sixth birthday. I remember exactly how we drove away in a truck, as well as the route. But I don't remember my childhood so well. We intended to travel to a certain location. We had Bahai neighbors, and they had a place called al-'Adasiya. They used to speak about 'Adasiya as an attractive place. They wanted to take us to 'Adasiya. We got into the truck, but along the way they told us, "No, you can't go to 'Adasiya because there is bombing and warfare there." So they changed the route to somewhere else in Jordan.
>
> My aunt took us, and father remained here with his mother and protected the city. He protected the city very well. Wasim Hakim defended Jaffa. They set up a committee and declared Jaffa an undefended city. Otherwise they would have destroyed it completely.

Documents bearing Wasim Hakim's signature as well as his intensive correspondence with Jaffa's military governor, UN representatives, the Red Cross, and the Arab League suggest that he did all he could to prevent looting and attacks by soldiers on the Arabs who remained in the city. The sisters are effusive in their description of the risks that their father took in attempting to come to the aid of the Palestinian survivors in Jaffa, and they recount at length his courage, determination, and resourcefulness in face of the horrors of the city's military occupation.

RANIN: He tried very hard to defend [the city], because all the houses had been abandoned. The mayor Heikal, for example, gave father the key [to the city] and said to him, "Mr. Hakim, I'm leaving for a week to escort the family and then I'll return." He left and didn't return. So father remained here, and they set up the committee, four dignitaries: Barakat, Abu-Laban, 'Abd al-Rahim, and father.[6] They did all they could. He endangered himself in order to protect the public. He went to the French hospital of the nuns to make sure they had flour and vegetables, everything.

When the army entered the city, it didn't know if it would remain, so the soldiers looted and stole. Father would make the rounds of the houses and lock the doors [to prevent looting]. Until they became fed up, and [then] they detained him in his home and placed a guard on him from the military government. He was not permitted to leave the house. His friends would come and talk to him from beyond the fence. Some years ago the soldier who guarded him met my brother and told him that he used to accompany him to the Qahwet al-Tuyus café, and my father would read the newspaper and explain [things] to them, and the guard was obliged to stick close to him. But how contented he was here! My grandma would prepare food for him. Father built himself an oven so he could prepare bread for himself. The guard said to him, "Mister Hakim, it is lunchtime. We should get a move on." Father said to him, "You can go. My mother will feed you. Are you hungry?" He replied, "Mister Hakim, who is the prisoner here? Me or you?"

In the midst of the tumult that descended on Jaffa, the father assumed the role of leader and peacemaker. According to his daughters, he was adept at settling disputes using his wisdom and common sense even at a time of lawlessness and disorder and inflamed emotions. The archival documents dating to the time of war and the subsequent years demonstrate that he did much to prevent looting and the division of the city into an Arab ghetto and a separate Jewish neighborhood. His vocal protest antagonized the armed forces, who broke into his house and stole his car and other property. But he was unrelenting in his efforts, commanding unreserved respect among the vestigial community as a moral authority.

NADIA: He had many stories to tell about that period. At the time, you know, things were in turmoil—people left, lost their children. Once someone brought him a Bedouin boy. They didn't know who his family was. Six, seven years old. And my grandma took him in, fed him, and put him to sleep. Gradually he recovered and began to go outside. You know, a Bedouin boy is accustomed to throw rocks. He grabbed a rock and threw it. There were Moroccan kids outside who were passing by, and the stone hit one of them. The child took fright, went to my grandma, and told her, "I'm hungry. I want to sleep." She thought he was ill. And that night there was turmoil. People came yelling—they rang the bell. My father went out and saw that they were all angry. My father had a way of talking to people, in a soft voice, he never lost his temper. They told him, "You have a kid here who threw a stone and injured our son. We want you to hand him over to us." He told them, "Kids play. Let me find out what happened." They said to him, "We want to see his blood. Like our son was hit, so we'll injure him." He spoke with them graciously and tried to explain that this was an orphan, but to no avail. He told them, "If you want to see blood so bad, injure me and you'll see blood." Eventually he decided what to do. He picked up a piece of iron lying next to him, lifted it like so, and they fled. Sometimes one has to use force against force.

Unlike the daughters secluded at home, the father was a public figure. Yet when the sisters feel obliged to protect the reputation of this man who was so involved in Jaffa's collective story, they touch on the national drama. Thus the traces of the collective story seep through the fissures in the private tale, and a moral that resembles an allegory between the private and the public spheres emerges.

My Father Refused to Go to the Ghetto

The father's strength is likewise manifested in his resistance to the attempts by the occupying power to remove him from his home, his castle. This struggle is documented in an official memorandum submitted by the Arab Emergency Committee to the military governor on August 20, 1948, that protests "the concentration of the Arab population in one area." According to the Hakim sisters, this resistance served as an example to their father's neighbors, who could not pluck up the courage to emulate him.

> FADIA: My father refused to go to the Ghetto. He said, "I won't leave home." We had neighbors. He told them, "Don't leave," but they [the army] took them away and put them inside the fence in 'Ajami. They surrounded all of 'Ajami and didn't allow people to come and go. They did all they could to get him out. They would come at night and shoot in order to scare him. He had sandbags on the roof. He would go up to the roof to watch them firing. He was a character and wasn't at all afraid. And that's how he remained here. He had a room in which he placed sandbags and wooden planks, and there he slept.

The fact that Wasim Hakim managed to evade the explicit order to assemble in an enclosed area of the 'Ajami neighborhood—an area known both to the military officials and to its residents as the Ghetto or the Fence (al-silek)—illustrates both a singular capacity for coping and the connections that Hakim maintained in the administration. The father's uncompromising national loyalty is displayed alongside his cosmopolitan traits, such as his command of languages and his image as a man of the world. Nadia extols his ability to mingle with both Jews and Arabs and to use his stature and knowledge to advantage in the service of the national cause and the general good.

> NADIA: His German was excellent, like his Arabic. He had studied at Schneller School in Jerusalem and was a good friend of Yitshak Chizick of the military regime [Jaffa's first military governor]. You know that all the Jews spoke German. He would listen in on them and hear what they had to say about the Arabs and what they planned to do in Jaffa. Once, in one of the offices, someone came in who knew that he understood, spoke with him in German, and that's how they found out that he knew [the language]. They asked him, "How come you didn't tell us that you understand? We said in your presence things that we shouldn't have said." The Jews often spoke in German, not Arabic. In my father's time, being a liberal, the house was always open to everyone, Jew or Muslim. Conversation and debate were always conducted in a good spirit.

RANIN: Father was very nationalistic [*watani*]—no doubt about it—but he was a good friend of Yitzhak Sadeh, a neighbor of ours, who respected father because he was sincere with him. They would argue. Zvi al-Peleg, who was the military governor of Taybeh, would come to visit, and they would be constantly arguing and talking. [His friends] wished to find out what the Arabs were thinking. It was in a good spirit.

Yet Wasim Hakim's ties with Jews, his familiarity with their ways and customs, and his quest for peace did not protect him against the state, which coveted his property and appropriated his lands—as described by his daughters with some bitterness, albeit ungrudgingly and with no desire to seek revenge.

NADIA: He died in 1972. He remained here to protect our property but didn't manage to preserve much of it. Those who used to work for him and left became millionaires abroad. But he stayed here, because he didn't want to leave. He had an orchard, the best in all Palestine, in Safaria, where [the ultra-Orthodox] Kefar Habad is today. Once he went to look at his orchard—he didn't know that everything had changed there. He drove there one Saturday, and the entire village assembled. They stoned the car and wanted to burn it, because it was the Sabbath. He talked to them, "You should have placed a sign at the entrance to the village that it is prohibited to enter on the Sabbath, just as the Ten Commandments defined what is permissible and what is prohibited. Isn't that what it says?" He spoke with the elderly among them. One of them said, "He's right, he's right, leave him alone. We don't want to burn his car, but don't come back here again."

We Don't Need a Jewish State

The father's nationalist legacy was bequeathed intact to his descendants. The ethnonationalist identities that the sisters refer to merged together in their family and opened up possibilities of identification and loyalty that were embodied in their father's multicultural figure but, given historical transformations, were realized only in the lives of his son and grandchildren. Their world is indeed a mosaic of bonds of affinity that proceed from Palestinian nationalism through Jewish-Israeli citizenship to a belief in "a state of all its citizens." The next generation thus becomes not only the representative of the stand-tall Palestinian generation but also signifies the complexity of the situation and the options available to the members of this group.

We should note that the sisters' niece, the daughter of their brother, espouses the principle of "a state of all its citizens." This principle has been adopted by her aunts, our three storytellers. This is an instance of how the third generation influences the retroactive fashioning of the Nakba generation's memories. The generation of youngsters thus provides a language and discourse that reframe the meaning of the foundational cataclysmic event that the old generation experienced. This is an inverse form of intergenerational cultural transference, in which the young determine the heritage of the old.[7]

> NADIA: He was the only member of the committee to remain in Jaffa. Fakhri Jday's father also stayed, but he wasn't on the committee. Other [upper-class] families began to leave in the '50s. At first things were very difficult for anyone who had children who wished to study or to marry, because there weren't suitable families [for an appropriate marriage]. Barakat left because of his daughters. Anyone who wished to study abroad encountered difficulties. Nowadays it's a little easier; everything's open. Everyone left during the '50s and '60s. We were together with these people at school and at work. Do you understand? My friends are still Jews. There wasn't anyone from Jaffa.
>
> My brother has a daughter and a son. He lives in Jaffa. His son is a lawyer, and his daughter studied to be a teacher. She is very critical of the people of Jaffa. When we meet and we say this or that, she replies, "I don't see that you're doing anything about it." We don't like to say things to shake the world. We keep what we think to ourselves, but she is not embarrassed to express what she has to say. Even the London Jewish Chronicle wrote an article about her. She said, "We don't need a Jewish state." That is, the state should belong to the entire people. She's right. We too think the same.

Like their niece, who does not hybridize identities but meanwhile enjoys the best of both worlds, the sisters adopt a position of almost postnationalist

observers who view the ethnonationalist conflicts from a genuinely humanistic perspective and, by virtue of Nadia's role at the British Embassy, even
a humanitarian one. They are aware of the fluidity of the tag of nationalism
and realize that identities can be malleable things in the hands of those who
seek to match the label of their affiliation to the circumstances of their existence. Their words reflect this stance also when the conversation turns to the
tensions between Christians and Muslims.

> NADIA: Some Arabs have a complex, and they don't like to say that they
> are Arabs. When I have anything to do with the Foreign Ministry,
> they always ask me about the origin of the name. And I always say
> that everyone should be proud of who they are. I was surprised that
> this happened with someone who works in the office, a Christian
> Arab lady. When the greens came to take the paper for recycling and
> bring us bags, she said to one of the workers, "But the Arab guy gives
> us the bags," and he replied, "Arab? Don't say Arab. Say Christian!"
> [both quotations in Hebrew]. She said to him, "What's the difference?
> He's an Arab and I'm an Arab." Today this is changing. How come?
> Is the Christian not an Arab? After all, in England there is a large
> percentage of Muslims who are not Arabs—from Pakistan.
>
> RANIN: There was someone who was at school with us and now lives in
> America. He's an Iraqi Jew, and he says, "I am an Arab Jew. My reli-
> gion is Jewish, but I'm an Arab," because he grew up in Iraq.

Nadia dismisses the difficulty of declaring oneself an Arab as a complex,
a psychological inhibition. When she talks of the Arab Jew, Ranin takes up
the challenge and raises the tone of defiance, as if to say the impossible is
occurring, but only in America. She nevertheless implies a form of cultural
Arabness that can be shared by those of other religions, and, like Nadia, she
stresses that one can and should take pride in it.

Always the Stranger

The upheavals that the family experienced between Jordan and Israel and the
perfidy of collaborators it came across on its travels have dissuaded the sisters
from becoming involved in politics and from making an explicit nationalist

commitment. In this respect they again commend their father's resourcefulness and valuable connections.

> RANIN: We stayed in Jordan for two years and returned in 1950 with the
> Red Cross through Mandelbaum Gate [in Jerusalem]. We tried to in-
> filtrate [*nitsallal*] across the border but didn't succeed. Once we went
> on foot from Tulkarem to Taybeh, half an hour. Father was under
> military rule; he couldn't come to Taybeh, but he took Chizick, who
> was a good friend of his, and told him, "I'll go get the children." They
> drove through the olive groves to get to Taybeh in order to bring us
> to Jaffa. In Tulkarem, the mayor was a good friend of his brother, and
> we stayed there overnight. When we got to Taybeh, not half an hour
> passed before someone informed on us.
>
> NADIA: We weren't smart. We didn't realize that we should dress like the
> locals. We walked around in the middle of the village, and the people
> saw strangers coming. You know, in Taybeh they are something else.
> They immediately went to report. Fadia played hopscotch next to the
> mosque. They asked her, "Is Fahima Hakim [the aunt] here?" She said,
> "I don't know. I'll go inside and ask." They said to her, "Come to the
> police station. Don't you know that Taybeh is in Israel?" She played
> dumb and said, "No, I've just came to visit friends." The police took us
> to the border and sent us back to Tulkarem. It was dark. They could
> have shot at us. Meanwhile my father came to Taybeh with Chizick.
> We missed him by a quarter of an hour. They told him we had been
> there and that they sent us back to Tulkarem. And they say that they
> had never seen him in such a state, because he knew how dangerous
> it was to return to Tulkarem.

The cost of the moves was paid in terms of a weakening of the national
bond, which resulted in a sense of alienation: alienation in relation to the
shiftiness of the components of their identity and their experiences, but
also the alienation of those around them, who could settle down among the
spheres of belonging through which they wandered. In the words of Fadia,
the Scottish School, where they work, like their home, constitutes a liminal
space that is not a part of Israeli cultural territory. It is a place of freedom and
satisfaction, but also one of otherness and exclusion. Among the Arab pupils

at the school this is manifested in the choice of foreign names, which point to a global sphere untainted by Palestinian Arabness.

> FADIA: When we returned, everyone had left. In their stead were Bulgarians and Iraqis, and later came the Romanians and others. To this day we correspond with our [Jewish] friends from the '50s. We were very content at school, but to this day many people think that Tabeetha is in Israel but not in Israel. Like our house, it's the same thing.
>
> NADIA: The bottom line is, you always, always, always feel you don't belong. You are always the stranger.
>
> FADIA: We were the only Arab family [in the school]. My grandfather, my mother's father, was a priest. My father's family is originally from Nazareth.
>
> NADIA: Look at girls' names nowadays: Nancy, Dominique, Crystal, Susanne, Jacqueline. Arab girls, Muslims and Christians.

Yet the alienation that the sisters experience is related not only to their place among others but also, and perhaps primarily, to their mental split between loyalty to the Palestinian national collective and their personal daily involvement with Jews. Nevertheless, by invoking historical memory, they are obliged to take a stand regarding the injustice perpetrated against their people and to reply to a question about the possibility of forgiveness.

> FADIA: As one person to another, I can forgive, but as a group it's very difficult. Religion has a great influence. You know, Christianity teaches us to turn the other cheek, perhaps that influences us. We have Jewish and Muslim friends; there's no difference. But to forgive all the Jews for what they did to the Palestinians, that's hard, not that we do anything about it. Many Jews are the same. They think they can live with Arabs as individuals, but the Jews as a unit say that that's impossible.

The characteristic liberal distinction between the individual and the collective[8] facilitates amicable neighborly relations while clinging to national pride and the perception of Jews as a mirror image: the Jews as individuals and the Jews as a collective category. The sisters are thus able to maintain a pragmatic existence, shunning extreme ideological solutions while leveling internal criticism at the "self-hatred" of the Palestinian minority in Israel and advocating the right of return.

> NADIA: I support the right of return even though it may not be realized—I strongly believe in the right of return. When Palestinians in the refugee camps are asked where they're from, they say "from Jaffa."
>
> FADIA: In the young generation there's an improvement, but for those who are neither here nor there, it's tough.

This generational reference raises the specter of old age, which the sisters are now confronting, and it transpires here that their desire to blur differences and to lower barriers in order to find solace at the end of the day is stronger than the nationalist imperative. Human fraternity is thus supported by memories that celebrate equality and comradeship. When Fadia addresses the coming of old age, she asserts, "It doesn't change. It's all the same. It's not a matter of a Jew or an Arab." Yet Nadia discerns differences: "Arab society differs from Jewish society. I've heard that there are those who bring [caregivers] from Thailand. That didn't used to happen before. If there was an elderly person at home, the family was responsible for caring for them." At this point she corrects her sister, adding the reservation that perhaps all was the same in the past, when Jews looked after their elderly just like the Arabs. She believes that caring for the old is merely a symptom of the differences between Jews and Arabs. According to the sisters, the political and cultural differences might be bridged, but this would require "natural" rather than staged joint action.

> NADIA: We too wanted to change the world. What I can't stand is when they hold Arab-Jewish groups. I find the "coexistence" groups very artificial.
>
> FADIA: It has to come naturally. We are natural without talking about it. We have lots of Jewish and Arab friends.
>
> NADIA: Perhaps one has to do this because many Jews have never met an Arab.

Thus, as they maneuver between the pragmatic and the ideological, between belonging and alienation, and between artificial and "natural," the Hakim sisters carve out a place that exists in Israel but is not Israeli.

Our Jaffa and Nobody Else's

What is the lived experience of that estrangement that wavers between nationalism and humanism? All three sisters have retired from their careers and are on the verge of old age, which is liable to exacerbate their alienation and marginality. The strategy that they use to remain shielded from the irresolvable dilemmas and uncertainty of their estranged position involves inflating their home on the hill, so to speak, so as to encompass and subsume Jaffa in its entirety, and looking at the city in the eyes of their youth.

> NADIA: We've traveled a lot in Europe, but nowhere is more beautiful than Jaffa. Jaffa used to be covered in orchards, and they built projects there. You could smell the orange blossoms. There were orchards on both sides of Yeffet Street, and then when the Jews from Europe came, they uprooted all the orchards and built projects. There were palaces in 'Ajami once. Wonderful houses. The Arabs don't like to live one on top of the other. Everyone wants a house with a garden. And they demolished them, turned them into a mountain of garbage, and then poured everything into the sea. Seventy percent was demolished.

Jaffa is depicted here through a sense of belonging and deep attachment as a private vista of a bygone life. And like many of the sisters' stories, here too the collective tale, despite its ostensive absence, is the pivot that arranges the description of the panorama and underlies the sorrow of destruction. The accumulative destruction of the city and of Arab urbanism has not dimmed their sense of place, which is molded through a personal point of view that refuses to conform to external frames of reference.

> FADIA: I personally do not regret that we stayed. I like living here, like to gaze at the sea.
> NADIA: Wherever we go, we must return to Jaffa. Sometimes we wonder what our life and situation would have been like had we traveled to Beirut in time. But we thank God that we didn't leave. We didn't budge. All those who used to be here are now professors and doctors. But they still come here and don't feel at home there. There is alienation. Sure, we would have studied more. We would have lived a different life. A month ago some family members came here and

searched for their house. We tasted the life outside, but our place is in Jaffa, our Jaffa, as we see it, and nobody else's.

In contrast to Fakhri Jday (Chapter 1), who regrets having stayed in Jaffa and frequently cites the criticism leveled at him by relatives and friends for having done so, the sisters do not regret their decision to stay, but neither do they associate it with the commonly evoked national formula of *sumud*. Their father's role in defending the city is key to understanding the sisters' attitude toward Jaffa as a private sphere that they are forced to share with the city's other residents. As our conversation draws to a close, Nadia seeks to reiterate the difficulty that the members of the National Emergency Committee faced in Jaffa in May 1948 and the following months.

> NADIA: There is one other thing. There is something that many do not understand. In '48 everyone left. There is no strength; there is no one, apart from the committee. The English left immediately on May 14th. Many say that the committee surrendered Jaffa. When people have public responsibility, they have to sit around a table and discuss what's best for them, for their people, for the people of Jaffa. That wasn't easy. There was much negotiating. We have drafts of the documents and letters that my father wrote. They resigned their position because they told the Jews, "You're not keeping up to your promise." "You said that you agree, and the next day all the houses are broken into and damaged." It wasn't easy. There was no surrender [*taslim*], in the sense that they handed over Jaffa [*sallamu yafa*]. They said that the city should have been an open city. There was nothing—no men, no army, nothing. What should they have fought for? They didn't hand it over.

> FADIA: We heard many stories from my father. We are only sorry that we didn't document everything he told us. It was only when he fell ill, I remember that he told us about his life. At that time in summer the Arab families would lock up the house and leave for summer houses, in the mountains, in Beirut. And they thought that that's what would be. The Arabs like to accumulate food. We have a teacher from Safed, a Jew, who was given an Arab house when the war ended, and she says that for months they ate cheese and olives from the home of those who left.

The sisters summon their historical memory to document the actions of their father, who remained loyal to the city. Their account is backed up by original documents that testify to the Emergency Committee's desperate struggle to protect the community's property and integrity. When these attempts failed, Wasim Hakim submitted his resignation from the Emergency Committee to the military governor of Jaffa on July 10, 1948. The document (written in English) states his position in no uncertain terms.

> In spite of all the efforts of the Members of our Emergency Committee and in spite of all the good intentions expressed by your good self and some of your good officials to stop looting, terrorizing, and destructions, conditions in Jaffa are getting worse from day to day. . . . Therefore I cannot see any good of being a member of the Emergency Committee any more and wish to hand over to you herewith my resignation.

We Are Like a Sorority, Like a Kibbutz

Having defined the domestic territory and the family's loyalty toward it, the sisters are prepared to tell us about how they run the household and divide tasks among themselves. The context of the conversation, which was conducted between the sisters on the one hand and a male Jewish interviewer and a female Palestinian interviewer on the other, brings their choice of charged metaphors into sharp relief.

NADIA: There are three of us, but each of us is different from her sisters, like a company. Everyone needs a role in the family.

FADIA: Many ask [about this]. With us it's natural. We keep no scores.

NADIA: Like a kibbutz. Each has a task in which she specializes: the minister of finance is Ranin; Fadia—the social secretary; and poor me—constantly having to make appointments with doctors at the hospital. It's as if they don't live in this world. If they are given a number in a queue and someone pushes ahead of them, they don't say a word. They're out of this world. This is Israel; you have to fight for everything.

FADIA: Nadia is the first woman in Jaffa to get a driver's license. She drives a Land Rover ever since she got a license, and the police constantly stop her. Once father bought us a sports car, a BMW with an open roof. Why did he buy it for us? Because they gave him compensation for land that they had expropriated from him, and he didn't want to keep the money, so he said, "I'll buy the girls a car." They wrote about us in the paper in Hebrew: "Three sisters in a car."

The use of the kibbutz metaphor, the quintessential symbol of Israeliness, might indicate a measure of detachment from the nationalist tensions that subsequently leads to conversion of political capital (expropriated lands) into individual capital (a sports car). Even though the nationalist refrain frames many of their descriptions, the dual discursive move of adopting a key Israeli concept and referring to being liberated of the burden of stolen lands leads the sisters further away from the political domain (land) and the city's general public and closer to the domestic and familial sphere.

The sisters' withdrawal into the home, which is run efficiently and democratically, enables them to conduct a fresh discussion of the emerging mixed city. The vision of the future city sparks a heated debate among the sisters, from which, as a continuation of the liberal approach reflected throughout the conversation, the American model emerges as an example worthy of emulation.

NADIA: What's most important is that they build schools at the same level as that of Jewish schools. But here too I have some criticism: Principals arrive who are not committed to the goal.

FADIA: I don't agree. I think that the schools of the Jews should be open also to the children of the Arabs. They should be allowed to study their religion. That's the ideal. Why shouldn't they study together? Like in America. There are Jews who don't know about our history.

NADIA: That's why we really do need a state of all its citizens. Like in America. Children will then also grow up together naturally.

FADIA: I say that people should live together. Why shouldn't they be equal? There are Arabs who are glad that Jews come to live here.

RANIN: When there are Jewish residents, the town hall takes greater interest and invests more. The Arabs can't go it alone. The Arabs are disorganized [*fawdawiya*], each for himself. But this leads to envy.

The eclipse of nationalist horizons, which are making way for rising local-ism, is manifested in transforming identities and the obscuring of boundaries, as in Nadia's closing story.

> NADIA: I frequently need to take a taxi. A taxi driver once asked me if I was afraid of the Arab neighbors, and then I told him that the neigh-bors were very good. When we arrived, he asked if I was an Arab, and when I said yes, he said, "but for sure a Christian." I said to him, "What should I be afraid of? I've lived here all my life." Some taxi drivers who, if they find out I speak Arabic, they say, "I'm Iraqi, I speak Arabic, but not Arabic like that of the Iraqis, but Arabic like me or you, like that of the Palestinians."
>
> FADIA: All the drivers used to be our neighbors. They all lived here in 'Ajami. Most of the drivers would say, "This is where my mother's house was, and here was my father's house."
>
> NADIA: If I ever write a book, it will be called *My Life as a Taxi Rider.* The taxi stories are amusing. Taxi drivers understand things and observe.

Thus localism and indigenousness enable one to circumvent nationalism and to create a common cultural domain that is at the same time a sphere of con-tention. Nevertheless, the amused reference to taxi stories adds a playful note to the narrative and goes some way to assuage its serious content.

A Story of Three Homes

By contrast to the diasporic discourse of Jaffa as either paradise lost[9] or a di-lapidated ruin, the sisters' home is located in three parallel spheres: the home of the father, which they depict as a nationalist stronghold that he defended and in which he entrenched himself; the autocratic, kibbutz-like matriarchal home; and the Jaffa home that is a local rather than a national home, planted in a city that reflects its image ("Jaffa as we see it").

These three homes converge in the sisters' estrangement, as they do all they can to defend their living and mental space. The integration of the codes borrowed from the British culture, according to which they were educated, and their Arab and gender heritage enables them to adopt an uncommit-ted cosmopolitanism and a cool equanimity that leaves them free to tour the world as they enclose themselves within the protective domestic sphere. The shared household expands into the professions that they follow, which consist primarily of caring for children and citizens in distress. A similar expansion is to be found also in the third home, which spreads its boundaries to include the Jaffaite place according to their perception. This understanding incorporates the city's population with all its nationalist shades and in this respect circumvents its exclusive national identification with the Palestinian territorial project. They indeed maintain amicable relations with their Jewish neighbors, but they are not prepared to forgive the injustice of the Nakba. Over and above their moderate nationalist discourse, they maintain a quotidian routine in which the here and now is suspended from the big time and place. The vacuum between the two is not filled by social networks in their close environment but by ties that nourish the source of their professional and cosmopolitan identity. Between home and nation extends a bourgeois social class sphere that cannot serve as a connecting link between them but likewise does not give way to the Jaffaite ethnonational community or to territorial claims to the place.

In the end, the absence of a big place of myth precludes a discourse of political victimhood and moral culpability, and the liberal distinction between the individual stranger and the collective Other facilitates adaptive conciliation in everyday life. Defense of family honor amounts to lauding the father's exalted stature. Nevertheless, the vitality of the following generation—manifested in the figure of the activist niece—enables the domestic economy of existence to take the place of the nationalist politics of identity, thereby both carrying on and replacing Wasim Hakim's legacy.

In Chapter 5, which relates the story of a Syrian Prisoner of Zion and mother of seven daughters and a son, gender-mediated nationalism undergoes a transformation from an exclusive and confrontational fortified outpost to a family temple in which the good of the children takes precedence over the good of the general national body.

CHAPTER 5

DOMESTICATED NATIONALISM

Nazihah Asis, a Prisoner of Zion

O Zion! of thy captives' peace take thought,
The remnant of thy flock, who thine have sought!
Rabbi Yehuda Halevi, "Ode to Zion"

Nazihah Asis was born to an indigent Jewish family in Aleppo around 1921. She was raised by her grandmother and lacked the means to attend school. At age 16, her grandmother arranged for her to be married to an elderly Lebanese man. The marriage ended in divorce within a few months, and three years later Nazihah was remarried to a neighbor. In 1967 she was arrested by the Syrian intelligence service, accused of aiding in the smuggling of Jews to Israel. She was jailed without trial for two years. In 1978 Nazihah escaped to Israel with her family, and since then she has lived in Jaffa with her second husband and eight children. Upon immigrating to Israel, she was recognized as a Prisoner of Zion and enjoys the attending prestige and rewards.[1] Nazihah's is a tale of successful immigration and realization of female autonomy under the auspices of the state. Her story portrays her husband, who longs for his life in Aleppo and his lost patriarchal stature, in less than glowing terms.[2]

I Have Neither Father nor Mother

Nazihah begins her story by depicting the circumstances of her personal life, which features family distress and lowly status combined with individual enterprise and artistic talent.

MY LIFE BEGAN BADLY. At a young age, when I was 6 or 7, my parents divorced, so my grandma raised me. No father; my mother fell ill. When

Hicham Chabaita

I was 8, 9 years old, I wanted to go to school, but we had no money. So my grandma said to me, "Come, I'll teach you a trade. I have no money. Come and learn a trade." She took me to a seamstress. I learned really well. When I grew up, they married me to someone aged 44 and I was 16, because I have neither father nor mother. After some months I got divorced and returned.

But I have talent. I have a musical ear. I hear a tune and go crazy. I listen to Umm Kulthum, Abed al-Wahab, Farid al-Atrash. Until then I was a seamstress at home. I abandoned the sewing—I said to my grandmother, "I want to buy a violin." The weddings in Syria were separate, men on their own and women on their own. I learned to be with the women. There among the Muslims there are two bands, all are women. A boy of 10 can't enter. In short, that's how it was until I was 25.

As she begins her life story, Nazihah makes no mention of the condition of Aleppo's dwindling Jewish community or of the Zionist ideology that would subsequently change her life. Her second marriage, to Leon the tailor, a neighbor of the family's, was a success. Nazihah gave birth to seven daughters and one son, apparently fulfilling her wishes as a normative Syrian woman. But life had much more in store for her: She describes her recruitment and clandestine activity on behalf of migration to Israel as a chance development that transformed her life.

> MY HUSBAND would bring me work for sewing and come to take it when ready. We were like friends. He is a cultured person, bashful, a jolly good person. He sent someone to ask for me, and we were married. I gave birth to seven daughters. We wanted a son and finally a son was born. Two years before I became pregnant with him, a woman from the neighborhood came and asked me, "Nazihah, do you want to leave?" I said, "I'm dying to get out of here," but I couldn't say in front of my husband that such-and-such families have fled. When he would come at lunchtime to eat or in the evening and we would sit together, we weren't allowed to speak together about families that had left for Israel. He didn't want to go. Above all he was a coward, and then his work in the market was in his father's store, and all those around were his clients. My home was full of meat up to the heavens, but the girls grew. Isn't that a pity [*haram*]?

Nazihah became enchanted with the idea of emigrating because she believed that it was only in Israel that she would be able to find suitable husbands for her seven daughters. Her husband, Leon, however, was apprehensive about leaving his social surroundings and source of livelihood ("above all he was a coward") and forbade her to raise the issue. It appeared that Nazihah had given up on the idea of emigrating, but she was prepared to lend a hand when the opportunity arose.

> ONE EVENING I was outside. It was winter and rainy. Someone appeared with an umbrella, walking slowly. "Are you Nazihah?" I told him yes. He says to me, "Go inside and don't close the door." A thief, a murderer, I didn't know, but nevertheless went in. He entered behind me. He said to me, "I'm Abu-Mahmoud. Esther told me that you wish to leave and your husband does not. Can I see him?" I told him, "He comes at one to eat lunch." The man returned on Friday. I told my husband, "Leon, you have a visitor." He asked him a few questions; he told him, "I'm not interested."

The man said to him, "You're not interested? At least bring two or three girls to take them. There they'll be married." My husband told him, "Not the girls, not me and not the family." He couldn't persuade him.

Two months later he came again, said to us, "There's no hope with you." He asked me, "Can you help me? I met a fellow in Turkey and he asked me to bring his sister to Israel." The sister of the fellow he met in Turkey is a friend of my daughter's. She's also an old woman, and she too has an only daughter here in Israel. Could I refuse to arrange something for her? That's how it began. That was in 1964.

That was the beginning, and it continued until they caught a group on the Turkish border. They interrogated them. They gave my name. My son was 8 months old. They took me for interrogation, underground, and you can imagine what they did to me. I was lucky to remain alive. Thank God I didn't go insane. After two months, I said to myself I have no choice. I told how I got to know Abu-Mahmoud and what I did. They closed the file and moved me to prison.

Nazihah had resolved to help the agent, "Abu-Mahmoud," who had knocked on her door, and to reunite her elderly neighbor with her only daughter in Israel. Just as her desire to immigrate to Israel stemmed from her concern for her daughters' future, so did her initial involvement in smuggling Jews to Israel stem from family sentiments. She was intent on reuniting families, not on the Jewish collective in Aleppo or Israel. She talks of being apprehended by the Syrian authorities as a matter of misfortune, the mirror image of the opportunity that came her way with Abu-Mahmoud's appearance on her doorstep.

I Agitated Against the Government

Nazihah had transgressed the holy of holies of the Syrian regime under Hafez al-Assad and was accused of treason. She made a full confession and was jailed without trial for two years, whereas the agent, Abu-Mahmoud, bribed his way to freedom.

NOT A SINGLE LAWYER would help me, even had I given him all the money in the world. Because I wasn't accused of theft, not of bad things, Heaven forbid, not murder. I agitated against the government. Treason.

They eventually caught the guide Abu-Mahmoud. Four years they searched for him. They took me to the men's prison, and I had a meeting with him. He said, "I don't know her." I said, "What do you mean you don't know me?" In the end he paid a bribe and was released. He was of Syrian origin. He lived on the Turkish border. He has ten children. I helped him. He would give me names all the time and I, *bint al-balad*, a local girl, knew them all, I helped him.

Nazihah's plight did not dissuade her. In jail she once again proved her resourcefulness and cultivated social ties with other victims of the state and even improved her sewing skills.

FOR TWO YEARS someone would volunteer to teach sewing in the prison over the summer vacation. I and the group that got caught were in a room of our own. Three Jews. The [female] commander came in, "Does someone want to learn to sew?" Everyone raised their hands, but in the end nobody learned except me. See how God is great! Once, before I was imprisoned in Aleppo, I went to an Arab neighbor to ask for a cup of oil, and that same commander was visiting. She saw me and called me, "Come, come, Um-Mussa." I couldn't sit with them, because I had to go cook, but she remembered me. The day I entered prison, she eyed me and said to me, "Nazihah, who brought you here?" I told her, "I haven't done anything, believe me." So she took pity on me. She knew I had many children, and I didn't know when I'd be released. In her room there was a sewing machine for anyone who wished to learn. She would lend me the machine twice a week. Children would bring me material, and I would cut. That's how I sewed for two years.

Nazihah was finally released just as arbitrarily as she was imprisoned, without trial and without explanation.

ONE DAY THEY CALLED ME, "Nazihah, you're free to go." I was afraid. I didn't want to leave. They told me, "Get going, get your things ready, get dressed, quickly, quickly." And outside, my children, my husband, friends, like in the movies.

My Clients Were Arabs, Jews—A Mixture

From here on it didn't take long for Nazihah to emigrate. The theme of the paterfamilias's resolute resistance to migrating runs through the story, but Leon was eventually persuaded by the argument regarding their daughters' future.

SO HOW DID I ARRIVE IN ISRAEL? When we celebrated my son's bar mitzvah, the daughters came: one who married in Damascus and another from Lebanon and all the others. Afterward my daughter's Lebanese husband said to my husband, "Don't you know? Everyone is moving out." My husband turned yellow all over, and asked him, "Who did this? I'll go to the *mukhabarat* [secret police] this minute." I told him, "Patience, calm down, what do you want? Do you want your daughters to be taken by Arabs? That seven daughters should go to the Arabs?" He gradually calmed down a little. But the matter was settled.

The meeting was at a *sabil* [public water fountain] in the large park. And we sat and listened to the radio. And every moment another group arrived; they didn't sit beside us. Until the guide came; he had come to our home beforehand—we knew him. We followed him, until we reached the car, without speaking. We drove until we reached Ankara in Turkey.

We were in a hotel in Ankara for three days. Each day someone came from the [Jewish] Agency, asked questions, and registered us. On the Friday they gave us tickets for a plane to Israel. We arrived at the airport, and my sister and my husband's brothers, who were in the country already, came to pick us up. They probably let everyone know. That was in '78. Thank heaven I'm here and thank God.

Nazihah proceeds to tell the entire story as a series of almost fortuitous events, yet a closer reading reveals tension between control and chance. What appears to be a haphazard development is in fact the realization of a scenario that Nazihah had in mind for a long time.

In Israel Nazihah took up residence in Jaffa, where she raised and married off her children. Jaffa was perceived as a suitable place that enabled the Syrian immigrants to live alongside Arab neighbors. She portrays her relations with her neighbors as peaceful and harmonious, thanks to the common Arabic language and her pleasant manner.

> WE SPENT two years and two months in an immigrant hostel until the building in Jaffa was ready. We were the first to enter the building. And how we were honored at the hostel! They gave me the nicest place, and what treatment! The neighbors said, "You have many children and you're a Prisoner of Zion. Of course they treat you like this." They asked us, "Do you want to live in Tel Aviv?" "No." "In Bat Yam?" "No." "Where do you want?" My sister said to me, "Why don't you want in Jaffa? I've lived in Jaffa half my life." Later she moved to Bat Yam. "Say yes, because we speak Arabic, know the language, and are familiar with the mentality." I worked in sewing at home, and my clients were Arabs, Jews—a mixture. Believe me, I have no problems. I have three Arab neighbors. I have one Christian. And you see them with a smile and talk to them in Arabic. Thank heaven, it's a present from God; we have it sweet here, and we understand and know how to talk with them. In Syria we were the only Jews in the whole neighborhood. Once, in Aleppo, the neighbor's son said to my son, who was called Moshe, "You're Moshe Dayan [a famous Israeli general]." I went to his mother and asked her if she didn't mind her son talking like that. He got a good hiding.

Nazihah refers to her status as a Prisoner of Zion as something that earns her the respect of her neighbors and affords clear financial benefits (a 70% reduction in rent and a monthly stipend). She positions herself within Jaffaite society as someone who provides sewing services to Arabs and Jews. Moreover, she has taken advantage of her priestly ancestry to create a further singular position.

> WHEN PEOPLE HAVE PROBLEMS, I bless them. My parents are from the Harari family, Kohens [priests]. At first one of my daughters made fun of this. Her son is studying in Safed at a college. He had an exam and I'm not Moses, but I've heard that a priest's blessing is good. My son couldn't for the life of him move apartments, thank heaven he moved. I blessed him, "My son, don't cry, God is great. You will gradually have a bedroom like you should. Thank heaven. You have an oven, you have a fridge, God is great.

The social role that Nazihah has assumed merges into the communal fabric of life in a manner that places her at the disposal of others and lacks the slightest element of political discord. She resolutely and modestly promotes her programs and secures her children's future. Nazihah has successfully implemented her plan, and all her daughters have married Jews of good standing.

> THE CHILDREN didn't stay in Jaffa; only we did. The daughters don't live in Jaffa, because the husband determines where they live. They didn't all marry Syrians. I wouldn't have minded them marrying Ashkenazis, so long as they were Jews.

The gendered logic of patrilocality dictates one's place of residence, so the daughters have followed their husbands to live in other cities around the country, from Bat Yam to Jerusalem; nor does Nazihah's son live in Jaffa. But to her this is less important than the fact that they have married Jews. Despite Nazihah's declaration that the ethnic origin of her sons- and daughters-in-law is secondary, her children have all married Mizrahi Jews. The family's success, of which Nazihah is so proud, ensures her continued vitality and affirms her gender identity and enhanced status as she enters her 80s. True to form, she stresses that her son makes a good living, having found a "jolly good" trade and married a girl from Aleppo.

> WE IMMIGRATED TO ISRAEL a fortnight after our son's bar mitzvah. At school he refused to study but eventually he learned a jolly good [*'ala keifak*] trade, speedometers. Thank heaven, he has a good salary; he makes ends meet. His wife's parents are also Aleppines. I was in the *ulpan* [Hebrew class] only two months. I was entitled to five months, but my husband fell ill and I had to help out. I can read, but not write. But I think in Hebrew. In Syria I learned from my children to read Arabic and French, just a few words, you know.

Nazihah commands a tone of personal empowerment that emerges from self-sacrifice. Although she was denied the privilege of formal education both in Syria and in Israel owing to her life circumstances, she complements what she lacks in formal education with help "from the children." She has reaped the fruits of her hard labor and sacrifice in the form of successful matches for her daughters, which is the principal yardstick she applies to her motherhood.

I DON'T WANT TO BRAG, but the civility of my children is second to none; they're well educated. We had just arrived—we were still in the immigrants' hostel—and we had a Syrian friend. She said to me, "Come with me this Sabbath. I want to travel to Jerusalem. I have family there." I said, "No, I can't leave my husband." The youngest said, "No, it's better if I stay." The older girl said, "Yes, I'll come." She went with her to our friend's cousin. They played the drum. My daughter stood up, danced. The head of the family was crazy about her. He had a son in the army. He called and said to me, "I want your daughter for my son."

This tale of matchmaking contains all the components that affirm the "good manners" of the Asis family daughters: Nazihah, who refrains from traveling with her friend because of her duty toward her husband; the daughter who enchants her host; and the happy end when the host who calls Nazihah—rather than her husband—to ask for her daughter's hand.

Here, Thank God, It's As If I Had a Father and a Mother

Nazihah traces the story of her life along kinship and gender lines. Having grown up in Aleppo without parents and with no husbands assured for her seven daughters, she has found her place and her home in Israel. Yet her husband, who pines for his friends and his stature in Aleppo, does not share this view and refuses to accept the prevalent permissiveness in Israel.

I FEEL BETTER IN JAFFA. If they were to say to me, "Take a bag of gold and we'll buy you an apartment in Syria," I'd refuse. When I hear Syria, I tremble. There I didn't have one clear day because I had seven daughters. Excuse the language, but there wasn't a dog that wouldn't knock on the door and say, "Do you have a girl for me?" Here, thank God, it's as though I had a father and a mother. In Syria the Jewish girls were fearful lest the Arab boys approach them. Here we feel as though it's our home. In Syria they used to cry. Here I have someone who comes to clean twice a week. Thank God, the Jewish Agency recognizes me. What more do I need? All my daughters have married. I have eight families, may they be healthy. What do I want of my life? I am 81 and a half years old.

But my husband isn't happy here. He wants Aleppo, his clients. He's always talking about how Abu-Jamil would bring him tea with the wagon each morning, for him and his clients, how people liked him in the neighborhoods. And I say, Let stone upon stone upon stone fall on Abu-Jamil and on them all. It bothers him here that he's not in command and also that he sees girls who wear shirts that reveal their tummy and kiss in the street, and he comes home agitated. What do we care? Let them go out naked—we don't care. My kids grew up with respect.

The narrative is not entirely devoid of nationalist vocabulary. Nazihah declares that she is willing to sacrifice herself for the general good in order to repay the state for its generosity. Before Syria and Israel gained their independence and enmity, Nazihah would visit her relatives who had left Syria and immigrated to Israel. But she was deported back to Aleppo because her cousin's wife felt that Nazihah was threatening her marriage.

I AM A ZIONIST HEART AND SOUL. I would die for the government.[3] I wanted to come for twenty-five years. My sister left Aleppo in 1942 and came here—what can I do? I wanted my sister, and I would weep. I was with my parents in '43. There was no Syria then yet. On every holiday they would come to us to spend the holiday in Syria and return here. My cousin wanted to bring me to the country. He came to Syria, the holiday ended, and he asked me, "Will you come with me?" I said, "I have a mother. I have a grandmother. I support them. I can't." He said to me, "Come see what your sister does. Every day here there is joy. She sings, she dances." I came to visit in '43, with my cousin. But his wife thought that I wanted to take him and marry him and informed on me. There was no state as yet, and they took me to prison here in Jaffa, because I came on foot without a passport. Then they put me in another place, and later transferred me to Syria.

Nazihah's slightly risqué relationship with her cousin adds a level of complexity to her map of loyalties: For a moment she wavers between one part of her family (her mother and grandmother) and another (her sister and cousin). It appears that, had it been entirely up to her, she would have preferred the sister and cousin. She dismisses the informing, prison, and deportation back to exile in Syria, however, as an inconsequential episode.

Like Rabbi Bachar (Chapter 2), who celebrates the patriotism of the supporters of the Maccabi Jaffa, Nazihah defines herself as "a Zionist heart and soul." In both cases nationalist-Zionist loyalty is perceived through a mediating object: the soccer club or the family. When Nazihah expands on what she means by "Zionist," she speaks of her desire to reunite with her sister, who had emigrated some thirty years before her. Her longing for Zion—like her motivation for engaging in the smuggling of Jews—is embedded in family sentiments rather than in a willingness to join the national project.

Whenever I Hear a Beautiful Singing Voice, I'm Moved

Toward the end of the conversation, Nazihah sums up the course of her life and her professional choices. The figure emerging from her story is that of a resourceful and courageous woman determined to improve her status in life. While still in Syria, she took advantage of her talent for playing music and singing to improve her financial situation and to enhance her independence. Although she continued to perform after she married, her musical career ended with her immigration to Israel.

MY CHILDHOOD WAS A DIFFICULT ONE. That's my strongest experience. My mother married, and after a few months was beaten by her husband. She delivered a son in the eighth month, took it to heart, and became paralyzed at the age of 28. I was just a girl; my grandmother raised me. I had an uncle who married me off at the age of 16 to a Lebanese man. But I came back from Lebanon to Aleppo. I wanted a good life. I worked for twenty-five years. I used to play the violin in Arab festivities. I used to sing. I had a good voice. I was very happy. I did what I liked. When an Arabic film would come out, I would go every day to learn the song. That's what swept me along. I gave up sewing and learned to play. There are girls who took two years to learn, but it took me three months. Also, after I married, I continued playing perhaps twenty years. I sold the violin before I came to Israel. I couldn't take it with me. Now I don't have the energy to play, as much as I love it. To this day, whenever I hear a lovely singing voice, I'm moved.

Yet Nazihah's financial independence and the capital she accumulated were taken up by the family. She gladly exchanged the spirit of freedom she enjoyed between her divorce from her first husband and her second marriage for the security of the family nucleus. Afterward, she would dutifully give most of her earnings to her husband and invest a small portion in her children's education.

> WHEN I WAS YOUNG, I would perform and also give private lessons. I didn't intend to remarry. I was happy. I earned a gold coin every night! And after I married again, I would get 33 Syrian liras. I would take 3 liras and give my husband the 30. With the 3 liras I taught my children.

I Call Myself a Hero

As a Jewish woman who maintains herself well by dint of a state allowance, Nazihah adopts a stoic and calm narrative that starkly contrasts with her grumpy husband's rigid outlook, expressed in his distaste for Israeli culture. With her characteristic tone of acceptance, she explains why "my life is not hard in old age."

> I'LL TELL YOU SOMETHING. My true nature, I call myself a hero. If something happens to me, I wait; I accept it patiently. If I can solve the problem, I solve it. I reach the solution patiently. I don't care how long it takes. I don't take much to heart. I'm patient. Because of that my life is not hard in old age.
>
> In the past, my husband used to really get to me. He would be very difficult. I wouldn't answer back, only listen; it's forbidden to answer back. He was very agitated. I would get angry, as if I was fainting, become agitated. And now I answer him respectfully. He wanted a son? I gave him a son.
>
> The happiness in my heart, if I'd share it out to people, would be enough for them all. My greatest joy is that I've come to Israel and that I'll die here. And people I had sent to Israel died here. That's a good deed that nothing can compare to. Who gets to die in Israel according to the Torah? That's why I'm not afraid to die. May God only grant me three days before death that I'll be *wa'iya* [Arabic for "alert"], with my wits together, not senile. I hope I won't fall, that I won't be bedridden. May God give me what I deserve. That's enough for me. There in Syria there's no

Agency, no National Insurance. I used to save money, and anyone in need, I'd give. In Syria someone who has nothing is as good as dead.

Nazihah longs to be buried in Zion. This mitzvah (religious duty), which she has also accorded others, establishes her as a righteous and devout Jew, protecting her against the finality of death and connecting her to the big place that has become a family site. From this perspective, the return to Zion is not a nationalist project but rather the privilege to join her ancestors and to die with dignity and in a way that was not possible for her in Syria. In light of this great privilege, Nazihah ends her story in the calm tone of someone who is prepared for what awaits her, sealing a narrative of multilayered metonymy in which the personal sphere is also the family one, and where the family is the nation, although the national domain does not encroach on the personal space.

Maternal Nationalism

Nazihah's primary commitment is to her nuclear family. The Zionist narrative dissolves in her story and acquires the form of a kinship ideology articulated in gender terms. If it exists here at all, nationalism serves Nazihah as a mere cover. Nonterritorial poetics constructs a sphere that extends in Nazihah's tale from family to neighborhood and to her Jewish and Arab clientele, without pausing to consider the sources of strife in the city. Jaffa space is presented as an enabling environment that facilitates the individualization of neighborly relations into an exchange relationship. In Nazihah's discourse the national logic loses its autonomous existence, becomes contained within gender and familial logic, and is controlled by codes of kinship. The symbiosis between nation and kinship locates Nazihah and her children in a multigenerational framework empowered by her special status as a Prisoner of Zion. Nazihah's husband, who eschewed this ethos and who migrated to Israel unwillingly, has paid a double price for his enforced immigration: He has lost his patriarchal status and is excluded from the collective identity that now embraces his wife and children. Nazihah's domestication of nationalism, like the domestication of religion by the Jerusalemite widows described by Susan Sered,[4] endows her with power and control over her life. Nevertheless, it turns her into a de facto matriarch who oversees the running of the house-

hold, keeps the family together, and marries off her children while practically
ignoring her husband.

This household, which is nourished by the nation's aura and resources,
can be considered a branch of the national home. In the reality of Jewish
Jaffa, in which national heroes are thin on the ground, this is an uncommon
phenomenon, and thus the title Prisoner of Zion constitutes a multipurpose
and valuable asset. Yet Nazihah's glory is not fully bequeathed to her descendants. Because of their country of origin, their ethnicity, and education, even
the mother's status does not enable them to join the bourgeois Ashkenazi
elite beyond Jaffa. This Prisoner of Zion thus remains alone in her glory, confined to the backyard of Israeliness, having no genuine claim to the symbolic
capital of the collective whose title she carries and upon whose generosity she
relies. She understands this and therefore sanctifies the family in the name of
the nation rather than vice versa. In her old age Nazihah is doubly rewarded:
She has rid herself of her husband's tyranny and has been able to establish
the lives of her children as Israelis whose identity is not dependent on an
existence in Jaffaite marginality, which is foreign to Zionism's political core.

Scholars of feminist and critical literature on the relations between nationalism and gender describe a persistent pattern of subordination of motherhood
and femininity to the ideology of national fertility. Nira Yuval-Davis, for example, defines nationalism as a gender project that generates a political order
in which women are bearers of the collective.[5] Shoham Melamed traces the
foundations of the Israeli national fertility policy to the 1950s, when it shaped
a pattern of worthy motherhood against the backdrop of the so-called demographic threat, a euphemism for the higher birthrates of non-Jewish women
in Israel.[6] Rhoda Kanaaneh similarly asserts that Palestinian women of the
Galilee "birth the nation" in gender discourse and practice as a strategy of
resistance to the Israeli Judaization project.[7] Palestinian children are presented
as key actors in the demographic economy of the Jewish-Arab dispute. In
these studies it is the citizen-mother who obeys the gender imperative to
produce citizen-soldiers, warriors in the service of the nation. Women who
operate within the private sphere are akin to secret agents whose participation
in the national demographic project is a necessary condition for its success.

Contrary to this ethnopatriarchal archetype, Nazihah's story collapses
the hierarchical relation between nationalism and motherhood by equat-

ing the Prisoner of Zion with Zion. Here it is Nazihah who uses the nation's resources for the good of her children and her relatives, no less than the nation benefits from her and her children. In this respect, Nazihah's position does not accord with the thesis espoused by the feminist scholars of Israel's reproduction policy. These scholars trace a pattern of distinctly hierarchical relationships between the state and the ambivalent recruitment of the fertility of Mizrahi women in the interest of the national cause, despite the "danger of Mizrahi expansion" that this entails.[8]

Nazihah's life story, which is related as a narrative involving gender, family, and tribe, does not regard the state or the nation as a lofty goal but rather as an obvious, almost natural tool to be used by the family. She interprets the relationship between citizen and state in the context of a gift economy and perhaps even as an element of the relation with a generous giving environment that unconditionally bestows its bounty.[9] The transformative power of this female narrative is located in the ability of the private sphere—in which Nazihah reigns supreme—to serve as a window onto the public sphere without compromising itself. Nazihah's status as a national hero allows her to unite three narrative strands of a single heroic tale: the heroic act itself, the nationalist-Zionist truth that it represents, and the female empowerment derived from it. As Tania Forte notes, "Heroes, even of the nationalist kind, are not produced in 'standard' nationalist narratives, but rather in the context of everyday life, in local social practices and conversations, in coexisting power struggles over the meaning of actions, purported truths and the legitimacy of histories."[10]

Because Nazihah is the figure who actively led the family's migration and because she has been recognized as a Prisoner of Zion and is now the principal breadwinner, her criticism of the gender order is leveled not at the state but rather at her husband, who represents the old patriarchal order, whom she accuses of cowardice and gratuitous inflexibility. Because Nazihah belongs to Israel's hegemonic Jewish majority, the merging of the state and motherhood can proceed fairly smoothly, and she is not required to shatter foundational myths or taboos. As we will see in the next chapter, for Palestinian women unable to fall back on such an institutionalized national status, this criticism requires far more forthright sacrifice and defiance.

CHAPTER 6

DISSOLVED NATIONALISM

Subhiya abu-Ramadan

and the Critique of the Patriarchal Order

That's who I am today. My hair is full of gray.
I'm an old woman. Today . . . I'm just living.

Marjorie Shostak, *Nisa*

In 1948 Subhiya abu-Ramadan was a girl of 14. She was forced to marry during the war because her family feared that the Jewish conquering forces would defile the honor of the young girls. Subhiya was born in a small well house (*biyara*) in Tel al-Rish, a Palestinian village that later became part of the Tel Giborim (Hill of the Heroes) neighborhood in Jewish Holon. Her parents were indigent tenant farmers who leased land from the al-Khalidi family; they sold their produce at the Jaffa marketplace. Her family had to relocate during the war to Jaffa city, where Subhiya was married and bore six children. After losing her husband and marrying his brother, Subhiya lived in Lydda for thirty years, bearing five more children. She was widowed again and returned to live by herself in Jaffa. Her story is a fascinating illustration of the link between political turmoil and oppressive patriarchal forces, shedding light on the welfare state's transformative potential in the life of a strong woman fighting for her family. We interviewed Subhiya in her home in the ethnically mixed Jerusalem Boulevard area. She was surrounded by her grandchildren, who were staying with her following her son's arrest.[1]

Subhiya abu-Ramadan grew up in Abu-Subhi's world (see Chapter 3), in which tenant farmers were totally dependent on their masters. Theirs is a story of patriarchal nationalism and the subaltern classes in Mandatory Palestine. Subhiya's narrative furnishes justification for a subversive perspective; she is unafraid to accuse Palestinian men of cowardice, hypocrisy, and treason, manifested in their collaboration with the Jews and leading to national calamity. She defines her identity in terms of utilitarian citizenship, the benefits of which she contrasted with the failure of Palestinian nationalism and its empty slogans, as she sees them.

Like Nazihah Asis (Chapter 5), Subhiya is positioned between the big place of collective myths and the small place of the individual's daily reality. From the confines of the domestic sphere, she fearlessly faces up to the terrible price she paid for the decisions of the men in charge of family and nation. In this narrative, so exceptionally caustic that it even angered the members of her family present at the interview, she dismisses several of the fundamental principles of Palestinian nationalism and feistily reveals the personal advantages entailed in the status of an elderly single woman on welfare in Israel.

I Was Maybe 14 When the Jews Arrived

Subhiya starts her life story by referring to local history as she recalls it. In her description, the fate of the land was sealed by the negotiations between the British and the Zionist forces, which took no account of her own people. The political and human implications of these relations—in which a colonial agent serves as the representative of the conquering power, or surrogate colonialism[2]—does not elude Subhiya, who nevertheless refers to it casually and uncomplicatedly.

> WE USED TO LIVE in Tel ha-Giborim [sic], in Tel al-Rish. In 1948, the Arabs called the place Tel al-Rish, and the Jews called it Tel ha-Giborim when they entered from Bat Yam. I was little then. The English ruled Palestine for 33 [sic] years. They gave the Jews the Balfour Declaration, and later they began to hand the country over to them "bit by bit" [in Hebrew].
>
> I'm 68 years old perhaps. I don't know exactly what year I was born. I was maybe 14 when the Jews arrived, and I got married in that year, '48. I remember the English after the Balfour Declaration: When they began to evacuate [the country], they brought boats. After all, they wanted to fulfill the Balfour Declaration! They promised it to the Jews here 200 years ago! This story began 200 years ago. Let's say I promised you some-

thing 200 years ago. Let's say I promised to give it you this year. So I want to keep the promise. That's what the English did.

Like Abu-Subhi, Subhiya clearly differentiates between three spatial-social categories: the urban area, farming land, and the *birawi*. The *birawi* were the farmers of the plain near the big city; they inhabited an area that was neither urban nor rural and defined themselves as a distinct group. Unlike the villages in the Galilee and other areas, which were composed of large *hama'il* (clans) and had a centralized economy, the families of Tel al-Rish were small and indigent and constituted the lowest tier in the citrus orchards' division of labor. The top of the pyramid was occupied by the Jerusalemite al-Khalidi family, whose local representative was a civil court judge.

> MY FATHER WORKED IN AGRICULTURE. We would plant vegetables and sell them in Jaffa. But we weren't fellahin [peasants]. The difference is that fellahin make a living from farming in a nonurban area. This is an urban area, not an agricultural area. Jaffa is a city. My father used to grow vegetables and sell them at the market. They used to call us *birawiye*, people of the village. We made a living from farming on the plain; we didn't live in the city. But we weren't fellahin either. That's something else.
>
> The land was owned by the al-Khalidi family. During the war all the landowners left for Beirut. Khalidi was a great judge in a civil court. When he passed a heavy sentence on someone, ten years say, fifteen years, he would break the pen after signing the sentence. He would say, "The pen sentenced him, not I." It would hurt him, but he continued to mete out justice. When someone was acquitted, he would stroke his beard contentedly. He had white hair and a beard down to here. He was a judge in Jaffa and lived in Tel al-Rish. His house was demolished.
>
> I once went to visit the place where I was born. The house is still standing, and the helmets of the Arab troops are still strewn in the empty pond. Iron helmets, to this day. Jews live below, and the upper part is partly destroyed. They produce shutters there. It's good to bring up memories.

The respect for the powerful by the simple folk is manifested in Subhiya's description of the judge, but she depicts this authoritative figure in the past tense. Subhiya does not elaborate on what happened to the judge in and after 1948, but she notes that his house was demolished, whereas her house is still standing. Contrary to Abu-Subhi and Fakhri Jday (Chapter 1), the proximity of destruction and construction, of presence and absence, does not seem to leave a traumatic impression on Subhiya, and she even cherishes the memories of the past that emerge from the rubble.

All Our Neighbors Left Except Us

The battle for Tel al-Rish broke out on April 28, 1948, as part of a Haganah operation designed to empty the area of Arab paramilitary forces east of Jaffa and besiege Jaffa from all sides. The Jewish forces sought to capture the former British fortified post (pillbox) on the hill, which offered a commanding view of traffic from Jaffa to Jerusalem and to the south of the country. By that time, most Arab villages in the vicinity had already been captured.[3] Subhiya describes the battle as she had experienced it from within her home.

IN THE '48 WAR we were close to Bat Yam. We stayed put, and the shells reached our home. In the lemon orchard next to our house the shell would hit a tree, uproot it, and make a crater in the earth. Some Arab soldiers fought, but there was no army to speak of. All our neighbors left except us. The Jews captured the water tower that the Arabs had built and fired on us. There was a group of Arabs who collaborated with the Jews. They would supply [the fighters with] bullets filled with fake powder. That was treason.

Subhiya's sense of betrayal is not confined to her collaborating neighbors, however. Its ripple effect extends far beyond Jaffa, and the disgrace of defeat is placed squarely on the shoulders of the perfidious Hashemite king.

WHEN THE ENGLISH CAME to hand over Tel al-Rish, they brought Jews along with them. They wandered about all the houses to check that they were empty, and no one reacted. They entered as if you were coming into your own home—all the houses were empty. The English army handed the place over to the Jews, got onto the trucks, and drove off. Meanwhile, Abu-Laban and Abu-Zir signed Jaffa's surrender agreement. Abu-Zir lived behind our house. He was the commander, an officer in the Arab army. We didn't think of him as a traitor for having signed, because there was no one to stand by him. It was the ones on the outside who betrayed. After all, an army from Jordan and from Syria arrived to defend Palestine. I saw them at Tel al-Rish. They had identifying marks: a red keffiyeh [headdress] for the Jordanian army and a black keffiyeh for the Syrian army. But they didn't attack. And what did King Hussein [Subhiya means King Abdullah] do in the end? They came and went. When they didn't find the locals, for whom should they fight? The locals had left.

There was fighting in Lydda and in Ramleh, but King Hussein helped the Jews. What did King Hussein do? He dressed the Jews in a keffiyeh and 'aqal and said, "Here's the Jordanian army come to fight with you." The Jews knew that this was a Jewish and not a Jordanian army. They entered. How could the Arabs make a stand? In Lydda there was fighting and many Arabs died. My brother-in-law was shot there and died. In Jaffa there wasn't. The Jews began shooting into the air. They said, "The Arabs are broken." They removed their keffiyehs, and it turned out they were Jews. This is the betrayal by King Hussein.

Once the village had been conquered and the Abu-Ramadan family lost its source of livelihood, its members went to live in an orchard adjacent to the Coptic monastery in Jaffa. In retrospect, more than fifty years after the event, Subhiya justifies the move to Jaffa as a natural step ("This is our city"), yet at the time the move signified the dire distress suffered by the most disadvantaged section of the population, for whom even fleeing was not an option. Anyone who could leave the city did so, but Subhiya's family stayed behind.

WHEN THE ARABS LEFT, the houses emptied out and no one remained. We went to the Coptic monastery [Deir al-Aqbat] in Jaffa. We loaded the donkeys and the wagons with what we had, and we all moved here. No one remained; they all left for fear of the shooting and the bullets. There was no one to fight; anyone who remained there was dead. We came to Jaffa because this is our city. We can't live anywhere else, here it's our city. I lived in Lydda for a time. When my husband died, we didn't bury him in Lydda; we buried him in Jaffa. Everyone who had money left first; only the poor stayed behind. There was hardly enough to eat. There was no money.

We rented from them an area beneath the monastery. There was an orchard there and a few huts, not good stone houses. We stayed in the orchard and began to grow vegetables. Life was hard. When the Jews came in to do a population census, they enclosed all the Arabs and began to count. They would enter a house and ask, "How many are you? How many children?" They would ask and make a record in order to issue identity cards.

Subhiya's first encounter with the state took place in the course of the general population census conducted on November 8, 1948. To carry out the census, officials imposed a curfew on all the country's residents from 5 in the afternoon to midnight. Fourteen thousand counters sent by the Central Bureau of Statistics went from house to house and registered all those living in them. For the Palestinian citizens of Israel this census was of crucial importance, because their presence or absence within the new state's borders sealed their fate for better or for worse. All members of the Abu-Ramadan family were fortunate enough to receive identity cards and food vouchers. For Subhiya, the encounter with the governmental logic also signified unprecedented gender modernization, presaging radical transformation in the status of the Arab Muslim woman.

LIFE WAS HARD. Every Thursday they would hand out meat. They gave us white bread and dark bread. Two loaves per family. Two liters of milk per family, a kilo of rice, macaroni, spaghetti, simple things. When the Jews arrived, first they made a census. When they came to count in our house, the women covered their faces with a black veil. The officer turned to my father, and what he said was true. The officer said to my father, "Hassan, listen to me, now they are veiling themselves?" My father told him, "It is our custom that they are not allowed to go out uncovered." The officer laughed and told him, "In a few years' time, they'll go out with nothing on." My father said to him, "There's no way a woman will go out bareheaded; whoever goes out, I'll slaughter her." The officer said to him, "You'll see, Hassan, in a few years' time they'll all go out bareheaded. You'll see your wife, your daughter-in-law, and your daughter—they will all go out with their hair bare." He spoke in Arabic, and it turned out that he was right.

They Defiled the Girls at Deir Yassin!

The gender concern is augmented as Subhiya continues to unfold her tale. In the wake of the Deir Yassin massacre on April 9, 1948, and its resonance in the press, the Palestinians in Jaffa widely believed that the Jews were defiling the honor of women (*kharrabu al-banat*) in the settlements that they had overrun. Consequently, there was a countrywide epidemic of hastily arranged marriages of young girls whose male relatives were anxious about their family's honor.[4] This was how Subhiya was married to her first husband, her cousin; and when he died, she was married to his brother according to the custom of levirate marriage. On the personal level, family honor explains the particular weight of the patriarchal yoke Subhiya was compelled to bear.

> MY HUSBAND'S SISTERS, who now live in Khan Younis, were here, but left in '48. What scared the Arabs? When the Jews entered, they passed through Deir Yassin, and that's what frightened the Arabs. They were scared they would come and slaughter us and would defile the girls. They defiled the girls at Deir Yassin! They massacred youngsters and killed mothers and fathers. We in Tel al-Rish heard about the Deir Yassin massacre on the radio. The Jews had not yet received everything and they entered village by village. The Jews filled trucks with uncovered girls and roamed around 'Ajami. They passed behind the orchard, where we lived, in order to scare the people, and anyone who had daughters, married them off—even at the age of 12 or 14—so that the Jews wouldn't enter and defile their honor. The Jews defiled many girls.
>
> I got married at the age of 14. We didn't hold a wedding. There was a war going on. We feared the Jews; we feared they would abduct the girls! Anyone who had a daughter married her off. They wrote a marriage contract and that was it.

The feminine experience of life overshadowed by war and the day-to-day struggle that followed its aftermath is mediated by the domestic sphere. When living in her father's home in Tel al-Rish, Subhiya worked in the field and also took care of household chores. Her father denied her and her sister, but not their brother, the opportunity of formal education. Subhiya recalls this discrimination in terms of harsh patriarchal domestic violence.

WHEN WE WERE IN TEL AL-RISH, the boys studied at the *kuttab*. Nowadays there's nothing like that. My brother also studied at the *kuttab*, and
after the world went upside down in the war, he went to [the private]
Tabeetha School [in Jaffa]. They studied in the *kuttab* for four, five years.
They would spread a mat on the floor and teach them Arabic and arithmetic. After school, my brother would come home and teach me and my
sister all he had learned. And then he would beat us up, even though he
was smaller than us.

When I was little, I dreamed of learning to read and write. It's hard for
me when I go to a bank and I have to ask someone to write me a check.
I say to someone, "Excuse me, could you write me a check" [in Hebrew].
Then they laugh and I say to them, "My parents are to blame. I'm not to
blame. They didn't let me go to school" [in Hebrew]. They didn't want
girls to study. They would say, "Better she doesn't study, so she won't have
a boyfriend." See those crazy people! Before the state was established, they
didn't send the girls to study. Girls would learn to sew and things like that.
When I told my father that I wanted to study, he beat me.

For me, life was the teacher. If I had been the way I am now back
then, neither my father nor my brother would have controlled me. I
would have gone to study despite them, for sure. Now my head is developed: Why didn't you let me study? What do you care? Had I brought a
boyfriend, they would have been entitled to say something. They beat us
badly. They had cows; if we didn't bring food for the cows, they would kill
us with blows. We lived a very hard life.

In the End He Had Neither Land nor Honor Left

In reference to the events of 1948, the language of gender and family mediates the subsequent discussion of the possibility of returning to the village.
Subhiya attributes the fact that the family continued to live in rickety huts
near the Coptic monastery rather than squatting in comfortable and elegant
houses, as so many Jews and Arabs did in the aftermath of the war, to the
cowardice of her father, who "went to live in a grave."

ONCE I WENT TO TEL AL-RISH to see the place where my father used to
tie up the cows. Moroccan Jews now live there below. Once I went, and

they made me coffee, I sat with them. I told them, "I was born here" [the entire conversation with the Jews is related in Hebrew]. They laughed and said to me, "Welcome." I don't know how long they had lived there, but I wanted to see what happened to the house after we had left. I entered the place where my father used to tie up the cows. There are stakes there driven into the ground to which he would tie the cows. And then they called out to me, "Lady, Lady, what's this?" I said, "My father drove these in. He used to tie up the cows here." They asked me, "What is this wall for?" I said, "Here he used to put food for the cows." It pained me. Your place of birth is half of you. I recalled the days when I was a little girl in the orchards, and how I worked the land with my sisters, and how none of the neighbors remained, and how everything was destroyed. It hurts.

Subhiya makes a distinction between her parents' home, to which she clings as a place of yearning, and the combination of patriarchal violence and political naïveté displayed by her father. She exonerates the new Jewish tenants of any wrongdoing, as they too were victims of historical events outside their control.

IF THEY'D GIVE ME THE CHANCE NOW, I would renovate the house and live in it. Would it were so. But they didn't let me. Had my father remained in the house, we could have stayed, but my father's crazy. He went to live in a grave. It's a pity. We would have stayed. The Jews wouldn't have driven us out. If someone was already living in a house, the Jews didn't say to him, "What are you doing here?" [spoken in Hebrew]. You could have entered and lived in any house you wanted. Even the houses of the rich, whatever you like. Jews and Arabs alike entered in this way. My father's crazy. He went to live in a grave. In the end, we remained in the monastery for over twenty years. My family moved out of the orchard not so long ago, in '75.

We also had Jewish neighbors in the orchard, and we had excellent relations with them. No matter that they're occupiers. After all, the owners of the houses left the houses and fled. The owners of the orchards left the orchards and fled. And we have nothing, and we didn't have any quarrel with the Jews who arrived. When we came to Jaffa, all the houses were empty. You could have entered the grandest palace. Open the door, go in, and the Jews wouldn't ask you any questions. The Jews wouldn't drive you out. They didn't know who the house belongs to. They didn't ask for the deeds. You would say, "This is my house!" They registered everything on a clean slate. We stayed in the Coptic monastery as tenants, with nothing. All because of my father, the coward. He was crazy. In the end he had neither land nor honor left [*la ard wa-la 'ard*].

The cowardice and lack of good judgment Subhiya attributes to her father are compounded against the backdrop of his dominance at home and in her early life. She interprets her father's response to the arbitrary historical events as an impromptu reaction driven by his feeble character, and she blames him for having left his family destitute. By using a dramatic inversion as she blames the victim, Subhiya places responsibility squarely on her father rather than on the perpetrator.

Why Did They Leave? They Shouldn't Return!

Subhiya abu-Ramadan's uncompromisingly critical standpoint extends to other facets of Palestinian life in Israel, to the point of even challenging the uncontested Palestinian right-of-return narrative. Rather, the part played by the state in the life of an elderly woman in Jaffa is illuminated in a complex and problematic light. Even though one can read this narrative as a story of Subhiya's surrender to the dictates of the state, such an interpretation would rest on the assumptions characterized in the Introduction as methodological nationalism. In its stead, we analyze Subhiya's story against the backdrop of her personal life story, the gender and class exclusion that she endured throughout most of her life, and her sense that "the Arabs left us to be humiliated" (*tarakuna la-lbahdala*). The accumulated failures of the identity agents responsible for Subhiya's marginal position feed into her distrust of Palestinian nationalism, which she regards as a false promise on the part of collective Arab masculinity—a mirage largely irrelevant to her individual status and life as an independent woman. Her disappointments and disillusionment have led her to discard every substantive or even declaratory vestige of loyalty and empathy toward her dispossessed countrymen.

THE PALESTINIANS WHO LEFT JAFFA don't deserve to return here. I'll tell you why. Had I left—and there are people older than I who left—God knows where I would have ended up, in Jordan, in Syria, in Libya. But where did I give birth to my children? Let's say I'd have gone off and left my home and borne six, seven kids. I gave birth, my children are there. "Why on Earth" [in Hebrew] should they ask to return? Return where? Do they know where my house is? Even my relatives in Khan Younis, let them stay there. Why should they come? Did they not buy houses and settle there? Even in a refugee camp, why should they return? Were they to put me in the government—be it an Arab or Jewish government— I'd say they shouldn't return. Why did they go away? It's their problem; why should they return? And if they do return, where will all the people who are already here go? Tell me, where will they go? Four million Arab refugees they want to bring back. That's like the number of inhabitants in Israel. Where will they go to? Who will build for them? Let them not come. Let them stay where they are. The Arabs left us to be humiliated [*lal-bahdala*], and thank God we were not humiliated. How come they didn't kill us? When Gaza was opened up in '67 [after the Israeli occupation], they began to covet what we [Palestinian citizens of Israel] have. Before the Jews came, what were we? We lived like dogs. If I had left, I would have died.

To the dismayed amazement of her nephew Moussa, who was present at the interview, and despite her enraged daughter, who phoned and argued with her, Subhiya persisted in deconstructing the nationalist discourse, enumerating the benefits of the welfare state and aiming her critical barbs at Arab despotism. As she spoke, Subhiya asserted a prenationalist identity similar to that articulated by Abu-Subhi and by the elderly Abu-George Hamati (see Chapter 10), according to whom identity is determined by "he who rules over you" (*illi hakimna*). As Abu-George puts it—in direct contradiction to Fakhri Jday's construction of Palestinian nationalism—"During the Ottoman period I was an Ottoman; during the time of the English I was British, and now Israel rules us, so I'm an Israeli." In a similar vein, Subhiya sacrilegiously states:

I'M AN ISRAELI. Where was I born? Here. Israel has ruled over us since before I bore my children. I'm an Israeli, and my children are Israelis. I'm not a Palestinian. He in whose land you live is the one who rules over you.

That's that. Even if the regime would change now, I would stay with the Jews. I'm happy with the Jews. I won't go to the regime of the Arabs. By God! The most oppressive regime in history [*azlam hukm*] is the regime of the Arabs. The Jews massacred in the war. You massacre me, I massacre you—that's how it is in war. People were massacred among them as well. That's why they protect the land. After all, they promised them the land here! The Jews bought this land. The English promised it to them, and the Arabs abandoned it.

This assertion is a further manifestation of Subhiya's rejection of the Palestinians' right of return, which she justifies by invoking her exchange relationship with the state that grants her rights rarely accessible to women in Arab countries. The geographic comparison with the Arab world is reinforced by a historical comparison with the inferior status of elderly people in "the days of the Arabs and the English" (*ayyam al-'arab*) before Israeli statehood. To drive her point home, Subhiya cites the allowance granted to her grandchildren while her son and their father were in an Israeli prison.

IF THE ARABS HERE HAVE ANY SENSE, they will cooperate with the state and won't go crazy and die of famine like the Arabs there [in the Occupied Territories and Arab countries]. There are no good doctors there, no proper treatment, and no sensible attitude—three things. Even if I were dying, I wouldn't go to Arab doctors. Here the medical treatment is good, the attitude toward children is good, there are schools for children, everything's clean. I receive social security. Should I rely on my children for support? Today they give me insurance and a pension, and I am admitted to the hospital for free. And not just me. They look after every old woman. Once an old woman would beg for alms and beg their children for money. Today you don't need favors. My money is in my pocket. The elderly live very well here, and anyone who says otherwise, I'll step on his face. Let the Arabs do to me what they will. Let them blow me up. Look, my son is in prison, and he has six children, and they receive an allowance and eat and drink and dress better than they did when he was working.

In the days of the Arabs and the English, when a woman was widowed, she would collect used clothes for her children and barely receive a little charity—rice, sugar, whatever they gave her out of pity. That's how widows were then. Today old women need neither work nor beg for alms. You're not dependent on your son.

Previously dependent on both older and younger men in her life before Israeli rule, Subhiya sees genuine benefit in living under the auspices of the Israeli welfare state, which liberates her from social practices of domination and, often, corporeal abuse.

It's Difficult for Us Under Arab Rule

Some might dismiss Abu-Ramadan's account as a narrative of betrayal and collaboration or as an unrepresentative story of an old woman whose age got the better of her. Thus Ted Swedenburg, in his study of the memories of Palestinian combatants in the Great Revolt (al-thawra al-kubra) of 1936–1939,[5] interprets such narratives as "collaborationist" and "accommodationist" rhetoric that "repeat[s] well-known Zionist ideologemes" and "cave[s] in to Zionist pressure."[6] Our concern here, however, goes beyond these initial dichotomies. Instead, anthropological analysis should seek to uncover the particular conditions of possibility of the social fields in Jaffa that are producing such counterintuitive and often paradoxical discourses.

These narratives, we argue, reflect a complex perception of identity in terms of both the Palestinian "self" and the Jewish immigrant Other.[7] As such, they express an ambivalent subject position:[8] subordinate Palestinian elders who are rights-bearing citizens of the same state that has occupied their cities and brought about their collective and personal ruin.

To Subhiya, the Jewish Other's responsibility for the Nakba is overridden by the pressing matter of her family's subsistence and the state's benevolent authority. Because this giving economy of citizenship is administered by Jews, the Jews turn into an agent of a positive transformation in her life. The transition from the inferior status of a poor woman in a rural patriarchal society to the official status of a citizen entitled to social benefits, as well as her life experience in a mixed city over a period of fifty years, have produced a nuanced perception of the Jewish Other. This perception recognizes difference while simultaneously rejecting it by virtue of a common civil status and in view of the prevailing local-communal fraternity.

WHEN I MARRIED and moved to 'Ajami, there were Jewish neighbors next door. We lived together. Here were my windows, and there the windows of the Jews. We were friends, but they moved out. God knows where they went. There was also a rabbi. We lived together for years. Israel was the rabbi's name, a very good man. When his wife would prepare food, they would bring us some, by God! The Jews, since they moved in here and to this day, we and they are friends. My son, the auto mechanic, has more Jewish friends than Arabs and Christians. That's how it is; it suits him. Once he was admitted to a hospital. It was a Saturday, and a [Jewish] friend of his came to visit him. I went to the hospital and found Shlomo with my son in the hospital. I said to him, "What are you doing Shlomo? It's the Sabbath today." He said to me, "This is my brother."

Recent events, particularly the 2000–2005 Second Intifada, only endorsed and reinforced Subhiya's viewpoint regarding the advantages of a pragmatic, conciliatory approach. The universal gender code of a mother's concern does not discriminate between Arab and Jew, and Subhiya mobilizes it to censure any violent solution. She wishes herself and her people a tranquil quotidian life. This, she has learned, could be led also with the Jews.

I'LL TELL YOU THE TRUTH: The Jews treat us well, better than the Arabs. Both those who were here before and those who are here now. It's difficult for us under Arab rule. There used to be good relations between Jews and Arabs here, but now [with the Intifada] they've spoiled them. They've gone awry. Today there isn't anybody who hasn't lost someone. If there is peace, everything will return to normal, but I feel that things won't be good between Jews and Arabs. If the situation deteriorates a bit more, it won't be good in Jaffa either. Everyone here has relatives outside, in the West Bank and in Gaza. Yesterday George Bush spoke, said that the Arabs must stop doing terror, disarm, and sit at a table and talk. But after what? Why didn't they do that before?

People are still dying. If not for this Intifada, Israel would have been a "top notch" [in Hebrew] place to live. That's why they now cut 400 NIS from the child allowance to give to the army deployed on the border. But they [the IDF] made a mistake by entering Ramallah. They killed people from here and they killed people from there, and four of them were also killed yesterday. Isn't it a pity? Doesn't everyone have a mother? Why? Because there's no sense! Why did they go into Ramallah? Because they [the Palestinians] made a "terrorist attack" [in Hebrew] in Haifa. When they did the "terrorist attack" in Haifa and in Netanya, the blood went to the Jews' head.

Having lived in Lydda and Jaffa most of her life, Subhiya takes issue with ethnic segregation, which in the end harms Arab residents because of their inability to live in peace with one another. As she observes everyday life and ignores the political-diplomatic arena analyzed in the previous quote, Subhiya severely criticizes the internal conduct of her fellow Palestinians.

WHEN WE FIRST ARRIVED IN 'AJAMI, it was full of Jews here [before the urban renewal plan of the 1960s]. Now, why are the Jews moving out? They've bought better houses than the houses here. What houses! I still have Jewish friends. In Lydda too I have friends. I call them, and when I visit in Lydda I see them. For sure. I lived with them well, really well. Today in 'Ajami people fight with each other [*bitqatalu*]. That's how the Arabs are; it's not good for them to live one next to the other. Jews and Arabs together "get along" [*mistadrim* in Hebrew]. Even now "they get along, they get along in the meantime." I hope matters won't get worse.

What Could I Do? I Have Small Children Who Need to Live

Subhiya moved from Jaffa to Lydda because she married a resident of the city, the brother of her late first husband, and when he also died, she returned to Jaffa, which she regards as her home. She depicts Jaffa's precarious condition through the hostile relations prevailing among inmates in the prisons and through the questionable reputation of the city's women.

JAFFA IS CALLED THE BRIDE OF PALESTINE. In the days of the Arabs there was no lovelier place than the Jaffa area. Whatever you desired, you could find here: a harbor, sea, good air. I love Jaffa. I lived in Lydda for thirty years and returned here. I moved to Lydda with my husband, and when he died, I came back here. It's better here, nicer. But I had good relations also with the people of Lydda. It's better not to mingle with the people of Jaffa. Most have become "informers" and "collaborators" [in Hebrew], trash. Many of Lydda's residents are Bedouins who came from the Beersheba region, from Kafr Qassem. But I "got along" [in Hebrew] with them as well. In Lydda they don't like Jaffa. Even in prison, the Jaffaite inmates are apart and the Lyddians are apart. Don't know why—perhaps because many of them are Bedouins. Jaffa's reputation is not good in Lydda. Not just because of the drugs, mainly because of the girls. They say that the girls are too promiscuous.

When Subhiya became widowed, she experienced financial hardship and was obliged to enter the labor market as a saleswoman, a seamstress, and finally as a cleaner in schools. By doing so, she assumed responsibility for her life and adopted an approach of personal empowerment.

WHEN MY FIRST HUSBAND DIED, life was very hard. I suffered badly, because I had six small children to care for. With my second husband I bore five. After my first husband died, I worked with my brother in vegetables, and even before my second husband died, I began to work at a school. I worked for the nuns. I used to clean there every Saturday, and I also worked in agriculture with my brother. Life was very hard then. I received welfare, but it wasn't enough. It was barely sufficient for shoes, not for clothes, food, and drink. But I did sewing at home. I sewed the blue school uniforms for the nuns. I was industrious. What could I do? I have small children who need to live.

Subhiya's subsequent work "at Jewish schools" led her to remove her veil, and her work cleaning houses of teachers from the school introduced her to the domestic sphere of Jewish women. This experience reinforced a strict work ethic in which she takes pride.

I USED TO WEAR A BLACK VEIL, but I removed it when I began to work. I was 35 years old and I worked at the Jewish school. How can you work with a head cover? I worked there for twenty years, and now I've retired. I go to the Lydda town hall, and when the clerks see me, they all get up to greet me, by God. They respect me. I like being honest. I worked cleaning houses of Jewish teachers. She would go off to school and leave me alone in the house. I would leave the key at the prearranged place, clean the house, and go. I also worked in a pharmacy for about three years. I would go in, change clothes and clean, and then take my bag and go home. They never asked me, "What do you have in the bag?" They never searched my bag. There, each bottle of perfume costs 300, 400 NIS. I never reached out to take anything. Never.

I'm Not Very Religious

Like many elderly Palestinian Muslims in Jaffa and in Israel in general, Subhiya has recently become more devout and resumed wearing a veil. Moreover, she refused to be photographed for the book on grounds of religious piety and humility. Yet she retains her critical spirit and vehemently rebukes the "deceitful" men of the frock (*mashayikh*) who exploit their position to repress women and to force them to cover their faces.

TODAY THERE ARE MANY who return to religion just like that. There are many girls who can't find a husband. All these religious men who grow beards, they're all liars. Girls who can't find husbands return to religion because they eye someone religious in order to marry. It's a false religion, and the sheikhs are liars. They tell you, "God said so, and Muhammad said so." I'm telling you, they're all liars, and I'm prepared to argue with them. My son prays five times a day; he listens to what the religious people [*mashayikh*] say in the mosque and comes and tells me so-and-so. I answer him, "You're a liar, and your sheikhs are liars. They don't tell the truth!" God didn't tell the woman, "Cover your face" or "Cover your hands." Our religion says that not covering the face and hands is permissible. These people tell you that it's not allowed and put on a veil and wear gloves. It's all a lie! I went on pilgrimage to Mecca, and I know the religion, but the religious people here are liars.

One might interpret the rediscovery of religion in old age as a strategy designed to bolster the precarious status of the elderly in Arab society, to gain recognition, or as a product of existential constraints. This self-labeling, however, is not a preterminal search for meaning in one's life, in culture, or in the transcendental, as the literature on the aging self suggests.[9] Rather than invoking charged concepts such as spirituality and meaning, Subhiya offers a social and individual explanation based on the relationship between people and between the individual and God. Subhiya the pilgrim is well aware of the primary and secondary benefits to be gained from religious identification, because a religious way of life is frequently complemented by pilgrimage to Mecca, granting the traveler the badge of honor Hajj, which confers important symbolic capital and social status and absolves one from having to account for one's past sins.

I HAVEN'T ALWAYS BEEN RELIGIOUS. It was only five years ago, when I went on pilgrimage to Mecca. I'm not very religious. I know God and fear God. That's it. I'm not a fanatic. I went on the hajj so that God would absolve me. Perhaps I've sinned in my time, perhaps I've lied, perhaps I've hurt my husband. I've reached a stage in life when I wanted to go on pilgrimage so that God would absolve me of my misdeeds. All the sins are erased. There are many elderly people like me who become religious.

My brother, for example, didn't know God, didn't pray. He studied at Tabeetha, at the Scottish school. He used to say that there is no afterworld and that there's no heaven and hell, God forbid. He was an infidel, like the Christians. Perhaps not altogether an infidel. Infidels were a long time ago; today there aren't infidels anymore. God belongs to everyone. My brother would say, "Here is heaven and here is hell, in this world in which we live." He would say, "What is heaven? Heaven is the life of the rich and happy, and hell is the life of the poor." We would all constantly tell him to pray, and he always refused. Now my second brother, who will soon be 80, tells him to pray, and he stubbornly refuses.

Subhiya rationalizes her piousness by associating it with a near-death experience she underwent, thus personalizing what seems to be a current cultural movement among elderly Muslim women in Israel and in the Arab world. At the same time, by adhering to the personal, she remonstrates the hypocrisy of clerics while upholding the authenticity of her own intimate experience.

BEFORE I BECAME RELIGIOUS, I wasn't aware of anything. But thank goodness, God opened my eyes. Four years ago I went through a period when I almost died. I had "pulmonary edema" [in Hebrew]. I suffocated from the water in my lungs and lost consciousness. They put me in intensive care for three days. I was unconscious. My son took me to hospital.

It was during the month of Ramadan. When I reached the emergency room, they put tubes into my nose, my shoulder, and my arms. I didn't feel a thing; I was on the verge of dying. When I woke up, the nurse told me that the children were crying all the time, because the doctors told them, "Your mother will die in four hours." I said to them, "Why are you crying? Are you crazy? After all, you're grown up and married and have borne children. After all I've done for you, now you don't need help from me anymore. I helped you with everything and that's it. Now each of you has a home, children, everything. I've lived to see all your children, thank God. So what do you want of me? If I die, do you want to bring me back? Let me go on my way." I worked hard for them. I was both a mother and a father to them. It all fell upon me. I have eleven children, not one or two, and I raised them all, and thank God they lack nothing.

I Don't Want to Grow Old

In Subhiya's discourse, existential matters are linked to questions of inter-generational relationships, old age, and forgiveness of wrongdoings that sons have wrought on their mothers. Time and again she describes the ongoing hardship and violence suffered by elderly women in the past.

THERE WAS A TIME when they didn't take notice of old people and didn't take an interest in them; they didn't respect them. My brother had beaten my mother because the cow trampled on the vegetables. My mother died still angry at him. They told her, "Forgive him." She told them, "I cannot." They said to her, "Say that God will forgive him. You go to Mecca on the hajj." She lived with him and was pushed aside. He would cast her into a corner. What a shame [*haram*]! Look at the Jews: They take the old people in a car and take them out and go with them on trips. They spend money on them. It's good that they put them in an "old folks' home" [in Hebrew]. There they wash them, dress them, cut their nails, feed and clean them. Today neither the daughter-in-law nor the daughter is pre-pared to carry the burden. Where will your mother go?

For Subhiya, the "Jews" serve as an idealized yardstick that contrasts with what she has seen in her family and society.

THE OLD PERSON remains abandoned in the home. If he wants to eat, they complain; if he needs a change of clothing, they don't change him. My neighbor is paralyzed in her arms and legs. Her daughters change her once a week and moan; they don't give her anything to drink so that she won't urinate; they don't feed her so that she won't make a mess. They abuse her. If I won't be able to walk, I'll bring someone who'll serve me. I'll give her money, and she'll come to help me.

Having tasted freedom from tyrannical kin, Subhiya is no longer willing to put herself at their mercy even if she needs help. She associates this crisis of values, of which the distress of the elderly is one manifestation, with the declining young generation and their moral failings, especially the girls.

THE YOUNG PEOPLE OF TODAY ARE DIFFICULT. They don't listen, do whatever they like, do stupid things. Not like it used to be, when you could tell your son, "Don't go with this guy. He'll put you in jail." Also today's girls. Most of the girls who marry get divorced in the end. They do whatever comes into their head. A girl falls in love with someone, and he wants her, or loves her lightheartedly, and when he's had enough of her, he gets rid of her. Nowadays not all the girls are good. But when I see a girl, I know immediately if she's good or bad. I know. A girl is to be known by her tongue. You can say that 50 percent of the women today are spoiled. Their husbands sell coke. They have a lot of money; they go out, dress up, walk about, drive posh cars, and the husband is in prison. What does the wife care? She smokes, drives a car, has fun; she has a spare boyfriend, goes out with him on trips, has fun with him. I tell you, most of the women are corrupt.

Subhiya has earned the power and independence she enjoys. Since moving back to Jaffa, she has lived on her own without relying on favors from others. She expresses apprehension about the helplessness that she associates with old age and comes to terms with the tension linked to her death. While she fears it, she reconciles herself to it and prepares herself for it.

I DON'T WANT TIME TO PASS QUICKLY, because I don't want to grow old. I want time to stand still so I won't get too old. The life of the old person is hard. I think about it a lot at night. Before I fall asleep, I think about the days to come. What is it I want? Only to be healthy and strong, so I can walk and retain my wits. But death will come. Every Muslim mentions death each morning when he prays. One mustn't fear death. Jews fear death more. But Arabs fear too. Those who don't think about the next world and don't think about the good and the bad things in this world, they fear death. But Arabs too become afraid when they grow old. They say, "Tomorrow we shall die." And when they fall ill, they begin to cry.

A Jew, a Muslim, the Same Thing

Unlike Fakhri Jday, who proclaims Arabic as the language of culture, and even by contrast to Abu-Subhi, who presents Arabic as a language that connects Jews and Arabs, Subhiya is proud of her Hebrew and her ability to use it to improve neighborly relations.

> I HAVE LEARNED HEBREW WELL, because we lived in 'Ajami with Jewish neighbors in the same building. They didn't speak a word of Arabic. I learned to speak Hebrew from them. I understand and speak Hebrew well. It's easier than Arabic. If I'd known how to read or write, it would've been easier for me in Hebrew. Arabic is complicated. The kids at school also find Hebrew easier.

Subhiya's observations about the benefits of learning Hebrew bring her back to her principal storyline: the pragmatic necessity to live "in accordance with the state." Although she does not attribute moral value to the state beyond its capacity to meet one's needs, she associates Hebrew as the state's language with the vital importance of communication with one's neighbor.

> ONE SHOULD LEARN BOTH ARABIC AND HEBREW, according to the state. If my children want to go to the bank or the accountant, they need Hebrew above all else. Where do they live? With the Jews. Is the Jew born after three months and the Muslim after nine? They're all the same. When I delivered in hospital, a Jew was lying beside me, and I'm a Muslim, and our kids are the same. They didn't say, "This is a Jew, we'll love him more, and this is a Muslim, we won't love him." The same. The nurse who brought her son to the Jew and the nurse who brought her son to the Muslim, the same, the same treatment. One can't deny God's grace! What are you, a communist?

To reinforce her argument, Subhiya tells about the friendship between her son the mechanic and his Jewish neighbor. As though to illustrate the validity of the proverb "Better a close neighbor than a distant brother," the neighbor lent her son his car while his own brother refused.

> MY SON, where does he work? With Jews! When he worked with Arabs, this one ate away his money from here, and the other robbed him from there. With a Jewish employer, the first of the month arrives, he gives him the salary, no problem. My son works at a garage, and the Jew who works for him told him, "If there's work and I need to stay another hour, two hours, I'll stay and finish it." Once my son took a vacation and said to our Jewish neighbor, "Give me your car, I need to go on an errand." The neighbor said to him, "Take the keys." He understands Arabic like we do. When my son asked his brother for the car, he refused. Our neighbor is like his brother; he's crazy about him. How happy we were when they released him from the army! He joined the army, and his mother works as a cleaner in offices, and his father is ill with epilepsy, so they released him. That was before the Intifada. We prayed that by the time they mobilized him, there would be no more wars. When they released him, I was very happy. They lived here for a long time—they grew up here. Moroccans. Good people. I like it when the neighbors are decent people. It's good that he's been saved from the war. Had something happened to him, I'd have gone crazy.

Feminine Protest and Honorable Exchange

Subhiya is not alone in voicing caustic criticism of Palestinian and Arab nationalism and society. Like other women in her position, she is well aware of her fate within a regime that Hisham Sharabi terms neo-patriarchy,[10] namely, the anomalous product of modernization of the traditional male domination regime. She refuses to relinquish her rights, and as a part of the "patriarchal bargain"[11] that involves negotiations with representatives of the ruling power, she deconstructs some of the foundations of her collective identity in order to accrue the personal benefits reaped from the occupying state. Yet, whereas the patriarchal bargain generally includes women who act as agents of repression toward other women, in this case Subhiya equates nationalism with patriarchy and relinquishes them both in favor of a concept of utilitarian citizenship. In this way, her sacrifice of components of collective-national identity serves Subhiya as a bridgehead from which to contend with the unfairness of sexism, classism, and ageism, as she puts the masculine domination mechanism to shame: "My father is a coward. . . . In the end he was left with neither land nor honor."

Subhiya proceeds along two parallel paths to secure the bargain whereby she exchanges her already lost national honor for two other types of honor:[12] dignity, namely, her right to protect her humanity and her universal human needs, such as the right to die with dignity; and respect, namely, the practical realization of her potential. The first step she undertakes is to berate Palestinian nationalism and to transfer her loyalty from ethnos to family, thereby repudiating her commitment to the politics of the nation. The second step, derived from the first, is to emphasize old age and gender as foci of existence. Once perfidious male nationalism has been abandoned, it will be replaced by belief in fairness, egalitarianism, and reciprocity between all humans. These are unconditional relationships, founded merely on the humanity of individuals and the right to welfare that the state provides. The removal of social accountability, implied by the attitude of "scratch my back and I'll scratch yours," from the realm of the imagined national community and its transfer to the boundaries of the neighborhood community turn the interaction between individuals into a generalized form of exchange. This relationship constitutes a gift economy that is based on dignity and is free of the limitations of identity and identification.[13]

The implications of this worldview for managing time in old age are far-reaching, because it metaphorically puts a halt to the transformations inherent in the aging process by anchoring Subhiya in the present and severing long-term social obligations. To this Subhiya adds her ability to confront her maker free of sin, thereby not merely ensuring an anxiety-free day-to-day existence in old age but also guaranteeing her future in the afterlife. Unlike Nazihah Asis, who is obliged to make minor concessions to gain the benefits of identity and the goods to which she is entitled by her revered status, Subhiya, the daughter of the Nakba, is required to pay an exorbitant price for her survival.

(CHAPTER 7)

OVERLOOKING NATIONALISM

Talia Seckbach-Monterescu In and Out of Place

> "So you want me to be your native. No, that's flattering but not
> good," he said. "I'm not typical. Get some of the others. . . . I'm not
> like them. I don't join clubs. I'm not Zionist. I don't believe in God.
> Find someone else."
>
> Barbara Myerhoff, *Number Our Days*

Talia Monterescu (née Liliane Seckbach) was born in Lyon in 1940 to ultra-
Orthodox Jewish parents.[1] Her father had escaped from Germany in 1933,
and her mother came from Switzerland. When the Germans occupied the
French *zone libre* (free zone), the family was forced to flee to Switzerland in
1942, where it found refuge with the mother's relatives. Liliane immigrated
to Israel at the age of 16, on her own, Hebraized her name to Talia, and lived
in a number of kibbutzim. After marrying a Romanian Jaffaite in 1964, she
moved to the predominantly Jewish Jaffa D neighborhood, where she lived
until the late 1980s. Since then she has lived in an ethnically mixed and violent inner city neighborhood. From a perspective of universal morality, Talia
unfolds a story that is critical of native Israeliness, which exposes the national
order as a repressive regime whose victims include Jews and Arabs alike. Per-
ceiving herself as a refugee rather than as a politically engaged migrant, she
identifies with the uprooted Palestinians and laments the decline of home,
neighborhood, and city.

In this chapter, which concludes Part II, we present the quasi-external
viewpoint of a woman who, ever since migrating to Israel in the 1950s, has
remained deliberately aloof and alienated from the indigenizing sabra cultural scene. Her story reflects gradual political disillusionment, which begins
in a frontier kibbutz and ends in a mixed neighborhood at the urban heart

Hicham Chabaita

of the country, whose decline she sadly witnesses. From a self-aware and declared position of universal humanism and cultural aloofness, Talia levels acerbic criticism at nationalism, which she regards as a force that dispossesses, defiles, and deceives rulers and ruled alike. Hers is thus a position of political and ethical reflexivity that combines recognition of the Other and moral identification with the Other's dispossession, though not particularly with Palestinian nationalism, and with constant engagement with the disintegrating urban space as a remnant of the historical alterity that has been expelled from its home.

From a house to which she is to some degree fettered, because of a muscular degenerative medical condition, Talia observes her surroundings soberly but without bitterness. Her story merges her self-definition as a refugee with recognition of her good fortune. The predominant theme is the great importance she attaches to the individual's own decisions and power to control one's destiny. Talia illustrates this awareness by referring to three major moves in her life: from France to Israel, from the kibbutz to the religious town of Bnei Beraq, and from Bnei Beraq to the Jewish-Arab city of Jaffa. She has no pretensions of being an Israeli or a Jaffaite or of representing her neighbors, yet she deeply contemplates the place in which she lives. She places herself in the position of a detached participant-observer: someone who is involved but does not intervene, who is located simultaneously within and outside, and who certainly fails to identify with the place.

Talia's life is a voyage of voluntary migration between key vantage points. Her journey has allowed her to consider alternative options of home and identity through which she passes without committing herself or pining for any. Each of these temporary anchorages offers a temptation to settle permanently in some big place that is likely to provide security and a sense of belonging by virtue of its being a collective representation; yet she is not tempted and proceeds along the path of her inquisitive strangerhood until arriving at her current Jaffa home, where she feels no urge to establish ownership. This house is the place of the Other, the uprooted Palestinian, whose dispossessed home she holds in trust until his return. This noncommitment to a well-defined and secure local-domestic identity is a fiercely guarded component of her right and ability to operate in and on the world as she sees fit. This is how she establishes her independence and realizes her freedom to move among available domesticated identities without fully adopting any of them. Her residence is only a place that obviously does not belong to her but that is worthy in her eyes to serve as an abode of borrowed time and temporary space.

The first of five stops in time that she visits as an explorer, tourist, or flâneur, is her parents' home in France, which she was forced to abandon during the Holocaust for the sanctuary provided by her Swiss uncles and aunts. This was followed by the kibbutz—a key site in the forging of the normative settler Jewish-Israeli identity. The third point was at her religious Jewish parents' home in Bnei Beraq, followed by the apartment block in Jaffa, where she found a community of neighbors for a while. The last stop is at the Arab house, where she waits as a custodian for the dispossessed owners to return and reclaim ownership. This is a path directly opposed to that trodden by the pilgrim, certainly according to the Zionist vision of immigration and integration in a national home. It thus denotes the dissolution of nationalism as a mythical expansion of the private home in time and space.

I'm All for Dual Loyalties

Some years before he died, Talia's father was urged by his children to write his life story. It relates his rescue "through divine providence" from a series of perils that lay in wait for his family and the recurring painful losses he suffered, such as his father's death in the Theresienstadt Ghetto and the death of his sister, brother-in-law, and their nine children at Auschwitz. Despite these shattering blows, the story that has become the family's metanarrative rests on the redeeming power of belief in the Creator and humankind's capacity to be worthy of God's love. Like her father, albeit from an utterly secular standpoint, Talia begins her life story by stating how fortunate she has been.

> I AM FORTUNATE in a number of respects. One is that I was born in France right before the Germans invaded and survived, and was also born to parents who didn't burden me in any way with the private or general Holocaust, and that they were lucky to have had at least two loyalties: first of all, my father's loyalty to Germany, and to Jewish tradition and faith. The same goes for my mother, perhaps in a less conscious manner. And it's very helpful this dual loyalty, to prevail when one of them is shattered. This is perhaps also my general conclusion; I would say: I'm all for dual loyalties.

As a daughter in a family of refugees, Talia's life experience taught her that belonging to a place is neither natural nor obvious. The young Talia converted her parents' dual loyalty to German or French culture and to Judaism into a dilemma between Israeliness and Jewishness.

> I WAS CONSTANTLY AGAINST SOMETHING. When I came here, I said to myself that I must choose, so I want to be an Israeli. I had no idea of what an Israeli was. I said, "I don't want to be a Jew." I had no idea of what it meant to be a Jew. You know, in adolescence you are searching, and you can easily say no, but today I can tell you, so many German and Austrian Jews committed suicide. Far fewer committed suicide when they didn't put all their eggs in one basket. They seriously believed one should be a good German and that one must obey the laws and speak correct German.

And nevertheless, they had another very important loyalty: religious loyalty. That gave them the opportunity to be independent in between.

This was how Talia learned that it was possible to counter local nationalism by means of a universal religious loyalty. This lesson laid the philosophical foundation on which her critical circumspection toward human authority in general was built. It stems from the position of a stranger who does not put all her proverbial eggs in one basket. And it has stood her in good stead throughout her life as an adaptive resource, enabling her to constantly recreate an "authentic" self. Talia likewise applies her critical spirit and freedom of choice to the manner in which she copes with the private sphere, such as when she defied the undisputed authority of the physician who sought to treat her chronic illness.

I'M LUCKY. Both because I'm stubborn and because I still have the capacity to think and draw conclusions. Had I been the type of obedient child who follows doctor's orders, I don't know where I'd be today. It began at an early age. It began the first time they hospitalized me and wanted to give me sedatives, so I wouldn't develop a spastic walk. I said, "A spastic walk doesn't bother me so much. Let me be. I won't take sedatives that would prevent me from driving." Not that I drive, but that's a sign. I refused. And to be able to say no, you must have some measure of self-confidence, which you acquire during the formative years.

I Grew Up Where Children Keep Quiet Unless Spoken To

The paternal household, as reflected in Talia's stories, endowed her with this self-confidence, the power to stand up to authority, to choose, to draw conclusions. Indeed, Talia attributes her characteristic skepticism and her ability to "draw conclusions" to the "formative years." From 1943 to 1945 her family lived in Switzerland with her uncles, who suggested separating the children from the adults for the sake of convenience. The young Liliane protested vehemently.

IN MY OPINION, the formative years for me were up to the age of approximately 5. The early years are decisive. I grew up where children keep quiet unless spoken to. But at some point, when we were refugees in Switzerland, when they separated me and [my brother] Mark from my mother and father and my younger brother, at some point, instead of being a well-behaved girl who does what she's told, suddenly I began to cry. And because I began to cry and repeatedly said, "I don't want to. I want to be with father and mother," probably because of this my parents found the courage to look for an apartment rather than live with the big brother. In other words, I suddenly found out, relatively very early, that it pays to speak up, even to scream.

Sixty years on, Talia interprets the demand to stay together as the first time she impinged on the world and realized "that it pays to speak up, even to scream." This foundational insight was seared on her consciousness and on the childhood memories that shape her story. Talia confesses that her cry emanated from an unarticulated need for singularity, which manifested itself later in her childhood as a kind of envy of God and even of the Sabbath, which for her stand as the principal bearers of meaning in the family. She analyzes the tension between the egocentric desire of a girl to be the center of attention and her parents' religious commitment as the factor that created the first fissures in her religious belief.

High School Was Fun, Because I Had More Independence

Talia describes her childhood in Lyon following the family's return to France as an ongoing learning experience and a time of expanding personal autonomy and intellectual horizons.

WE ARRIVED IN JUNE '45, I was 5 and a half years old when we returned to France from Switzerland. But I understood nothing. I went to kindergarten and didn't understand a thing. Later I went to school, and I remember the moment I understood what multiplication was, because minus and plus are self-evident. Multiplication was a mystery to me. Until I realized that in fact it's a plus and another plus and another plus. I remember the feeling of "Hey, I didn't know, didn't understand. Now I know." That felt real good.

High school, on the other hand, was fun, because I had more independence. In the afternoons my mother worked with my father, so I used to go to a café and order coffee and a roll and lay out all my exercise books on the large table.

The more Talia learned about the world, the more confident she became, the more adept she became at creating independent spaces and times for herself—such as the café on the way home. Her criticism and skepticism grew as well, alongside her sense of knowledge. She therefore found it difficult to accept a life of religious dogma, and she now dismisses it as an "obsessive-compulsive" lifestyle.

> I GREW UP AS A RELIGIOUSLY OBSERVANT GIRL, but that didn't bother me. That was not the problem. But at some stage I said to myself: "It is impossible that this God is interested in what I put on my plate." There's something obsessive-compulsive about Jewish dietary laws. I remember my big brother's children, Mark's. I would bring them books with all sorts of pictures of animals, and each animal they would ask if it was kosher or not. And I'd say, "No, it's not kosher, thank God." At some point you realize you will never manage to match the ideal, and then you suddenly open your eyes, and also go to school and open books, and you say, "Hang on, there are also other things."

Once she realized that she would not be able to live up to the religious ideal set by her parents and brothers, she fashioned her own view of religion and anchored it in the general concept that she gradually developed: freedom of thought and the need to draw conclusions independently. Having migrated to Israel and settled on a kibbutz, Talia began to apply this critical approach to the local political sphere as well.

It Took Me Seven Years to Develop Serious Political Awareness

Like many Jewish immigrants, Talia was not motivated by a coherent Zionist ideology but rather by a romantic and adventurous desire "to be where the action is" and, perhaps paradoxically in retrospect, to distance herself from the "racist atmosphere" that prevailed in France at the time of the Algerian War. It is with obvious pride that she relates how her parents followed in her footsteps.

> I WAS 16, and in France one was legally considered an adult at age 21. One of the reasons that drove me to migrate was that I heard that here you come of age at 18. So I said, "Gee, I can gain three years!" I left because

I wanted to be where the action is. I didn't want to regret afterward that I didn't do it. In my opinion, that's also luck. In my own way I somehow managed to persuade my parents to come here. My brother was already here, but I think that it was because of me that they decided to come, and many good things happened to them here. First, to reunite with the family, and without the dark memories of our time of refuge in Switzerland. When you're a refugee, you are at the mercy of someone else. The internally displaced Palestinians in Jaljulia must have felt the same; despite being only a few miles from home, still they were seen as strangers in the village they were forced to move to. Perhaps I was also searching for something new, free of European baggage, without being aware of it. I left France in the midst of the Algerian War, which was a nasty war, and there was a very racist atmosphere on the streets, and to move from there to here [for that reason], in retrospect sounds a bit funny. But really when I came here, I began to study a little Arabic. I got to know the country by hitchhiking.

At that stage of her life, Talia had not yet articulated her series of personal decisions in political terms and still regarded them rather as a process of individuation and separation. Seeking to connect to the new place, she studied some Arabic and toured the length and breadth of the land.

During her early days in Israel, Talia was still caught between her loyalty to her parents and her search for an alternative identity. In the beginning she tried to join her sabra (native Israeli) peers in the kibbutzim. At her parents' request, she settled in the religious Kibbutz Sheluhot, but subsequently moved to the Hashomer Hatsa'ir's Kibbutz Horshim.

I TOLD MY PARENTS that I wanted to go to a kibbutz, so they said, "It must be a religious kibbutz." I said, "All right, as long as I can get out of here." Now I realize that I felt, without being aware of it, that this was a confrontation with the parents and that I didn't want to confront them head on, but at the time I was totally unaware of this. At first I was in Kibbutz Sheluhot, a religious kibbutz. And I did ordinary farm work— absolutely no discounts for the youth groups! Eight hours straight. Later, in the youth group there was a girl who got pregnant from a guy who was a soldier, and they threw her out but not him. I didn't like that. I didn't know her well, not at all. I would walk around all the time with a note-book asking, what's this and what's that in Hebrew.

And later I went on my own to Tel Aviv to Hashomer Hatsa'ir, and I said I wanted to go to a kibbutz, and they mulled it over until they said that in Beit Qamah there's a French-speaking group. And then I said that I wanted to know where my group would end up, and that was Horshim, and then I was alone for a while with those animals, the sabras, who seemed so messed up to me. Messed up on the one hand, and on the other, I tried to assimilate with them. And then I said to myself, "What? Braggarts! Who are they?" They didn't even move their butts. They grew up here and stayed here. And then there was the Sinai Campaign, and I didn't realize then that this meant linking up with the new colonialists. As if linking up with the old colonialists was better.

Once Talia despaired of integrating with the sabras, she articulated a critique of the arrogant indigenous kibbutz members, who remained in the place where they were born, bereft of self-criticism. In the wake of the 1956 Sinai Campaign and following a series of events at the kibbutz, she began to regard kibbutz society as chauvinistic and discriminatory, anchored in the colonialist context. Talia attributes the process of political disillusionment to her life on Kibbutz Horshim, which had expropriated the lands of the Palestinian village of Khirbet Harish. As a young woman, she could not reconcile her uncompromising commitment to the principles of communality and equality in the kibbutz with what she witnessed within and outside it. The reaction of kibbutz members to the land grab gradually led to disenchantment with the ideals that had guided her thus far.

IT WAS ONLY AFTER I HAD LEFT THE KIBBUTZ—it took me seven years to develop serious political awareness. To understand that a kibbutz is an economic enterprise like everything else, on land that they grabbed. You know that Kibbutz Horshim, there was a village there, and Palestinians were displaced from there and now they're in Jaljulia [a nearby village in Israel]. And they told me that, and I said, "How can that be? How can Hashomer Hatsa'ir do a thing like that?" Then they told me, "If we hadn't taken the land, then Mapai would have taken it." I remember that sentence to this day and exactly where we were standing on the path.

In retrospect, it's fortunate that I left. Even though I left my entire library there—and I had no small a library—apart from two books: Shakespeare's collected works and a history book.

Despite her abhorrence of what she had learned about the kibbutz history and way of life and the sabras' provincialism, what eventually drove Talia to leave was in fact the naïve ideal of total commitment to communal labor. Loyal to the communal spirit, she left all her possessions to the kibbutz and moved to her parents' home in Bnei Beraq.

IT TOOK ME SEVEN YEARS to wake up from adolescence, from foggy political conceptions, sort of general ones like equality, justice, unclear loyalty, and suddenly realize that nothing is simple. I decided to leave because I felt that I wasn't providing enough labor power. I suddenly felt that I had no energy. I didn't like it. And then I said, "What am I doing on the farm when I'm not producing labor?" It took me time to change my ideas.

We Used to Walk from Bnei Beraq to Jaffa and Back

In Bnei Beraq Talia began to do odd jobs while completing her matriculation exams. Her studies in the Israeli education system and university added a further tier to her critique of Israeli frivolity. She stayed in her parents' home in Bnei Beraq, but only temporarily until she managed to move elsewhere.

I STOOD IN LINE AT THE EMPLOYMENT BUREAU, and there was this couple or someone looking for an au pair, and I was very glad. They spoke French; they were Turks. You understand that me and housework are not the perfect match, but they were patient. I told them my parents weren't here—I didn't want them to know—and later I told them they had arrived. I began to attend night school. I learned most about the [conventional] Israeli school when I got to the university, however. What a shock! To meet the products of the Israeli school system. There was someone who asked me to let her copy my paper. It sounded totally crazy to me! Or there was someone else who said she hadn't written this and that because she thought the teacher may not like it and give her a lower grade. I considered that beneath contempt! It angers me to this day. The French school gave me an advantage. Today I feel that even more. They took studies seriously.

In the course of her studies at Tel Aviv University, which was located at the time in the former Palestinian village of Abu-Kabir, Talia got to know Jaffa and her future partner, an electrician who immigrated from Romania in 1951. They married and moved to an apartment block in Jaffa.

I REMEMBER HOW WE USED TO WALK from Bnei Beraq to Jaffa and back [more than 4 miles]. There were trees and frogs on the way. The first day we met, Father came with a yellow shirt and light brown waistcoat and said that he had just then been in a lottery and won an apartment in a housing project. It seemed so funny that he should talk to me about it. At the lottery one could choose between a home in Ramat Aviv [now an upscale neighborhood in northern Tel Aviv] and a home in Jaffa. It's very fortunate that it was Jaffa in the end.

They Called Me the French Woman

Life in the apartment block gave Talia a taste of something quite different from what she had known in the kibbutz or in ultra-Orthodox Bnei Beraq. The people who lived in her neighborhood, Jaffa D, were young couples and working-class families, most of whom had moved from Jaffa's older neighborhoods. The residents addressed this multicultural mosaic by using ethnic categories based on country of origin.

IN 1964 WE MOVED TO JAFFA D. In the beginning it seemed so strange to me, so backward, that people would speak of the Bulgarian woman, the Romanian woman, the French woman; at first it sounded to me like they were saying "the Jewish woman," as though it was some forbidden word. It was only later that I realized it had something to do with seeking identity, because who could remember all those complicated names? They called me the French woman. It was kind of strange, but in those projects there was some sort of an elite, in the sense of people who had extricated themselves from [old] Jaffa and managed to take control of their lives. Hardworking, well-organized, and enterprising people with a social life, interactions. I remember there was a neighbor on the third floor, a large Bulgarian woman, who was always asking me, "Well, are you pregnant?" It embarrassed me of course. I felt that was a private matter. And she felt it was a public concern.

The unavoidable close multicultural contact in Jaffa D, built on the ruins
of Palestinian Saknet Darwish and its orchards, brought Talia face to face
not merely with a blurring of boundaries between the private and the public
domains but also with the Palestinian presence. At first she took comfort in
the knowledge that the land on which she lived had been privately owned.
At the same time, in the emerging neighborhood Talia discovered a "community life" and mutual support that charmed her.

> WHEN I CAME IN '64, there were still some remnants of a transit camp.[2]
> There was an almond tree, a hill, and a few remains of houses. And there
> were chicken coops below. And there was a greengrocer and some kind of
> grocery store and the houses where we were, the first five blocks. They de-
> ceived us. They told us that this was privately owned land. And I thought
> that this was not houses that they took, that it wasn't loot, and I didn't
> understand that they had grabbed all the land.
>
> But there was communal life. Once, after you were born [meaning
> her son Daniel Monterescu, who is conducting the interview], and I was
> holding you and fell asleep, and your sister had enough, she looked for
> something to do—she was 2 and a half years old—she opened the door
> and went down. And then a neighbor came and took her by the hand and
> brought her home and she yelled at me and I was so happy. It was so nice
> that someone cared. A real neighborhood. I liked it.

In contrast to Tel al-Rish in Holon, where Subhiya abu-Ramadan was
born (see Chapter 6), in Jaffa D an orchard owned by the Abu-Seif family
remains to this day. Although she does not portray the relations with the
Abu-Seif family as hostile, Talia speaks of the aversion on the part of some
neighbors to living in "an Arab's house" and their desire to live "in some lousy
cramped project, but a new one!" as a part of the refugeehood complex of the
recent immigrants.

> THE ARABS WERE PRESENT, but as I see it, all people are the same. Now-
> adays it's the boundary between Bat Yam and Jaffa, because Bat Yam
> suddenly took another piece of land. And some of the residents really
> wanted to be a part of Bat Yam and not of Jaffa, as part of this busi-
> ness of moving away from refugeehood. Because probably they weren't

all happy to settle into a home that belonged to someone else. And on top of that the message that wasn't all that explicit was that Arabs were primitive, so why should we live in an Arab's house? Better some lousy cramped project, but a new one! Don't forget that many of them, both Bulgarians and Romanians, were not that long ago part of the Ottoman Empire. They wanted to feel new in Israel, so everything had to be new, particularly the walls.

It Took Me a While to Get Involved in Israeli Life

Talia's familiarity with Israeli society gradually broadened, as she grappled with the identities to which she was exposed, committing herself to none. She slowly gained a sense of her ability to position herself at the existential center of her world, using her experience of Israeliness merely as a nonbinding repertoire and a toolbox with which to construct her selfhood.

MY THINKING SLOWLY CHANGED. Not so much at the university. It was a matter of connecting one thing with another and another. Beginning with that story of the internally displaced Palestinians, which was in '57. But until you absorb and connect and hear and learn Hebrew, it took me a long time. At a certain period I was in the Communist Youth Alliance [BANKI], and I was expelled from it. Because at that time in Europe they founded the Common Market, six countries, and there [at BANKI] they said that the situation was awful and that it was the end of capitalism, and I said that from what I heard from France, I did not gain that impression. So they said that was provocation. They really persecuted Communists here. I worked in some place and demonstrated because of Lumumba's murder, and they fired me. I worked in all kinds of places. I was pregnant and went to a demonstration [with the radical Matzpen organization], and they arrested us, and that was when I lived at the university. We went out with paint to write on the walls, so they confiscated it.

The birth of her children and the need to take responsibility for raising and educating them brought about a transformation in Talia's life. She no longer devoted herself to hazardous and uncompromising activity in the name of ideals but settled in an environment that would enable her to ar-

range her daily life around schools and health institutions and to foster a
sense of stability and tranquility, alongside her work at the Jaffa Mental
Health Center and ongoing contact with the afflicted and suffering.

I Thought That Jaffa Was the Very Essence of the State of Israel

After she was diagnosed with multiple sclerosis, Talia wanted to live closer
to work and moved to the Arab house in the heart of Jaffa where she still resides. Here too her experience of multicultural encounters and ethnic mixing
continued to shape her interpretation of the refugee way of life.

> ALL THROUGH THIS PERIOD my political awareness grew deeper, be-
> cause I met all sorts of people. First of all, I thought that Jaffa was the
> very essence of the State of Israel, the same thing only more concen-
> trated, in the sense that if you're a refugee and come to a different coun-
> try, you meet people whom you would most probably not have met had
> you remained where you were. The second thing is multicultural encoun-
> ters: not merely a different language, different tastes, different habits, not
> merely different classes. A mixture. It seemed to me like the State of Is-
> rael. But more concentrated because there were also more religions here.
> In most of Israel there were only Jews, of all kinds. But in Jaffa there were
> also Catholics and Pravoslavs and Maronites and Muslims, although I
> initially noticed the Christians more than the Muslims. They were also
> less prominent on the street. We're speaking of '89.

Talia's multicultural experience is accompanied by an awareness of the
universal meaning of refugeehood, as well as awareness of the particular in-
justices of the Nakba and the Holocaust. Talia is given the opportunity to
speak about the two events in the same breath through her place of work,
which brings her into contact both with Palestinians from Gaza and her
personal family memory.

> PEOPLE FROM GAZA who remembered the French hospital that closed
> down in 1970 would come to the Community Mental Health Center in
> Jaffa. Up to 1970 this had been a general hospital that admitted everyone,
> with no strings attached. And they looked for this and said how good
> it had been. I think it was only in the midst of my work at the center—

twenty-five or thirty years ago—that the meaning of the Holocaust gradually began to dawn on me, and the fact that I had lost a grandfather . . . You push it aside until you feel one can cope with it.

This recognition is not expressed as an emotional account but rather as a sober observation of the twists and turns of human fate and their impact on her own experience: "Life in Jaffa didn't affect my perception. My life affected it. That is, meeting all kinds of people who underwent all kinds of experiences, meeting people who returned to Jaffa after '67 after not being here so many years because they were pushed into Gaza. Jaffaites ended up in Gaza." Having to cope with everyday woes pushes the past's shadows aside and underscores the need to survive in the present, which has no time for memory and testimony, for humiliation, guilt, and shame, because their burden would only hinder one from realizing the existential moment.

THIS STREET is very representative of Jaffa. It's something between the underworld and the fringes of society, but one must make do. It's about constantly practicing what to do and what not to do, how to avoid, what you can dare do and what not. It's very complicated. You have a car? So don't register it in your name, because you may not receive some allowance from social security. If you take a car from someone else, then you'll pay him but won't take it on your name. There are also stories I've heard that I won't tell you because they're not mine, but life is heavy.

There are family quarrels. Every second Arab will tell you, "You're like a brother to me, you're like my grandma," and so forth, but the confrontations within the families are so harsh. It's simply frightening. So, don't take this "you're like a mother to me" too seriously. There's tension here: The family is terribly important. It's the only thing there is. On the other hand, because it's so important, it's so charged.

The refugeehood reflected in Talia's story and her street is a result not merely of war but also of exile from time. It is a withdrawal from parental and communal responsibility resulting from one's inability to meet its normative demands, which compel one to remember the past and anticipate the future. This disrupted timeframe, in which one lives the present without reckoning with the past and the future and without committing oneself to

binding normative principles ("there's no such thing as laws"), manifests itself in a range of social and educational problems.

> FROM TIME TO TIME there is yelling here. All in all it's terribly sad what's
> happening here. I see it in the little bored children, who try to do some-
> thing, to play, to arrange all kinds of boxes, and then one comes along and
> kicks, and that too is part of the game. And one has a bicycle and another
> takes it, and the other one cries. There's so much boredom here among
> the kids, that there's no structure, and there are no parents who think one
> should give structure, which is very important, no less than you're giving
> love to kids and food and all you need—it's also very, very important to be
> able to say no to them, and the world won't collapse if one tells them no.

The Jaffa experience of a casual timeframe, lacking duration and continuity—"slack time" in Talia's words—does not deny the place its historical time,
but this history too is that of sojourners, refugees who are not permanent
residents and who fail to generate a local historical continuum.

> THERE IS HISTORY TOO. On this street there is also Sarah, there is an-
> other Jewish family, but right now I don't recall who, but there are many
> people who come and go. At one time there was an elderly immigrant
> couple from Russia. There is always some elderly person or woman who
> disappears, because the children don't have the energy or don't feel like
> taking care of her.

The delinquent world of Jaffa's streets is a further marker of this contemporary, immediate, untenable, and unpredictable temporality. Talia indeed
depicts Jaffa as a conflicted and anarchic place whose routine is determined
by turf wars, because territory is the principal resource in this crowded and
cramped space.

> IN THE ARAB UNDERWORLD, they won't kill a Jew mistakenly in self-
> defense, because they know very well that if they kill a Jew, the police will
> wake up. But both sides feel that they are persecuted. Arabs are certain,
> and with no little justification, that the police don't care and don't take on
> the drug dealers, and don't deal with all kinds of things and with Arabs
> who kill each other, because they don't care, and even maliciously gloat.

The Jews say, "Anyone who can, gets out of Jaffa because the Arabs are taking more and more control." And that's true. Everyone tries to find a place to squat and take over, because the entire legal system is a mess in this respect. So if you live for a certain number of months or you can produce neighbors who will say, "Sure, he's been here five years already!" and he actually arrived yesterday . . .

In short, this is a world full of lies that merely complicate life, mine at any rate. Sometimes I say, I don't lie, not because of any great moral virtue but simply because it would complicate my life. How can I remember the lies I told yesterday or the day before yesterday or two months ago? The problem—as I see it more clearly in Jaffa—is that there's a dual conflict here: social class conflict and the nationalist conflict. And of course, the one nourishes the other and vice versa.

Talia's Jaffa is an arena in which a dual ethnoclass conflict is played out in frequent street skirmishes. The Jaffaite trap, she maintains, generates an urban economy of power and domination that holds both ruler and ruled captive. The political labyrinth translates into struggles for control over space, religion, and identity, which ultimately escalate into all-out war. The "unfortunate" Ottoman heritage, as she sees it, has left "the entire State of Israel a collection of refugees."

WHAT THEY DID HERE TO ALL THE ARABS is what they did in England in the nineteenth century and in France and in all kinds of places. They closed places that were open in general to all. Anyone with power said, "This is mine," put up fences around it, and people no longer had space. They came to the cities and began to work in factories, in poor conditions, with all the frustration and the revolting stuff and the drinking and all that goes with it. It's the same here. In the past, in the early Middle Ages, there were the Normans and the original English, and there was a conflict of power, but here there's a terribly similar confrontation to the colonial confrontation between a different people and a different class, those who have power and those who don't, that is. In other words, those who'll be simple laborers will mainly be Arabs, because they took their land away. The combination of the two things makes it far more charged and harsh, that's the first thing. The second thing, just like in the United

States, the poor whites are the most obnoxious: They're the nastiest; they are the most racist. Here too you'll find this among the Jews. And in addition to all these things, there's the continuous stupidity of the Jewish regime, which cannot accept emotionally that there is also an Arab national movement, just like there's a Jewish national movement. They said, "No way, that's illegal," and this led to the development of other forms of expression that seemed less dangerous, inheritances from the Ottoman Empire such as religion and religiosity, and suddenly they wake up to a more radical reality and say, "Hey, what's this? What barbarians! They're waging religious wars." Excuse me?! You have done your best to draw this out of them. You were stupid enough to fear religion less than nationalism!

I now perceive the entire State of Israel as a collection of refugees and as the hapless heirs of the Ottoman regime, which was a clean regime in that it showed absolutely no interest in the quality or the type of life of its subjects. It was a very focused regime, and what interested it was money and power. Ultimately this is a regime that promotes anarchy, and this anarchy persists to this day. Even if the Jews had not come here, it would have been the same.

Because Walls Are Not Just Walls

Talia's story ends with an insight into the link between personal biography and the boundaries of understanding. Although she does not regret finding herself in the eventful Jaffa where "the action is," perhaps getting more than what she had bargained for as a young French Jew, she claims to have learned to also accept what she fails to understand in order to maintain peace and quiet in this neighborhood at odds with itself.

I DO NOT REGRET COMING TO JAFFA. Because what I had at age 16, I also have now, the passion to be where the action is. But today I also know that I won't travel anywhere, because I'll take myself wherever I go. So I don't have to travel. There are tensions everywhere, but here they are more pronounced. I'll give you an example. The solar heater belonging to 'Abed, the neighbor below me, whose heating element I replaced at my expense because it was short-circuiting. I thought to myself, if this had happened to me, and I had seen this, I would have said, "How much does it cost this thing you replaced? I'll pay you." It simply didn't occur to him. And Ramzi said, "It's not worth it. We'll replace it so there'll be peace and quiet." And that was very wise. So he put in a new one—let's say it cost him 200 shekels. But for the peace and quiet, it was worth it. I don't understand, and I admit and am aware of this. And that's also the wisdom of the elderly to know what you know and what you don't know.

This insight soothes her, enabling her to survive in the contested Israeli space. From a position of introversion and emotional circumspection, Talia manages to find some cautious optimism in the choices that have led her to the present point.

I FEEL THAT I'M FAR WISER NOW than I once was and am suffering far less. I remember, for example, that Sarah the neighbor would come over after all sorts of events that were blown up by propaganda—the bus explosions, the war, and things like that. "Dear me, such things. We don't have a shelter, we don't have this." So I told her, "Listen, I'm not worried at all." Why? There's nothing I can do here. If I'm responsible for something and I haven't done what I should, then I'll worry and I won't sleep and that will prey on me. But here there's nothing I can do, so why should I waste my nerves on it? But in order to arrive at this, one needs time, I think, and also a minimal capacity to think. Because, really, what? The world is really shit! Must I add things that will burn my heart for nothing? If there's something that's happened and I can do nothing about it, then I want to know, yes, but to eat my heart out? For what? In general I know that the world is shit, but still, I'm not sorry that I came into this world.

Despite the secularized fatalism that commands her view of the world and confers on her the equanimity that accompanies liberation from responsibility and commitment, it is precisely because of the significance she attributes to the personal realm and to authenticity that Talia views herself as someone who has accepted the mission of guarding the realms of domestic and personal memory that Jaffa's Palestinian refugees have left behind them.

SEE, I've insisted on looking after this table I received as a gift from Yvonne's son many years ago. It's dear to me because it's personal. Something that's not personal cannot be dear. There's a further problem among the Arabs, which is very complicated. That is, What gives you the feeling of being what you are? Now I'm somehow living in a house of someone who lived and who was expelled from here, so I'm telling you that I'm looking after the property because there's an investment here that goes beyond money. They didn't build a house in order to make a profit, in order to invest. They built a house, and you can see that the house was built with great attention and passion, because walls aren't merely walls. It's not just a piece of property. It's something very meaningful to many people. So at least I can look after it. All this street from here to there, it's gone. It's not like it used to be, at least this floor should remain.

For Talia, the essence of the building, which is "not just a piece of property," takes precedence over the arbitrary legality of ownership determined by the laws of the state. Therefore right of possession is not invalidated by any change in the land registry. When asked if she would hand over the house to its original owner, she replied in the affirmative, on condition that the authorities gave their approval; and in any event, as for her, she would even encourage the owner to squat. This hypothetical encroachment, albeit antithetical to orderly urban procedure, is nevertheless commendable so far as distributive justice is concerned.

TODAY WHEN THEY BEGIN TO TALK, when almost everyone talks about ownership, about protecting property, I wouldn't give it up. Tell you why? Because if I were to give it up—not return it but give it up—then in the end the state would take it over, and I don't want that to happen. I preserve the building like it was, try not to betray the contours and so forth. I think that I'm not a bad neighbor. First of all, I wouldn't have come to this had it not been for the illness, probably. But once I saw that they were demolishing and demolishing in a stupid way, mainly Chich [former mayor Shlomo Lahat], yes, that was important. When I came here, a neighbor said to me, "Why have you come here? This building should be demolished!" I said, "I don't think it should be demolished. It's beautiful." Today I think that it's a luxury to think about esthetics and about history. But I don't think that she now wants them to demolish the building.

For Talia, persuading the neighbor that the building should not be demolished is her way of performing her role as a self-appointed custodian of the abandoned property. It constitutes the rescue of a building in Israel so as to return it to its original Palestinian owner, should he return. Returning the apartment rather than relinquishing it is an active measure that will prevent the state from appropriating it in the event that it is handed over without the authorities' permission.

A Refugee from Nationalism

In a biographical dialogue on Ephraim Kishon, a celebrated Israeli satirical writer, Kishon the ultimate migrant-refugee is portrayed as follows: "His alienness was his forte. . . . Only the eye of a stranger could have discerned the grotesqueness of the ordinary Israeli. Only a recently arrived stranger could question the logic of arrangements sanctified since time immemorial."[3] Like her better-known contemporary who shared her fate, Talia finds herself in the permanent status of an observer, who, from the existential position as a refugee, eyes the culture she has come across with a curious, astonished, and primarily distant and unyielding eye. Like Kishon, Talia also understands that the choice of identities offered to her is merely an illusion of belonging and that only by maintaining her autonomy and keeping her options open can she hope to retain her capacity to act and to act upon others. Her insistent refusal to yield to the temptations laid before her at the places where she temporarily resided indicates her will to preserve the authenticity of her path, despite her tortuous life journey through stations, none of which she planted roots in.

Talia indeed does not feel at home among the groups of people in which she was or is immersed: European Christians in France; European Jews who chose to immigrate for ideological reasons; Israel-born parochial sabras; her neighbors, the present Palestinians; and the dispossessed denied the right of return. Refugeehood is the fundamental condition that defines her life, from which she knowingly and ironically eyes the bearers of firm, uncompromising identities, which to her are merely a passing shadow. From the position of someone who has not been betrayed, who does not feel like a victim, not even of her diseased body, and who in fact has not been uprooted from her own land, she steadfastly rejects all the sanctuaries available to her. She prefers to safeguard her singularity as the molder and exclusive interpreter of the reality of her life. Her refusal prevents her from accepting the burden of any particular inclusive identity. She identifies neither with the Zionist state nor with the Palestinian people, despite the sympathy she displays toward them, and she fails to view her neighbors as representatives of the oppressed collective to which they belong.

Like Subhiya abu-Ramadan's outlook (see Chapter 6), Talia's worldview is a-national; yet unlike Subhiya, Talia does not seek consolation in religion or in the security of the household to cope with ongoing hardships. She looks the trials of existence squarely in the eye, clearly aware of the relations between necessity, ability, and will. In her eyes, her dwelling place is the sphere within which all these elements vie for power, in the midst of which stands her figure, which requires no extraneous affirmation or authorization.

Talia appears to have consciously and deliberately made herself homeless. She embraces her refugeehood as a condition of strangerhood by choice[4] in relation to both Israeli and Palestinian society. Her wanderings among her various homes indicate that she has no desire to settle down and control a permanent physical sphere that regulates and administers patterns of routine time and meaning, which are metonymically subordinated to the ethos of the national home. Within a culture that straddles borders, populated by refugees and the uprooted, migrant workers, tourists, ramblers, businessmen, and ordinary travelers, the home and its customs—this embryonic, microcosmic form of human life[5]—are not confined to a particular territory and timeframe.

The domestic time-space chronotope[6] disintegrates in the wake of the incessant movement of passers-by, who come and go and do not always return.[7] The domestic haven is replaced by codes of behavior that people carry with them wherever they go,[8] such as customs, characteristic gestures and manners, values, and cultural regimes of justification. These private homes, which contemporary nomads carry on their back, belong to those individuals whose choices are guided by enduring meaning.[9] Although Talia certainly orders the movement of her life in the way of someone who anticipated the global era of movements and transitions,[10] at the heart of the Jewish and Palestinian Israeli melting pot of nationalism, she is aware of the disparity between her way of life and her environment. She observes the landlords and their tenants and those who long to return to them with a pinch of irony while adopting an explicitly moral standpoint. This moral position determines her attitude toward her place of residence as a house rather than a home to the Palestinians, whose spirit, aspirations, and rights fill it and the time within which she is placed—a time of waiting until the dispossessed return to their land and houses.[11] Unlike them, Talia is not homeless in the social order in Bhabha's terms.[12] In fact, she does not even accept the hybrid category between homeland and exile, of which the homeless are the extreme and most distinctive case.

One might maintain that if the hackneyed and vilified concept of authenticity retains any meaning, then Talia, who engages with herself, views her world and her life in its terms: "I'll take myself with me wherever I go." Yet this humanist and idiosyncratic authenticity is a double-edged sword for her. She invests it with the inner conviction that she serves as a pawnbroker of the past of her residence, which is destined to return to its owner at some unknown, almost messianic future point; at the same time, she clings to the existential present, whose demands on her powers of survival are becoming ever more strident as she grows older and her illness progresses.

As time passes, Talia's center of gravity indeed turns toward ongoing needs and recognition of the vital importance of quotidian relations of reciprocity and assistance within her immediate surroundings. Hence the voluntary gaze is turned into a circumstantial social participation. In this respect Talia finds herself alongside Jaffa's other elderly people, such as Subhiya, who place their trust in one another and cast supportive safety nets that transcend the differences of identity that divide them. It is in fact her universal thesis of refugeehood that makes it easier for Talia to join this contingent modus vivendi, and despite insisting on her own singularity, she is ostensibly prepared to relinquish the position of a subject conditional on nationality, ethnicity, and kinship, which has in any event never been her lot.

⌒

In this respect Talia presages the third chronotope, in which this book's remaining protagonists reside: the threshold toward which those devoid of identity stumble purposefully or otherwise. The links between the signifiers of identity remain strong, and in time vanish, as though they had never existed. Their test lies in their maintenance, which is conditional on their immediate utility. In between the period of limbo, in which the elderly who are ruled by present hardships are locked, and the period of refugeehood, which is likewise an intermediate time, one finds an existential proximity of episodes that constructs Talia's existential space and that of others like her as an experience devoid of historical time despite its historical circumstances. The annulment of past identities and disregard of the terrors of the future that typify the behavior of the elderly[13] lead us toward Part III, which deals with the total decline of the spirit of nationalism.

Although nationalism is certainly a formative force in the women's stories of Part II, it not only plays a marginal role in their self-perception and consciousness but is also obscure and lacks a mobilizing political focus. The women's stories revolve around historical events, but seen through their eyes, these events appear to be a secondary narrative framework that merely forms the backdrop to the dramatic script of their lives. Their interpretations do not ignore the nation's history, but neither do they commit themselves to it. In terms of the interlocutory pattern that evolves in the stories, the gap between the storytellers and the national agenda is broader than the fissure that emerged from the men's stories in Part I. The more the women suspend mythical time and move further away from the big place of the nationalist city, the more they realize resources that are embedded in their daily lives and in domestic, family, and neighborly exchange relations.

PART III

NIGHTFALL

CHAPTER 8

SUSPENDED NATIONALISM

Moshe (Mussa) Hermosa and Jewish–Arab Masculinity

Every man is the architect of his own fortune.

Appius Claudius Caecus

Moshe (Mussa) Hermosa was born in Haifa in 1923 to a family from Hebron. He grew up in the impoverished Shabazi neighborhood of Tel Aviv on the border of Jaffa.[1] Throughout his life he moved between Tel Aviv and Jaffa and between the social worlds of Jews and Arabs. Hermosa's story is one of financial success and class mobility, as he progresses from a boy dependent on his patriarchal father to the owner of a thriving meat-processing plant. Nowadays, Hermosa lives in the upscale Bavli neighborhood but spends his mornings in a Jaffa café. He defines himself as an Arab by custom, manner, and comportment and renounces Israeli culture and his Jewish neighbors in bourgeois northern Tel Aviv.

Hermosa shares his story as he sits in the Arab café where he passes his time since retiring from his business. Here, where time stands still, he weaves the strands of his yarn and tells the story of his life devoid of history and myth. Each morning he comes to Torsina Café in Jaffa's 'Ajami neighborhood, where he meets with friends, listens to music, discusses current affairs in Arabic, and smokes a hookah to his heart's delight. The café's clientele is made up of Arab men of varying ages who live in the neighborhood, elderly Jews, mainly of Lebanese and Syrian extraction, and occasional tourists. Apart from Fridays, when he shops for the Sabbath dinner, Hermosa spends nearly every day in Jaffa. At midday he collects his things and returns home to Bavli, which practically belongs to a different universe. This daily

Danniel Monterescu

crisscrossing between Tel Aviv and Jaffa is emblematic of the functional and symbolic schism between the compartments of his life.

Having grown up on the outskirts of Jaffa during the 1920s, Hermosa is an Arab Jew.[2] Jaffa enables him to preserve his cultural Arabism without relinquishing the ethnic-Jewish component of his identity. His narrative, which skips effortlessly between his native Arabic and Hebrew, is coherent and shaped by a total division between the municipal and global north and south. He lives in two social worlds and suspends any potential contradiction in his multicultural milieu, which bears closer affinity to the Ottoman *millet* than to the contemporary Israeli culture that he renounces.

Hermosa is a *homo faber*,[3] a self-made man who displays a form of suspended nationalism. He relates a story of personal and financial success in terms of total control over the events of his life and leaves no room for myth or history. Although certainly aware of the events, he ascribes no importance to them with regard to his own life story and the construction of his identity. Hermosa presents an apolitical and humanist ethics focused on his gender role as a normative male, head of a large family, and husband to a woman of valor, whom he lauds as upholding the best of Arab traditions (*bint 'arab*). He does not engage with nationalism through the idiom of land or the comfort of religion but rather through the language of normative masculinity.[4] His patriarchal masculinity, evoked in terms of Arab culture, establishes the values of honor and courtesy as a common denominator that defines his social world and guides his way through life. This outlook facilitates pragmatic, reciprocal relations between Jews and Arabs as an alternative to the territorial conception of nationalism, which Hermosa considers a folly of little consequence.

I'm No Thief. I'm a Working Man!

Scholars of narrative set great store by the way storytellers choose to start their tale,[5] because the foundational event they choose as the starting point of their life's voyage reveals much about their frame of reference. Fakhri Jday (Chapter 1) chose mythological Jaffa; Rabbi Bachar (Chapter 2) began with his immigration to Israel, and Subhiya abu-Ramadan (Chapter 6) started with the 1948 war. By contrast, Hermosa chooses to begin with his personal experience as a working youngster, making no reference to the tempestuous events that troubled the country at that time. In response to the question of how he would choose to describe his life, Hermosa recounts a tale of success and social mobility that celebrates his autonomy and extols his entrepreneurial virtues.

AS A CHILD I WORKED FOR MY FATHER, of blessed memory, he had a slaughterhouse. One day I asked him to give me 5 liras per week. He wouldn't hear of it. I went to tell my mother. She began to yell at him. Nobody could talk to him. He said, "If he doesn't want to work, he can leave." At that time the mayor of Tel Aviv was [its first mayor] Dizengoff, of blessed memory. On Salame Street, on Herzl Hill, there was an ice-cream factory. I told him, "I don't have a penny." He said to me, "Can you sell ice-cream?" I said, "I can do anything." He gave me a three-wheeled bicycle, put three drums on it. Until now I can't forget: lemon, white, and red. Where Dizengoff lived on Rothschild Boulevard there was a guy selling all kinds of soft drinks, named Robnenko, born here. I took the bicycle and went to a funeral, before the funeral parade started. It was summer, hot, hot. Within an hour and a half I sold out the three drums.

I went and filled another three drums. I remember it to this day, three times. Nine drums I sold. I made a whole lira that day. A family of ten could live on a lira for two weeks. I went to my mother. I told her, "Take it, hide it for me." She said to me, "Where did this come from? Did you steal it?" I said to her, "I'm no thief. I'm a working man!"

The modest beginning to Hermosa's long career as a working man and entrepreneur was followed by a series of similar random opportunities that he skillfully exploited to enhance his capital and his status. His quest for financial independence was motivated by his defiance of his father's patriarchal tyranny, hence his choice of entrusting his hard-earned money with his mother for safekeeping. As Hermosa developed his own career, his mother interceded with his father, a successful cattle trader, urging him to take Moshe back into the family business. His father eventually relented and suggested that his adolescent son serve as his foreman. Hermosa portrays this as a great victory, celebrated in public.

MY PARENTS MOVED TO TEL AVIV, to Shabazi. My father was a Hebronite, from Hebron. They smuggled them out during the pogrom of 1929. Twenty-eight laborers worked for my father in Tel Aviv—all of them Arabs. In Haifa he was a cattle trader. Here they would bring him mutton, sheep, goats from all the villages. I had already saved about 11 or 12 liras by that time. Whatever I earned I would give to my mother for keeping. One day my father came to my mother, says to her, "Look." She said to him, "Didn't you throw him out? Because you didn't want to give him 5 liras?" He said to me, "Come back." I was 12 years old. He said to me, "I won't give you 5 liras. I'll give you 15 liras per month." That Friday he called all the laborers, every Friday was payday. He says to them, "Do you see my son? He's the head manager here. If you disobey him in the slightest, he can pick up his clothes and go." I reached my bar mitzvah. He threw me a bar mitzvah that lasted seven days.

Hermosa's description of his financial success is a story of self-taught adolescence and masculinity. As befits a Jewish youngster in traditional society, his adolescence is marked by the normative religious and social rites of passage (bar mitzvah, driver's license, and wedding). Throughout the interview,

Hermosa constantly celebrates his early life and the symbolic disengagement from his authoritarian father.

I CAME TO HIM AND SAID, "Put down money, put." I'm now a man of 13, right? He gave me 20 liras a month! A good time. I was rich. In my neighborhood I had seven, eight friends, I would take them out. There was an ice-cream parlor on Allenby—it was called Whitman. I'd take them all with me, ice cream and soda for half a lira. Ice cream as big as this. That's sixty-nine years ago. Now I'm 82. I was 14 then; going on 15 more or less I wanted a car. Only the mayor had a car. He had a car and a horse. I told my father, "If you don't buy me a car, I won't work." He said to me, "What kind of vehicle do you want?" I said, "A truck." He said, "A truck? You don't have a license." I had a friend, and he told me, "A license, five minutes. Put half a lira inside an envelope. The English sergeant will see it, hand it to him, you have a license." I told my mother of blessed memory, "Wait for me." I put half a lira in an envelope. I walked up from here to the second corner. He said, "Come back and you'll have a license." I came to the old man, of blessed memory, the old man said to me, "Where did you get a license? Is it illegal?" I told him, "Read! Is it illegal?" He said, "You've brought a license. I'll buy you a car." I told him, "I won't be working at the slaughterhouse any longer." I began making deliveries. At the age of 17 I had 150 liras. For a hundred liras you could then buy five houses with deeds, with land, with everything. For 20 liras you could buy a house, and what a house, four, five rooms.

One day my father came to me and said, "Lend me 50 liras." He made fun of me. He wanted to see what I was made of. I told him, "I have 150 liras with my mother. Go to her, tell her I said she should give you." He said, "I should go and ask your mother to give me money?" No two ways about it. I was about 16. On Herzl Street there was the Halva Ahdut factory. I walked over there. "Hello, hello, who's the owner?" He said, "You're a boy." I told him, "I'm not a boy. I'm a young man. I'm 16 years old, what do you mean a boy? I want to work." He said, "Are you prepared to take a horse and cart and distribute goods?" I would go and park next to every store. Whatever was in the cart I emptied out the same day. Money, money, money. No installments, cash down only. People then didn't know what installments were. I came to the owner after about three weeks. I told him, "I want 50 liras a month." He gave me 50 liras.

That Neighbor's Daughter

The story of Hermosa's passage into adulthood is incomplete without the symbolic act that establishes his status as a normative family man: a proper engagement and wedding held according to "customs like yours."[6] Strictly adhering to the patriarchal manner, Hermosa selected a close neighbor for a bride, a Sephardic girl from a good family, "a daughter of Arabs" (*bint ʿarab*) originally from Tiberias. She lived in a building owned by Moshe's father. His mother was asked to act as the matchmaker.

THE DAUGHTER OF MY NEIGHBORS—her parents live over there in my father's building. I came to my mother. I said to her, "That neighbor's daughter, I want you to go and ask for her hand in marriage." She began to laugh. I was already 17 or 18. You know our customs; you must bring her gold. I said, "How much money do you have?" She says, "Three hundred liras." I told her, "All these 300 liras, if they're needed to ask for her hand from her father, you can cross them out. I'm working, what's the problem?" They went and asked for her hand. Her mother and her father came to my parents. They said, "We want the boy, but what have you got? Do you want to buy a horse or a mule?" Her father exclaimed, "Whatever you put down, we'll match it." We were engaged. It was permitted to take her out for a stroll from 6 o'clock; by 7 she had to be home. We strolled along Allenby, on the seashore. By now I was a grown lad, at 20, and she was 17. I'm married to her sixty years. May you have grandchildren, great-grandchildren I wish you like I have today. Two great-grandchildren I have, twenty-seven grandchildren.

Having established himself as a patriarch in his own right, Hermosa's narrative proceeds to the desired class transition to a penthouse in Tel Aviv.

HER MOTHER HAILS FROM TIBERIAS. The uncle of her mother's brother was Mayor of Tiberias—Elias Dahan was his name. Her father is a Yemenite. They are of Sephardic origin. They were the fifth generation in the country. We are sixth generation. The children seven, the grandchildren eight. I lived in Shabazi, next door to the parents. Later I bought a house in Yad Eliyahu. I sold the house in Yad Eliyahu and moved to Ezra Ha-Sofer Street near Ge'ula. From Geu'la I've been thirty years in the house where I live now, in Bavli. I have a penthouse. Thirty years ago I paid 455,000 liras, cash down. By then I had a factory—my father's trade—the meat industry. I had a factory for forty-five years.

Like his wife's family origins, Hermosa's real estate history affirms and glorifies both his economic resourcefulness and entrepreneurship and the management of his masculinity that facilitated the family's social ascent.

The English Made Us Quarrel

Up to this point Hermosa has focused on the story of how he established himself. When asked how he came to Jaffa and about the relations between Jews and Arabs at the time of the British Mandate, he relates the events surrounding the expulsion of his family from Hebron in 1929. Even when addressing the political context and the Jewish-Arab conflict, however, he refuses to point the blame at the "Arabs" and notes that before 1949 "people were civil" and that an Arab neighbor had in fact saved his father's life. Like Abu-Subhi (Chapter 3), Hermosa mainly blames the British for stirring conflict.

AT THE TIME OF THE ENGLISH we were together constantly. Twenty-eight Arab laborers worked for my father. We lived through the riots like everyone else. My father was wealthy. Four streets, five dunams of land—all of it my father's. Nothing is left. Not in Hebron, nowhere. In Hebron Arabs are living on my father's land. It's worth nothing. What can you do? Throw them into the street? *Haram* [God forbid]. These days I'll never return to Hebron. Things were different then. They smuggled us out, my father, from Hebron before 1929, when all the riots began. An Arab who worked for my father there, he smuggled us out. Lifted us onto mules and took us to Jerusalem. From Jerusalem to Tel Aviv. We were like brothers.

In Shabazi an Arab wouldn't walk next to a Jew while smoking a cigarette [as a sign of respect]. There was civility. Arabs lived in my father's building. My mother used to cook, brought them food. Like family. The English made us quarrel.

Hermosa bears no grudge against Hebron's Arabs, nor does he wish to reclaim the family land. He recognizes that circumstances have changed but regards the historical processes as something detached and incongruous in the dominant and coherent trend of his personal life experience.

In the same breath he proceeds to describe the military manifestation of his masculinity: his enlistment in the Israeli Defense Forces and service in the navy during the 1948 war. Despite his unconcealed personal pride in his exploits, his story is devoid of nationalist fervor. In a similar vein, he dismisses the Palestinian tragedy as a tactical error ("They had no brains"), while portraying the erstwhile functional relationships between Jews and Arabs as a social system unsullied by politics. Above all, Hermosa vehemently rejects the notion of any overarching national identity: "I wasn't a Zionist. I consider myself a decent person." From his perspective as a "decent person," he observes his neighbors' fate and laments the world that has disappeared forever.

THEY RECRUITED ME TO THE 8TH BRIGADE in the '48 war. Later I moved to the navy. I was in charge of supplies: food, cigarettes, everything. I enjoy remembering things. But I didn't enjoy fighting—I wished they would live in peace. We have a saying, "You don't spit where you eat."

I'll tell you about '48. There were laborers working for my father—all were Arabs. Each day they would kiss his hand when they went home. During the war they left. They fled, the asses; they had no brains. To this day the children of the old people come to visit me at home from Taybeh, from Tira, from Qalansawe. Eighteen Arab laborers worked for me and eight Jews. The Arabs would listen to my every word; the Jews won't. There are good people among them. They say, "In every home there is a toilet." After '48 I would buy animals from them, sheep, everything, for my factory.

In Shabazi they were mingled together. They lived as one family. I wasn't a Zionist. I consider myself a decent person. There wasn't a wedding of the Arabs in which my father didn't pay for the whole thing. That's what my father was like. A neighbor wished to marry off her daughter; she would come to my father, "Biddi ajawiz binti" [I want to marry off my daughter]. He would tell her, "Kul al-farah 'ala hsabi": All the celebration at my expense.

Arabic Is Our Mother Tongue

Alongside his total rejection of every form of nationalist identification, Hermosa carefully constructs a narrative based on the logic of Arab honor and ethics, which regulates relations of trust between people. In his mind, reciprocal relationships and mutual responsibility overshadow the roots of the political conflict. Hermosa returns time and again to his personal experiences to stress the futility of ideological struggle. He sees no point in dwelling on what he calls "hatred" and "nonsense" and proceeds to describe the idyllic relations between his Palestinian associates and himself with typical optimism.

ARABIC IS OUR MOTHER TONGUE. There were people who appreciated what I did for them. Nowadays people spit where they eat. Shabazi was part of Jaffa. The mayor was then the one after Dizengoff, Eliyahu Sasson.[7] He also lived in Shabazi. One didn't see the difference. Many Jews also lived in Jaffa. The hatred and the conflict—that's all the English's doing. They would come and say to you, for example, "These people are bad. Keep away from them." Divide and rule. You see Abu-Muhammad the fisherman sitting there? I've known him for over fifty years. He's 64 years old. That's why I believe there's a chance we can live together. But what's the dispute about? Neither these nor those understand. If they understood, there's no country in the world like Israel. Hatred, they put hatred into them, and it's all nonsense. Don't they know that no one takes anything along with him? After a long life, every person, whatever's written about him in Heaven.

The Arabs have no brains. They could have lived like kings. Not because I'm a Jew. You know, you go the Triangle [an area populated by Palestinian citizens of Israel], see houses there—they didn't dream in a thousand years what they would have.

They used to be envious in my factory that I liked the Arabs better than the Jews. The Jews were envious. I had a shepherd with whom I entrusted the cattle and the sheep in Lydda. I had a butcher shop for fifty years. One day I had enough. I gave the shepherd all that I had. Just like that! The children come to me to this day. His children would take my sheep out to pasture. He would say to me, "If the tail of a single sheep is missing, all my fourteen kids I'd slaughter them. There was good faith then!

The local patriotism and nostalgia prevalent in stories narrated by elderly men who tend to glorify their own ethnic[8] or national[9] community emerges, paradoxically enough, in the context of Hermosa's personal services to the local Arab elite.

> THE MAYOR OF JAFFA, Abu-George, every Sunday I would slaughter a sheep for him, dismember it, and bring it to his house. He lived next to the hospital of the late Dajani, who also bought meat from my father. There was also Sasson, the mayor. There were 400, 450 Jews in Jaffa. I knew them all. They were like a gold lira. Once there were people speaking good Arabic, respectable, decent people, who helped one another. Where are they now? Where have they gone? Nowadays a person won't bring a glass of water to his own brother! God forbid. The world has gone topsy-turvy. To this day my friends are Jews and Arabs. I haven't counted them, about the same. If there's peace tomorrow, let them return to Jaffa and to Haifa—why not? They also have their houses in Syria, property. If they give them up, they'll get something in return. One can't just receive.

Hermosa makes no distinction between Jewish and Arab notables in historical Palestine and identifies himself as an emissary who serves the upper class as such. He refers to the possible return of refugees with characteristic resignation that indicates a utilitarian logic of exchange and negotiation. This is not a matter of generosity as far as he is concerned but rather the appropriate reward for the offer of peace and reconciliation.

I've Been Here in Jaffa All My Life. This Is Home.

Hermosa is able to suspend nationalism and neutralize its content by separating his place of residence in northern Tel Aviv from Jaffa, where he meets companions and spends his leisure time. He renounces any affinity to northern Tel Aviv, declaring that "I have nothing to do with them. I live like an Arab."

> I'VE BEEN HERE IN JAFFA ALL MY LIFE. Nowadays Jaffa is different: drug addicts, thieves, criminals, murderers. But I keep on coming. I live at the world's end in Bavli. But don't you see me here every day? Every day! I've lived in the same house [building] for thirty years, four floors, in my

penthouse, [and] I don't know 80 percent of those who live there. Don't know them. I have nothing to do with them. This here is home. I live like an Arab. Same thing. No one believes I'm a Jew; they don't believe it.

I've learned a lesson in life. It's the best school. Don't you notice that I never sit next to people? I sit alone. People come to sit next to me. Let them sit! What's this, my father's house? In my father's home Arabs ate breakfast, lunch, and dinner. They [the café's clientele] don't interest me, don't share my opinion. People sometimes sit and talk nonsense. For example, during the war, they leap up, talk, "Eight were killed." I don't want to hear about it. That's idle talk. These who talk are not people. Once there were respectable people. They had manners; they had respect. I've smoked a hookah for fifty-six years. I don't smoke other stuff, only tobacco. I have thirteen lovely hookahs at home. Whoever comes is welcome.

In this Jaffa café, a liminal place of leisure, Hermosa considers political incitement to be inappropriate, something that spoils the ethos of honor and civility, which to him are the core of one's identity that cannot be compromised. Moshe Hermosa is a self-declared Arab Jew. This position is not a manifestation of identity politics but rather part of a cultural and gendered fabric that has no need to apologize for refusing to hop on the nationalist bandwagon. The cultural world in which Hermosa chooses to live moves along the axes of patriarchal familial attachment and the Arab code of honor and respectability. This conception enshrines the traditional division of labor between men and women and comforts Hermosa in his old age. And it gives rise to the greatest accolade he can confer on his wife.

ALL MY CHILDREN GIVE ME JOY, thank God. All my grandchildren give me joy, each and every one of them. If everything goes smoothly, one forgets about God. My mother died at age 96, my father at age 105. There were hard times, but those who endure, prevail. A man finds it more difficult to grow old. All his life he runs about, worries, the wife stays home. My wife is nearing 80, may she reach 120. My wife cooks only Arab food. What is she, a French woman, my wife? An Arab woman, the daughter of Arabs [*bint 'arab*]. There's no one like her in the entire Middle East. My wife doesn't work—a woman is made for housework only. Why on earth should she work? Yesterday she prepared *mulukhiya* for me. There's an Arab proverb that says, "If your beloved is made of honey, don't lick him all up."

Although Hermosa considers himself and his wife as members of the Arab culture, he insists on maintaining the separation of religious categories and his wife's kosher cooking.

I HAD A MEAT FACTORY in HaTiqva neighborhood. Before I had a factory, I used to trade in meat. My father had a slaughterhouse, behind Abu-Kabir jail. The whole area belonged to my father. They would bring him *halal* meat [suitable for consumption according to Islam] from the Triangle, from Syria, from the villages. Those were the days! Each according to his religion. We cook the *laban* [buttermilk] dish in a kosher way, without meat.

The Arab patriarchal imperative imposes the continuity of patrilineal kinship, which is manifested by naming the firstborn after his grandfather. This is an important component of the symbolic capital of the extended family's paterfamilias, and Hermosa shows it off, emphasizing furthermore that all his children understand Arabic and that he has nothing in common with Israeli culture.

ALL MY BROTHERS' AND SISTERS' CHILDREN are named after my mother and father, and now all my eldest grandchildren are named after me, without exception. All are Moshe Hermosa. My children are all well off, thank God. My eldest son is a flight engineer for El Al. My eldest grandson works for Microsoft. He too is called Moshe. We, the sons of Arabs, are obliged to name the first grandson after the grandfather. As the saying goes, "There is no loved one like the son of one's son." They know Arabic, understand every word. I listen only to Arabic music. Don't understand anything else, don't understand Israeli culture.

In a manner that well illustrates Hermosa's focus on his entrepreneurship and personal achievements, his life story closes with the end of his business career. After fifty years of hard work, he decided to sell his business, persuaded by his children to retire. As far as he is concerned, having sold the meat-processing plant, he has ended his activity and concluded his story.

I STOPPED WORKING SIXTEEN YEARS AGO. I sold the business. I would
go to the plant each day at 4 in the morning. The kids badgered me constantly, told me, "Why do you come home every day at 8 in the evening?
Take the mattress and sleep there!" They would sing a different tune each
day. What did I do? One day someone came to me, "Do you want to sell?"
I said, "Yes, I'm selling." He said to me, "Go to the lawyer and take the
money." I went to the lawyer, went home, "I've sold the plant." They didn't
believe me. I started working at age 11. Bygones are bygones. Who'll em-
ploy me? I've always been self-employed. Ever since my father died I've
always worked on my own. Now you have it all from beginning to end. I
might have forgotten 50 percent.

Hermosa's lifetime achievement is a whole greater than the sum of its
parts. It is an indivisible substance. Every detail, notwithstanding the "forgotten 50 percent," metonymically represents the whole—and perhaps also the
ethical wholeness that he offers the listener. No particular detail can alter our
understanding of the metonymic frame of his life's structure as he displays
it: a cultural conception of urban life explained according to a well-defined
thematic code that remains constant through time and is not subject to the
whims of contingency and circumstance. Before us stands a man whose
narrative figure corresponds to Sharon Kaufman's[10] insights regarding the
existence of an ageless self whose unchanging consciousness stems from
the deep cultural structures that determine his being. Hermosa is guided by
themes of popular prenationalism,[11] which is independent of the vicissitudes
of any particular national community.

Coffee-Time Nationalism: An Arab Jew in a Liminal Space

In his book *The Arab Jews: A Postcolonial Reading of Nationalism, Religion,
and Ethnicity*, Yehuda Shenhav describes the conspiracy of silence responsible for the fact that "Israeli society had placed a taboo on any discussion
of the *Mizrahi* question as a political issue."[12] The encounter between the
Zionist movement and the Jews of the East, Shenhav maintains, generated
the categories that facilitated discussion of the Mizrahim, in particular, the
separation of imagined nationalism into categories of East and West, thereby
stifling the category of Arab Jews and obfuscating religion and nationalism

within Judaism. The twilight zone between the national and the ethnic becomes a site of denial that does not enable the circumvention of ethnicity and sets in stone a uniform national Israeli identity: "The Arab past of the Mizrahi Jews threatened to affect the coherence of the homogeneous Israeli community and to blur the boundary between Jews and Arabs."[13]

The processes of dismissal and exclusion that Shenhav traces find no place in Hermosa's life story. On the contrary, not only is Hermosa disinclined to delete the hyphen between his Arabness and his Jewishness, but he takes pride in it and, in fact, lives from and within it. With a perspective of over half a century, Moshe Hermosa has created a world of his own in which the individual is measured by the ethics of his conduct, by his successes, and by honor and civility. This worldview may seem naïve, romantic, and far removed from the modern ethos of nationalism, yet it should be appreciated as the product of the historical period in which Hermosa grew up and of the social context in which his worldview evolved.

Between the two World Wars, Greater Jaffa was a multicultural and binational Mediterranean city in which the implicated relations[14] between Palestinians and Jews established a social reality of political and territorial confrontations; yet it was also a city of quotidian reciprocal relations. The boundaries of the imagined community were not aligned with those of the extensive social networks, and collective political spheres did not confine the area in which private agents operated. Jaffa and southern Tel Aviv were the locus of a growing struggle for territorial control between municipalities and paramilitary organizations, but they also constituted—in particular, in the border neighborhoods such as Shabazi and Manshiya—an environment that allowed for a hybrid identity, in contemporary terminology, such as the Arab Jewish one. This identity is the organic product of the fabric of life of that time and place, and as such is not a part of the current discourse of collective rights or identity politics. And yet, because this hybrid identity renounces hegemonic Israeli culture, it challenges its fundamental premises.

In many respects Mandatory Jaffa was a remnant of the prenationalist Ottoman city in which Jewishness and Arabness were not mutually exclusive categories.[15] Although this urban form has become defunct, Hermosa's adherence to it against all odds is an act of political critique; he anachronistically anchors himself in a Levantine culture founded on reciprocity, courtesy, and a man's word of honor. It is a culture that regards nationalist affiliation as a mere secondary derivative of colonial syncretism that fuses together a mish-mash of fragmented identities. Suspension of nationalism is perhaps a way of defying nationalism's impositions and its transformation into the be-all and end-all of identity. Hermosa thus dismisses political discourse and territorial conflict as inconsequential and mean-spirited.

In the wake of the 1948 war, the spatial and cultural boundaries between Jaffa and Tel Aviv crystallized according to a cognitive and political map drawn in terms of north and south, Arab and Jew.[16] As befit his economic status, Hermosa chose to reside in northern Tel Aviv. Nevertheless, true to his hybrid identity, he skips between rich and alienated Jewish Tel Aviv and the indigent Jaffa that is dear to his heart. Moshe (Mussa) Hermosa's choice of a hyphenated way of life indicates that he is located beyond the ethnic, national, and social class order. From this perspective, Hermosa's narration is an apt preface to the striking liminal persona of the next storyteller.

(CHAPTER 9)

MASKING NATIONALISM

Amram Ben-Yosef on a Tightrope

Where are you from, brothers, originally
From the nest of a bird
In Givat Aliya in Jaffa
Where are you from, sisters, originally
From a whorehouse

I don't talk to foreign whores
He who won't talk to strangers
Has a problem
He's alone, but I dance
Look at me, I move my body
I'm dancing
But it still sucks
To be alone

Shmuel Shohat, "I'm Dancing"

Amram Ben-Yosef was born in 1934 in Casablanca, Morocco, to a poverty-stricken family. He immigrated to Israel on his own in 1950, at age 16. After moving from one kibbutz to another, he settled down in the crime-infested area of Jaffa formerly known as the Large Area (ha-Shetah ha-Gadol), adjacent to Clock Square. During his time in Jaffa, he made a living as a pimp and a trader, and he divorced his second wife. He now lives in Ramat Aviv in a public housing apartment that he has squatted, but he spends all his time in a café in Clock Square in Jaffa. Amram represents the generation of Jewish squatters evicted from the Large Area after its renovation. His story is one of failed absorption of an indigent immigrant who clings to the last vestiges of communal existence on the outskirts of Jaffa's old city.

The plot of Amram's life could have been copied from a Hollywood movie. His bastion, located in the northern section of the Old City near Clock Square, has a history of its own and is a portrait of a cultural space of exceptional ethnic and class features. This is the ultimate slum. Its residents refused to bow to the dictates of the Municipal Planning Inspectorate in the 1950s and early 1960s, and the area took on a cultural otherness that has gained notoriety in Israeli popular life and culture as a symbol of neglect and licentiousness, violence and marginality, alongside a saccharine scent of gutter exoticism. Even before the founding of the state, but primarily in the decades that followed, the Large Area was a location of casual sexual en-counters, a casbah of crime, drug dens, and gambling.[1] As such, it became a nuisance to both the Palestinian and the Israeli municipal authorities. Under the auspices of the Tel Aviv Municipality, the Large Area became home to orientalist fantasies and ethnic demons that created a place of contamination and revulsion, which is the Jewish antithesis to the White City of Tel Aviv, a UNESCO World Heritage site.

Like neighborhoods such as Wadi Salib in Haifa,[2] the Large Area is one of the "designated" districts on the cultural map of Tel Aviv and Jaffa. This is the place where creators of musicals, theater performances, films, books, and exhi-bitions offer a romantic, conservative, or critical reading of the Israeli and local way of life.[3] In Israeli public imagination, the Large Area is presented in terms of folkloristic orientalism. Cultural agents such as Menahem Talmi and Yigal Mossinsohn populate the place with flamboyant types who display a boastful masculinity, impulsive Mizrahiness, and an insatiable craving for mischief.[4]

The Large Area is likewise the prime arena in which Jaffa bears the brunt of the Tel Aviv town hall project of acculturation, which seeks to suppress any spatial and social order that fails to comply with its modernist planning regulations. And indeed, in the 1960s the so-called Artists Colony was built on the ruins of a large part of this area.[5] Yet Menahem Talmi's orientalism is by no means an innocent folkloristic show. Talmi celebrates the demolition of the Large Area, which serves as the setting for his protagonists' story, as a desirable case of creative destruction,[6] out of which "the pearl of Jaffa" will hatch. By so doing, he turns his orientalist nostalgia for place into a weapon used to destroy it.

Hicham Chabaita

THE MISTS OF LEGENDS, rising out of the obscure dawn of history, hover here transparent and invisible. Here, above the roofs, between the yellowing stone lanes, the mists of legends and ancient sensations, gliding on the salty scent of the nearby sea, whose white foam laps over the darkened rocks, transparent mists that caress the roofs of old, and the spires of inward looking churches. Above Old Jaffa's hill the ancient sensations merge with historical rustlings, which have, after all, permeated the cool paving stones, as they hum in the murmur of the south-westerly breeze, which carries the scents of Jonah the Prophet's shore. . . . Yesterday this was the old, shunned Jaffa, *The Large Area*, a heap of rubble and waste; the home of marginal people and the narrow-eyed arena of traders in white meat [a Hebrew euphemism for pork] and overwhelming smoke. Today—a refreshing island of charm, anchored in authentic depths. . . . There, on the rebuilt hill of the thousands-year-old city, a new gate has opened, leading you to a small and beautiful legend.[7]

All My Life Has Gone Astray

It is against this sociocultural backdrop that Amram presents the story of his life, flirting with the orientalist representations that envelop the place.[8] His tale begins in the form of a dense and entangled melodramatic script, in which he stars as the sole protagonist: a betrayed victim, a leaf dangling in the wind.

> MY STORY—if you hear it, you'll want to weep. I have lived for fifty-two years in the country. I've worked for only four years, and the rest is all from Allah. My story begins in the year '50, when I came here, to the Large Area. Here it was all dead in 1950; it was sand here. There was nothing. It was full of prostitutes here—miserable girls who came here without parents. They tricked them to come here. They didn't come as prostitutes; they had to live. I stayed here a while, not for long, until '51. I have no parents. I have nobody. I went to join the army. They didn't want to take me either. I pleaded with them; I made a commotion. I entered the army; they accepted me. But during the leave, I defected. I came here and stayed to this day. Until I got married. I met someone in Tel Aviv, a rich family. I was a handsome guy. I have six kids. She was a good wife. They sent me to Habima theater to be an actor. I could neither read nor write—I still don't. All my life has gone astray.

The sentence "All my life has gone astray" sums up the narrative that Amram unfolds. It is a circuitous tale of economic disadvantage, exclusion, and evasion of normative social shackles, a failed marriage, and, above all, a talent for acting that enables him to hoodwink those in power. Amram had the misfortune of suffering a series of mishaps, and he began his career as a pimp. This was his first step toward "the world of shit." In his view he did not choose this authoritarian and violent role either; he was driven to it by necessity.

> I'LL TELL YOU WHY. I got married, two children. One day I was sitting there, along came this amazing chick. She said, "Get up, get up." I got up. That was my first time in the world of shit, the world of filth. She put me in a cab. She tells him, "Drive to Ramat Gan." She roped me into this, Ramat Gan, a hotel; she paid the hotel. In short, I slept with her, and she was a whore. She took out a wad of bills and said, "Amram, put this in

your pocket." I took half of it. I gave it to the wife and told her, "I work as a waiter at the Khalif Club." And she bought it. And it went on like that perhaps eight years together. Until the wife went to the Rabbinate to get a divorce and asked for alimony. I don't know what it means to pay alimony.

The temptation and easy money served up to him as if on a platter led Amram to spin a web of lies, which eventually deteriorated into divorce and neglect of his children. Amram depicts the course of his life as a series of events that inadvertently "transpired," and all he could do was accept them. Yet he does take pride in one particular area, namely, the acting talent that extricated him from the clutches of the military police.

SHE GAVE ME MONEY BECAUSE I WAS HANDSOME; she loved me. And that's how it was. Eight years later I quarreled with her. She worked here, upstairs. I had a house that I bought with the money from this filth. I bought a house upstairs, and this house was full of whores. I would get lots of money, half to me and half to her. And I told my wife there are many tourists, there's a lot of work, they give me tips aplenty. And that's how it was, until this one, the girl, tells me, "You must get divorced. I work for you. I bring you money. I'm your whore. I'm everything." I said to her, "You do all this for me so that I'll get divorced?" "You must." What do you know, I too went to the Rabbinate to open a file to get divorced. We divorced after ten years.

After ten years they noticed that I hadn't been in the army. I went to release my brother from the law court, and they asked me, "How come you weren't in the army?" So he put the military police onto me. I didn't know what to do. It was hard for me. In short, they taught me what act to put on, how to get released. A little crazy, a little this—I don't know what. But during that time I was an addict. The money made me an addict. They would do drugs, so I would shoot up. I too shot up. Whatever they did, so did I. I had lots of money. I didn't know what a bank was—I still don't. The pocket is my bank. That's when I became an addict. In the army, at the recruitment office, I asked how long I'd have to spend in prison for being a deserter for ten years. They told me five years. I was really afraid. I began to tell my girlfriend bring drugs when you visit. I began to get dope also through kissing, and to get everything. And they saw that I really wasn't cut out for prison or for the army.

Having spent a short time in military jail, Amram returned to Jaffa and to the underworld. Through his story he conveys a thief's ethics, a moral code that considers pimping a legitimate source of livelihood. In contrast to his weakness for drugs, which he concealed from his friends and family, Amram shows off his normative achievements.

I WAS IN FOR TEN DAYS, and they released me after ten days. Just like that, no trial or anything. They even gave me 5 liras and some toothpaste, a gift. I gave it to the driver from military police who brought me here. I arrived and entered the underworld. Worse. I never was a thief, God forbid. A swindler I never was. I was never a robber. Just prostitution, that's what I dealt in. I didn't deal in anything else. Not a drug dealer, nothing. No one knows I was an addict here. To this day. I always did it quietly. And now, we're through with it. I've given it up, because of the shame, for the kids. And today I thank God, I've married once again. The first wife died and left two kids. Good ones, I have a daughter, assistant to a manager. A big rank—Naomi is her name. I have one who's called David. He has two taxis on Levinsky Street. I've never received a shekel from them. I paid alimony for ten years.

Yet this new beginning was likewise tainted by deception. Amram could not find the strength to make a living, and a further attempt to hold down a job ended in failure.

AND THAT'S HOW I DIVORCED. I married this one, a girl of 17. A good family, innocent, doesn't know about the drugs. And I began to work—I worked at the municipality, in sanitation. Eleven months. They threw me out of that job. I went to look for work once again. They sent me to the [Israel] Aerospace Industry [a manufacturing plant] in Lydda. What a job: in the dining hall, a guard, a supervisor. From 11:30 to 14:30. There were 13,000 employees then. Today it's more for sure. They told me to clean a bit with a broom, to replace the trash cans. A real job. But they really liked me there. And that's how it was, until I left that place.

I Get Divorced Because of Other Women, and Then They Dump Me

Amram does not elaborate on the failure of his second marriage. He hurries
on to a further tale of conquest that was likewise founded on deceit, temptation, and false promises.

> BUT I WAS NEVER ALONE, never in my life. I always had someone. Right
> now I love someone. I dated her for two years, a woman aged 60. She
> doesn't look 60; she had a facelift, everything. Everyone who sees her is
> amazed. Rich as well. She worked at the Sheraton Hotel, thirty years.
> Now she's retired. And I loved her, and I had to get 600 shekels for her
> every week, no matter what. And I'm just a pensioner, get 1,800 shekels
> [a month]. When I'm with her I have to help her: rent, electricity, water,
> two packs of cigarettes a day, dairy products for the week, two kilos of
> fish each week, whatever she needs. And I have no money, so what do I
> do? I go to my friends: Give me 500 shekels, until tomorrow. The next
> day I go elsewhere, to another friend: Give me 600 shekels. And then I
> return 400 to the first one, and that way I have 200. And I got along like
> that for two years.
>
> But eventually perhaps she noticed that I had nothing. She said, "Ei-
> ther you leave me alone, or I'm going to the police." And I lay out a table
> for her in a restaurant each week, 200 shekels. She said, "You deceived
> me. You said you have money." I said I have my own apartment in Ramat
> Aviv; I'll sell it soon for 270,000. She hears money, and I'm still stringing
> her along. I told her that I get 5,000 shekels per month through various
> government offices, and all that's a fib. I deceived her, in short. So those
> [people] must have told her that I, Amram, am the pits.

Amram portrays himself as a womanizer, with women constantly falling
at his feet. His demanding love affairs are his Achilles' heel. When his most
recent lover realized that he had deceived her and he threatened to harm her,
she turned to the police and broke off the relationship. This parting left him
heartbroken and led him to drink.

> THEN SHE TOLD ME, "Either you leave me alone, or I'm going to the po-
> lice." And I'm really crazy about her, to this day. It's been forty days since I
> last talked to her. She went to the police and filed a complaint that I threat-

ened to murder her. I've never in my life hurt a fly. Perhaps I once said to her, "If you leave me, I'll kill you." I said that casually in jest. I was stoned, and she took it seriously. She went to the police, and I was bailed out. God is my witness that I've never done anything to her. Every day I cry for her. I'm facing up well. But every evening I'm flat drunk. All because of her.

The recurring pattern of Amram's failed affairs adds up to a tragic and inevitable chronicle of dissolution of an ongoing relationship because of a new woman, who would also eventually leave him upon discovering that he is unfaithful.

THE FIRST WIFE PASSED AWAY, and I was divorced from the second after thirty-five years, because of this one. I get divorced because of other women, and then they dump me. It's like a calculation. Get divorced, and then "so long." It's very hard. I wanted to commit suicide more than once. Just because of my kids. With the last one I had it good: She took care of me, brought me back to religion, I don't smoke on the Sabbath, everything. She did only good to me: to sleep well, love, a warm home. I've never had a warm home. I met her here, in the café. She just looked at me, I looked at her. That was it. I took her on the spot, two years. She took me to the whole family. She told everyone, "This will be my husband." It's all a lie. She wanted to get married. I too wanted to, but suddenly she heard I was stone broke, that all I had promised her was a lie. What could I do? I have to lie to her. Today is her birthday. The whole family is at her place today. Whatever she's doing, I know about it, and whatever I do, she knows. How come? I don't know.

It had appeared as though Amram's latest lover would put an end to the trail of destruction, but he squandered this opportunity as well by making false promises. Amram believes that lying is a necessity, because had his girlfriend known that he was "stone broke," she never would have started the relationship.

If You Belong to the Haves, You're a King

Amram presents the story of his life through the prism of masculinity. As he sees it, he, the man, is victim to the wiles of women and subject to their constant surveillance ("and whatever I do, she knows about it."). He reproduces a familiar image of women in Mediterranean cultures as possessing occult powers and the capacity to domesticate a man and emasculate him.[9] Faced with such power, the masculine gender ideology in these cultures leaves the victim no option but to follow the path of deception and violence to maintain an appearance of power and control. Whereas at first it appears as though Amram is driven to lie against his will, as the tale proceeds, he reveals that lying is also a successful seduction strategy.

> ONE HAS TO KEEP GOING. I have another one. The same stories I told that one, this one also buys them. Someone really attractive, a nice young thing, 54 years old. Both pretty and a Moroccan. Every day I have women, but money I don't have. Take a couple of bites, take something to drink, that's 50 shekels. If she smokes, start to bring her a cigarette. This one wants me to buy her a pack of cigarettes every day. If you belong to the haves, you're a king. If you don't, forget it. Whatever I had is gone.
>
> I've also been in prison because of that one, who gave me money, who worked for me. I got nine months in prison. And there things got even worse. The nine months became forty-two months. It was lucky that the Six-Day War came along. I was pardoned. To this day I thank God. The prison warden told me, "Take care not to return." I said to the warden, "If I return, take my balls and hang them on the door." I'll go and work in shit. I've never worked. It doesn't suit me to work in garbage collection. I need something special. I am spoiled to this day.

My Friends Are All Worthless

To conclude the personal chapter of his life story, Amram presents his social relationships in the form of a forlorn triangle, whose three points—friends, women, and children—have all let him down. The betrayal by his friends, the women's scheming, and his abandoning children complete the profile of his victimized figure.

> THE WOMEN SPOIL ME—only the women. My friends don't. All my friends are worthless. I had many friends. Everyone was my friend. They knew that I would pay a lot of money. Once it was gone, they all kept their distance. I had a friend for five years. We would travel to Morocco, Canada.

Every feast, we're the first. The best drinks, the best food. Back then I had it all. One day he came to me and said, "I have a video player for you to buy for a hundred dollars." I bought it, took it home. I put in the cassette; it got stuck. I returned it to him, "It doesn't work." He said to me, "You damaged it." Since then we don't speak to this day. He comes by every day hoping I would make up with him. I don't want to, because of the deception.

Then I had a little money. I wasted it on this one. I showed her that I was wealthy. Until it came to an end. She used to say, "I want a dress." I tell her, "Next week I'll bring you one," and wouldn't bring. I stole two rings from my wife, all for her love. To tell the truth, I'm now heavily in love. I sit in the café; then I go to the flea market and wander around just to get rid of the thoughts. Come home crying. My children are fed up by now. They know that I'm in love, because I have a videocassette of her. I just watch it and I'm burning my heart out. Don't know what to do with it—I want to throw it out, my heart aches. I can't carry on like this.

Three of the kids live with me. A married son plus three kids. I have a bachelor son, and I have a daughter who's done the army. The three of them live with me and don't give me so much as a shekel, and I can also never ask. They know that "Father gets by." They live with me, but none of them has ever knocked on my door, asking, "Dad, do you want a glass of water? Do you want coffee?" No such thing. Only if there are utility payments. When I did have, I paid all the time. Now I don't have. They are observant, but not truly observant, actually fraudsters. Religious, but he won't knock on his father's door and ask, "Dad, do you need anything?"

In Casablanca the Arab Is Like a Brother to You

Having established his image as someone who has fallen victim to his quarrelsome wives, his perfidious companions, and his disrespectful children, Amram proceeds to describe his birthplace in Morocco.

I WAS BORN IN CASABLANCA. My father too was born there. There the Arab is like a brother to you, not like the stinking Arabs here. There, the Arab eats with you on the Sabbath. He lights fire for you on the Sabbath. The Moroccan Arab is something special. Today too there is a king who loves Jews. Morocco is something special.

The two types of Arabs that Amram invokes mark the difference between "here" and "there." Having delineated the boundaries between the communities while highlighting the otherness of Jaffa's Arabs, he bridges the political gap in terms of cultural affinity illustrated by language. Yet he is quick to deconstruct this affinity as well.

> IN THE LARGE AREA THERE WAS NEVER AN ACT OF SABOTAGE, never in your life. You'll never find someone attacking the Moroccans. We speak their language. Here at the mosque, we greet them, they greet us. We have good relations with them, because we know their language. But we don't trust them. You can't trust them. In Morocco he can eat and drink with you. Here he'll eat with you and then stab you. They have hatred, because we conquered them. We really did conquer; that's why we're tolerating them. I understand them, but not in Jaffa. In the Territories, not here. Here it belongs to us. Where can we go? Give them all the Territories. Give them Gaza, give them the lot. Not here. Not Israel. For a start I hate them—you don't want to know. Not here and not of Morocco. I don't have Arab friends. And I'll never have. All the Arabs who were in Jaffa now live together with the Jews in the projects.

The close physical proximity between the bastion of the Moroccan Jews in the Large Area and the Great Mahmoudiya Mosque across the road, where hundreds of worshippers pray every Friday, creates tension that Amram expresses in terms of treachery: "Here he'll eat with you and then stab you." This tension does not allow him to ignore the nationalist aspect of life in Jaffa. Although he is prepared to understand the origins of Palestinian "hatred," he nevertheless draws a clear line between the Occupied Territories and Israel. His words imply recognition of the need for a solution, but this should be applied "there," not in Jaffa. For the first time we can discern in his language a nationalist separation between "us" and "them." As did Rabbi Bachar (Chapter 2), Amram Ben-Yosef presents an ambivalent and convoluted narrative as he portrays his relations with Jaffa's Arabs. In this story pragmatic and reconciliatory logic alternates with hate-filled slogans. Yet immediately after noting the potential threat that this neighborliness presents, Amram portrays a reconciliatory picture of de facto coexistence, whose stability is assured through the generosity of the welfare state.

SOMETIMES ARABS who have come to work here from Morocco sit in the café. There are many here who have married Arabs here. There are no terrorists here, no troubles. Many Israeli Arabs live here. We see them every day. For years they've grown up with us, we've grown up with them. What can one do? You'll kill me after I ate with you? Abu al-'Afia also throws in a good word on Fridays in the mosque: "Don't make trouble. These are brothers." Here they do nothing; there's no reason to fear. Over there in 'Ajami, we can wander about at 2 at night. They are good—not all of them. Some hate us. But they don't hate us ourselves; they hate the government.

They get welfare money. They've all bought cars on the kids' account. Ten kids, they receive loads of money each month. Where would he get this? In Egypt? In Gaza? They have all renovated their homes. Each of them now has a house. What was once a ruin is now a villa. All from welfare. They also sell drugs freely, and the police don't check. Once I went to buy. The undercover squad stands there, they see how I take it, and they catch only me because I came to buy. Why only me? I'm ill. They said, "We got him." I swallowed it. I had to swallow. If you don't swallow, you'll end up in jail. That's an old trick.

I've Been Through All the Hardships

As noted, Amram immigrated to Israel alone at age 16. His father, who according to Amram "wished to get rid of" him, sent him to a youth group on a kibbutz. But Amram was considered a misfit and wandered from one kibbutz to another. He caused a commotion wherever he was.

MY FATHER HAD SIX CHILDREN, and he wanted to get rid of me. And perhaps I was a misfit. At first they sent me to a kibbutz. After that I moved to another kibbutz. I stayed there for ten months. I made trouble. I would go wild in the animal farm. My big brother came along, said to me, "Come with me to Kibbutz Manara." I was there perhaps three months. I got into a brawl. They took me to Kfar Szold. I was agitated then, not like now. When I'm agitated, I fall down and I froth at the mouth. Like epilepsy. Nowadays thank God, I've been through all the hardships. Tortures, worse than a ghetto. I used to eat from the garbage. I have no one—no father, no brothers, no one.

Amram unfolds the story of his poverty-stricken family's migration as a tragedy that extended from Morocco to Jaffa and that led to the death of his parents from a broken heart.

> LATER THEY BEGAN TO COME ONE BY ONE. Also when they came, they were in a worse state than me. We were a needy family. Father used to work as an upholsterer. What he earned in a week, we would eat up in two days. The brothers began to arrive, one by one, until they all came here. Here in Jaffa two of them died on me, addicts. One with an IV, and the other a champion alcoholic. The police knows him. Everyone knows him. Father and mother also died because of the worries.

Amram takes responsibility for having gathered his family in Jaffa, which appeared to him as a natural place for "the Moroccans." Yet his description is replete with feelings of impotence and inevitability, encapsulated in the phrase "there's nothing else."

> THEY ALL CAME TO JAFFA. I brought them one by one. The parents lived on their own with my brother. Now he's sick. I have another one, got a stroke. The youngest got a stroke. That's what there was in Jaffa. There's nothing else: whores and addicts. The Moroccans came to Jaffa, because Jaffa was like Morocco. The Turks went somewhere else; the Iraqis went somewhere else. Nowadays the Moroccans don't get along. The one curses the other. Once they used to get along with them all, all the ethnic groups ['edot]. Today there's nothing. They're all gone. Only Moroccans and Arabs remain. There's nothing else.

Amram brought his family to Jaffa, where they lived in poverty, illness, and sorrow. Like the history of his marital life, the family history is trapped in the tension between individual initiative and the twists of fate, superior forces, and powerlessness. The tragedy of Amram and his family is a product of the social-structural conditions that prevailed in Jaffa, where conceptions of cultural intimacy[10] came face to face with feelings of strangeness and constant crisis. As a marginal area, Jaffa became the only place that enabled the most ostracized and excluded populations[11] to share a common social life. As in Amram's story, this is frequently a minimalist existence, which entails a constant struggle for survival.

The Large Area Is Our Place. We Don't Have Any Other.

Lacking any other place with which he could identify, Amram settled in the Large Area. This, however, is not the big place of myth and autochthony[12] but rather a place of refuge, a voluntary ghetto teeming with tourists and cafés. Amram does not address the place's political or social history but views it from an entirely personal perspective, molded in the shape of his life story.

I DON'T KNOW WHY they called the place the Large Area. Perhaps it is large: full of whores, full of pimps, full of alcoholics, full of addicts—so it is large. It is large. Not today. They changed the name. Destroyed the place. Tricked all the Moroccans out. I had a house. They took it from me, gave me a project apartment. Here they sold for $2 million, where they took the house from me. The government and the municipality fooled everyone. All the Moroccans used to live, each had his house. Now all the wealthy people are coming: painters, actors . . . This house was sold for a million dollars. Today it's worth 2 million.

The Moroccan residents saw the apartments they sold for a pittance turned into spacious dwellings well beyond their means. The area's gentrification has exacerbated their sense of victimhood. But Amram nevertheless declares that "we have nowhere else to go." Many of the Large Area's original residents have scattered in all directions but continue to spend their days there.

THIS IS OUR PLACE. We have nowhere else to go. But no one lives here anymore. I've lived in Ramat Aviv for twenty-eight years now. But I return home drunk every day. When I wake up, I come here straightaway. I would stroll around in Ramat Aviv. I took the wife for a stroll, said to her, "Come see this house for sale." No key, I kicked down the door. We broke in. We demolished, improved—we renovated the entire house. I replaced everything, one month, and no one knew about it. After a month and a half passed, they told me, "Go ask who it belongs to." They said to Halamish [public housing agency]. They told me, "We'll send someone. If the apartment is to our satisfaction, it's yours." We renewed everything, and now I've been here twenty-nine years.

Amram squatted the apartment in Ramat Aviv and was permitted to remain in it, yet Ramat Aviv is a hollow and meaningless nonplace to him. He
thus lives on the fence of detachment and schism between Tel Aviv and Jaffa:
Tel Aviv, where his successful children live, and Jaffa, "my place."

> I WENT TO RAMAT AVIV not for me but for my children, who were little.
> I'm in Jaffa each day, but this is for the children's future. My kids are no
> criminals, don't drink, don't smoke. From work back home, from home to
> work. They went to school 'til twelfth grade. My girl here studies law at
> the university. Thank God, it's for the children's future. I'm now fucked
> up, can't be fixed. I'm crazy about Jaffa. I can't look at Ramat Aviv at all.
> Once they invited me to ice cream in the center. I felt like I was in prison.
> I love it here. This is my place. I've grown used to it. Come what may. I
> love it here.

Today There's No One to Tell About Jaffa

Having rolled out his escapades and described his surroundings and family,
Amram resumes his personal vein and seals his tale with a tear. His life, he
maintains, is a stage, and behind the scenes lie his true feelings. Like the
other weaknesses that the male survivor cannot afford, old age too marks
a personal decline and invites a hostile takeover by younger and stronger
men. To survive into his winter, Amram is obliged to don the mask of his
lost power and youthfulness. He thus comports himself in his old age in a
manner quite the opposite of that portrayed in the literature regarding the
mask of old-age[13]—a mask of gray hair and lines that society imposes on
the elderly, beneath which hides a true, ageless face.

> I PUT ON AN ACT. Carry on, play cards. Get by, this way and that. If I
> think of myself as an old man, I'm finished. I'll get depressed. One must
> keep up appearances. If they see you falling, they'll gobble you up. You
> must be stronger, act normal. Laugh each day, chat. Each day I weep be-
> cause of her. If I could return to work, I would work. If I could return to
> be younger, I would go all over Europe.

The condensed conclusion of Amram's story is rife with guilt feelings and
self-deprecation. In his mind, the Large Area, this aspect of Jaffa, should be

wiped out. Amram therefore concludes that the young would do well to keep their distance.

MY KIDS HAVE NO CONNECTION TO JAFFA. Not one of them ever comes to me in Jaffa. I've kept them away since they were little. Here they mess up kids. Here there are addicts; here there are murderous people. Today there's no one to tell about Jaffa. The generation is a goner. It's better that way. A generation like this had better end. A dirty generation, believe me. It's a pity we came to the country in the first place; perhaps I'd have been a different person. All my life I've worked maybe four years, maybe. Self-employed, buy this, sell that. Ever since I met this one, I can't even buy a shoelace. She bewitched me, for sure. It's all written down in Heaven. I've been tormented all my life. Only at night I'm a different person. Drink, drink, fuck up my head. I take a pill, get high, I'm in another world. I'm in serious depression. Can't do anything about it. In the end only God knows. It will end well. Perhaps my wife will come back to me . . .

Liminoid Space for Playful Identities

As far as the urban and national authorities are concerned, as well as the Israeli cultural imagination, the Large Area and everything associated with it are doomed to oblivion among the pages of folklore; they are devoid of any sustainable sociological remnants. Following the establishment of the Artists Colony and the evacuation of the veteran residents in the 1960s, the Large Area became a symbol of social neglect and an object of slum clearing. This prevented it from turning into an arena of struggle between the Mizrahi delinquent residents at the city's periphery and the founders of the White City threatened by them. The exclusion of the enclave, even from the "social" discourse conducted among the city's resident well-wishers, means that only a handful of local social activists have come to the defense of the area's occupants. According to the geographer Arnon Golan, the crime culture attributed to the Large Area can be explained in terms of rituals of resistance that claim legitimate autonomy and that will thus inevitably be erased and dismantled.

SOME OF THE RESIDENTS OF FORMER ARAB AREAS endeavored to establish local communities, an initial step toward autonomous urban communities. National and local governments and sectarian institutions suppressed these attempts, which jeopardized their dominance in former Arab areas. Unable to be integrated into Israeli society on their own terms, residents of these neighborhoods turned to strategies of resistance defined officially as illegitimate—violence and crime, and rituals of resistance. These included latent symbolic forms including various styles of dress and patterns of verbal and non-verbal behavior, implying an attitude of resistance to those in power.[14]

The Large Area is the epitome of the Mizrahi stigma encompassed in Jaffa's otherness. Seen in this light, the crime and violence associated with the place are the product of its exclusion from the national, ethnic, and class identities and power centers that are a mere stone's throw away from the city square. These identities and identifications impede and fetter Amram's survival skills and his versatile self-presentation, and he can therefore not afford to adopt them, even if he were so inclined. Nevertheless, their presence in his life infiltrates his silences; he ignores their existence, though they permeate the strategies of resistance he uses in the illegitimate existential and cultural space that is the Large Area. Amram makes no attempt to combat the negative representation of this unfamiliar and unconventional place and of those who reside in it. On the contrary, he lives in a shrinking space that does not accept the burden of the national, religious, and even urban big place.

Even though Amram does not conceal his opinions about Arabs in general ("We don't trust them"), he portrays his Arab neighbors in familial terms ("We grew up with them"). They are associates in the day-to-day struggle for existence, to the extent that he understands their aspiration to return to their occupied homes ("I justify them, but not in Jaffa, in the Territories"). Yet the Large Area remains free of nationalist stirrings, and Amram speaks fondly of the complete absence of commitment inherent to it, but at the same time he wishes for its annihilation. He does not recreate its past glory, nor does he call on the quarter's residents and traders to take action to protect their communal rights. Instead, he entrenches himself at the Jaffa café in a protective bubble with which he is associated and identifies and which includes a support group of aging Moroccan men like himself. Yet this sanctuary likewise emerges as a cockfighting arena—a sphere of violent strife—in which the ugly face of both masculinity and companionship is exposed. This is an individual struggle for survival devoid of the politics of ethnic identities.

The temporary detachment from his surroundings that Amram experiences in the Large Area is not merely a matter of clinging to the way of life of the place; it likewise helps him to come to terms with his futile predicament and meets his need to separate this unworthy life from the world of his children and their future. Amram's juggling act is set aside when it comes to his children's well-being. Elimination of the Large Area will dispel the threat of defilement or temptation to his offspring and will facilitate their assimilation with the Israeliness that plays no part in their father's life. His greatest wish is to eliminate the slightest risk of intergenerational continuity. Contrary to Moshe Hermosa (Chapter 8), Amram does not seek to display continuity of the family's status and identity. To Amram, the vestiges of the Large Area constitute a playground that awaits the final whistle.

Urban spaces such as the Large Area illustrate what Victor Turner called liminality.[15] The liminal space is defined as a renunciation of the social structure and is portrayed as an antistructure that removes its occupants from historical time and from any normative routine. The liminal stage serves as a mechanism for the management of communal crises and the marking of status transitions through rites of passage and social dramas. Toward the end of his life, Turner proposed the term *liminoid* to describe social activity occurring on the margins of society that challenges the social order by means of artistic criticism or by proposing to reorganize power relations. The liminoid sphere is characterized by playacting that challenges the normative order by its very lack of seriousness, which enables it to speak the truth. This is a no-man's land that lies betwixt and between and, as such, makes room for narratives that are repressed and silenced at the center and even serves as a mouthpiece for them.

The contradictions, compromises, and evasions that emerge from the lifestyle of the men in the Large Area invoke conceptualization of the enclave in terms of play. By approaching play as a practice that mediates between both political and gender-related social identities, we can observe the complexity of Amram's deceptive narrative as a playful motility among essential elements. The cultural and spatial predicament in which the men of the Large Area find themselves pins them between Jaffa and Tel Aviv, between their

Moroccan identity and hegemonic Israeliness, between the private and public spheres, and between principle and practice.

> PLAY-ACTING not only permits the existence of worlds with different
> value systems, but also enables its participants to position themselves on
> the boundary between these worlds, to cross it at will, and to commit
> themselves to none of them, or to remain in an intermediate position
> without having to expose themselves or to adopt a forthright standpoint.
> Attitudes toward both the worlds, and toward the play that mediates be-
> tween them are likely to evolve from within each of these worlds, or from
> the game. This multitude of possible responses creates considerable free-
> dom of action, and releases the participants from the tension that exists
> between conflicting value systems. Those among them who are familiar
> with the mechanism may also harness it to their needs . . . as a way of
> coping with the proliferation of contradictions in culture.[16]

From this perspective, we can view Amram's identity play as a strategy that
orders actions and meanings and as a form of communication anchored in
Jaffa's contradiction-laden social milieu. He wanders between one world of
meaning and the next, and through his presence both in Jaffa and in Tel Aviv,
as victim and victimizer, powerful and powerless, sentimental and rugged, he
is able to maintain the conception of his masculinity as he absolves himself of
its consequences for his wives and children. This is a paradoxical strategy that
reflects the liminal and crisis-ridden position of other men in Jaffa whose
social attributes are similar to Amram's. The turn toward playacting attuned
to contingency as a coping strategy is thus not fortuitous but stems from a
structural correspondence between the attributes of this strategy and the signifiers of the context of crisis in the Large Area. As Don Handelman writes,
"Predicated on premises of amorality, doubt, and falsity, with a voluminous
capacity to comment on the immediate, play is tailored more precisely to
express the contours of public anomie and personal alienation, than it is
to express the lengthy durations of collective integration and harmony."[17]
The double meanings that play helps transmit are the product of a paradox
of identity and the marginal position in which Moroccan men in the Large
Area find themselves, namely, the product of entrapment in a liminal position
of "neither this nor that, both this and that," between the poles of identity.[18]

Entrapped in his narrow and dire straits, Amram nevertheless refuses to commit himself. He subordinates identity, ethnicity, and locality to a disappearing act devoid of the politics of identity and loyalty to supralocal categories. The playfulness, deception, ambiguity, and juggling that are part of his deep play are an existential refuge from the lack of resources, but this refuge is not a source of political empowerment because it belongs to a deprived, silenced, disenfranchised, or emasculated class. Unimpressed by the city lights, this representative of the lumpenproletariat, whose class consciousness has been silenced, uses his playacting skills almost shamelessly. Amram creates a world of simulacra,[19] an impression of representations, the very shallowness of which grants him leeway to exploit his survival-oriented creativity.

In God's little acre that the denizens of the Large Area preserve, political planning policies have led to the establishment of an artists colony that has brought the curtain down on Moroccan communalism's rearguard action in Jaffa. Like other processes of gentrification, this project has gradually put an end to Amram and his companions' waiting time. Thus is the Large Area transformed from an expired place that still clings to the remnants of flimsy houses, petty trading, and cafés into a desirable upper-middle-class neighborhood. In the midst of these waves of change, Amram remains as firm and dejected as Andromeda's rock, remote from the system of stratified mobility: an anarchist who overturns every form or order, including that determined by nationalist imperatives, as he defies their agencies and deserts their ranks. He has no part and parcel in the state, in the city, or even in commercialized Jaffa, nor has he any material interest in them. He is an implant who makes a virtue of his strangerhood and spurns any sign of belonging and permanence as foreign to his rebellious spirit.

Amram's strategy of self-representation is one of masked nationalism, which conceals him as a political subject. Amram is a truly marginal man who aims barbs of anarchistic criticism at the heart of the national and social order, thereby precluding himself from belonging to any unifying framework. He perceives his life as a melodramatic series of personal betrayals and unfortunate decisions from which he has emerged by the skin of his teeth. Amram is Moshe Hermosa's alter ego, because he presents his own survival not as an ongoing operation of individual morality and cross-cultural fairness but rather as a succession of cunning deeds through which he deceived the agents of illusory nationalism and the powers that be, namely, the army, the police, and the tax authorities. Having deserted from the army in his youth, in later life he has deserted normative nationalism, adopting a principle of wary egoism devoid of morality. He exposes Ashkenazic Zionism as a disenfranchising brand of nationalism and ensconces himself in his Mizrahic masculine and playful identity, which eventually also fails to sustain him.

Amram is a juggler of identities who treads a triangle of tightropes strung between his perfidious companions, the repressive state, and his estranged and demanding wives and children. In his own elusive and playful manner, he rejects every collective identity and indeed every form of collectivism as such. The Large Area as a cultural no-man's land that is neither a part of the Arab Jaffa to which Hermosa comes on pilgrimage nor a part of Tel Aviv, in which Amram resides, facilitates a sustainable liminal existence. This is a way of life devoid of the challenges and benefits of collective affiliation. Amram floats in a spatial bubble that lacks mythical-historical memory—a bubble whose wretched and glorious days are coming to an end.

CHAPTER 10

SPEECHLESS NATIONALISM

Abu-George on the Edge

Vanity of vanities! All is vanity.

Ecclesiastes 1:2

The play over, each of them throws off his gold-spangled robe and
his mask, descends from the buskin's height, and moves a mean ordinary creature. . . . Such is the condition of mankind, or so that
sight presented it to me in Hades.

Lucian of Samosata

Abu-George Hamati was born in Acre around 1900 to a Greek Orthodox
family of menial workers. Until the outbreak of World War I, he attended
the Greek school in Jerusalem, and as a young man he began working in
Haifa on the railroad line to Port Said, Egypt, and as a janitor in the local
Greek Orthodox school. Abu-George lost his son in the 1948 war, and his
sister and her family became refugees in Syria and Lebanon. Having survived
the death of his wife and two children, he remained alone and moved to Jaffa
to live with one of his sisters, also widowed. Despite his personal loss and the
exiling of his extended family, Abu-George, potentially the ultimate witness
to the tragedy of 1948, refuses to bear witness and remains a storyteller who
relishes on fabrications. He retired in 1965 and spent his time lounging on
the threshold of his home in 'Ajami and strolling in the public park. Living
in effect as a willingly displaced person in a strange and unfamiliar Jaffa, he
maintained hardly any social ties, failed to learn Hebrew, and died in 2005,
at age 100 or so.[1]

Abu-George is a man of dialogue and is the most flirtatious of our interlocutors. The conversation he holds is constructed of a long sequence of

Hicham Chabaita

anecdotes that cannot be strung together into a consecutive narrative. More than any other interviewee, Abu-George is an elusive figure who defies representation. Mikhail Bakhtin's assertion that "there is neither a first nor a last word, and there are no limits to the dialogic context (it extends into the boundless past and the boundless future)"[2] aptly describes the course of Abu-George's life and the type of discourse in which he engages. Yet, although Bakhtin portrays "great time" as an eternity invested with religious solemnity, Abu-George renounces the possibility of such eternity as he dissects his past into opportunistic slices and portions, exuding irony, parody, cynicism, joking, and frivolity. He is the carnival type who occupies the tiniest, microscopic unit of temporality, turning his back on the collective.

Whereas the male storytellers in Part I tended to depict their activity against the backdrop of the city, the community, and the national project, and the women in Part II tended to position themselves within the confines of the home and the security of the private sphere—all expressing what Bakhtin terms the co-being of being—Abu-George plays no part in this universal or national social world, nor does he act out the biographical illusion.[3] He eschews the responsibility involved in joining any kind of association and eventually gives the impression of being the ultimate outsider to Jaffa's Palestinian society and to history at large.

In generational terms, Abu-George represents the fourth age,[4] and his story is thus devoid of vision and lacks an exalted heroic or tragic *telos*. At the end of the day, all that remains is the echo of his mocking victimhood. His is a negative consciousness that undermines both Fakhri Jday's nationalist subject (Chapter 1) and Moshe Hermosa's integrative individualist subject (Chapter 8). Abu-George's narrative elusiveness is revealed in a disjointed discourse in which he vacillates between options without committing to anything. He makes no fiery speeches about the city's past and his own, and even fails to unfold a coherent personal tale. The conversation with him bears no resemblance to a linear narrative, for it proceeds circuitously in a manner that casts Abu-George in the role of the jester who performs to an empty court. His story is fashioned from knee-jerk responses to the questions we unsuccessfully tried to put to him and from spontaneous but uninitiated repartee. This discourse is not driven by a narrative urge that seeks to leave a coherent impression, and the story is thus displaced, present in its absence.

They're All Good for Nothing

Abu-George spends much of his day sprawled on a mattress on the threshold of his home, neither inside nor out. He begins complaining from the outset, and following some perfunctory formal greetings, he mutters, "Life is a nightmare," adding, "It's good that you've come to see the way I am, cast away here like a dog." When we tell him about our project, he immediately rises and declares, "I am very unhappy with the people of Jaffa. They're all good for nothing [*al-fadi*]. I lie ill here, and no one comes to inquire about me. No one says, 'This is a fellow townsman. Let's go see how he's doing.' You don't see them. In Haifa, if they didn't see me for just an hour, they would start looking for me. I'm from Haifa; I have no relatives."

Abu-George portrays the people of Jaffa as vulgar and rude and depicts Jaffa itself as an inhospitable town. Although he ostensibly longs for Haifa and feels that he belongs there, when asked whether anyone from Haifa visits

him, he mutters that even his long-standing acquaintances from that city fail
to look him up. He came to Haifa from Acre, his birthplace, after marrying
and starting work on the railroad line to Egypt in the 1920s.

> I WAS BORN IN ACRE. I lived in Acre twenty years and moved to Haifa
> when I got married and began working on the railroad. I would travel to
> Egypt, for three days at a time. You won't believe this, if I didn't arrive
> in Egypt as expected, they would come to the station to ask about me:
> "When will Abu-George be coming?"

Abu-George pronounces his name in the Egyptian dialect with a pronounced hard G and bursts out laughing.

> I HAVE ALWAYS MADE FUN OF THEM. I once sat with an old barber who
> was familiar with my jokes and asked me for a glass. I said to him, 'Here
> you have a cup. Your hand is grasping its handle and your moustache is
> thrust in its backside.' He got up and tried to stab me with his scissors,
> saying, 'What kind of a joke is that?' Eventually we made up.

Abu-George retired from his railroad job after 1948, when the Haifa-
Egypt line was closed down and "the days of the English" (*ayyam al-ingliz*)
were over. The closure of the borders put an end to the trips he used to take
in the region: "We lived like the English. We were happy. I would go on
trips, travel to Egypt, to Ismailia, to Cyprus." Contrary to his contemporaries, Abu-George does not use the usual expression "the days of the Arabs,"
which implies nationalist pride. Whereas for Jday and Abu-Subhi the founding of the State of Israel marked a new and painful chapter in Jewish-Arab
relations, Abu-George refuses to view the transition in political terms and
confines history to his personal story: "Arabs and Jews got along with each
other. Life in the days of the English was sweet. There were Jews who worked
at the railroad station, but they didn't travel to Egypt."

For a while Abu-George tried his hand at painting and construction: "I
worked in construction in Tira for a Jew who spoke Greek. I spoke a few
words of Greek with him and he gave me a pack of American cigarettes. A
friend of mine went to ask him for cigarettes too, and he told him, 'As long
as you don't speak Greek, I won't give you any.'" Abu-George learned the language at the Greek school in Acre, from which he moved to the Patriarch's

school in Jerusalem. The interest we take in his fragmentary life story affords him an opportunity to relate anecdotes about jokes that got him into trouble and fights. His eccentric behavior led to a beating on more than one occasion, but the two sides always made peace at the end.

Abu-George refuses to commit himself to the place and time of the events related in these entangled anecdotes. He skips between Haifa, Acre, and Jerusalem and between past and present. In Haifa, where he lived next to the Catholic monastery (*deir al-rum*), he reasserts, "We lived like brothers in Haifa, Christians and Muslims. I lived with Muslims all my life. There was no anger or resentment between them. Good friends. At that time there were not many Jews yet." But immediately thereafter he asserts that "Acre was full of Jews."

Surprisingly enough, given the tragic personal price that Abu-George paid during the 1948 war—the death of his son and the exiling of his sister's family—he replies to our inquiry about his activity during and after the war in his usual prosaic manner: "When Israel conquered, I was 60 years old. I used to smoke and drink." He dismisses our attempt to extract a historical testimony from him: "Look, nothing happened; nothing happened in Acre. We were friends. Life in Acre was good. We had no relatives in Acre apart from my mother and sister." His niece now lives in Lebanon, yet he dismisses her exile in similar fashion: "I have a niece, the daughter of my sister, who lives in Lebanon. I haven't gone there; it's difficult for me to get to Lebanon. I have no [refugee] relatives other than in Syria."

Let's Go for a Walk

Abu-George's war of 1948 bears no resemblance to Jday's tragic transformation or Abu-Subhi's trauma. To him it is no more than a historical footnote that once again speaks of the Arabs' political naïveté. When asked why the Palestinian residents left Haifa, he likens the great exodus of April 1948 to a walk in the park (*shimmet hawa*) as he alternates between innuendo and explicit assertions: "They are stupid [*aqelhum khafif*], man. We, the children of the Arabs [*awlad al-'arab*], our brain is small. What did the government tell them? It told them to go, so they went. They went, got stuck there and couldn't return."

Abu-George is the counter-*samed*, the mirror image of the nationalist type praised for his steadfastness (*sumud*).[5] Even though he did remain in

Haifa in 1948, he makes no attempt to claim that he did anything to protect his home. He refuses to draw a moral or to relate to historical experience, as did Abu-Subhi in declaring that "exile is a humiliation," or Subhiya abu-Ramadan (Chapter 6), who stated that the war was the outcome of political failure and betrayal. In fact, Abu-George attributes his remaining in Haifa to his wife: "I didn't go. My wife didn't want us to go. I said to her, 'Let's go for a walk and come back.' She said to me, 'No. I don't want to go.' I told her that I didn't want to go either, and in the end we didn't go, me and her." The banality of refugeehood and staying put is manifested not merely in the casual conversation between Abu-George and his wife but also in the choice of the verb *to go*, which denotes no sense of coercion or urgency and is conspicuously unlike the terms usually used in the Nakba discourse, such as deportation, escape, fleeing, and expulsion.[6] Abu-George does not present his decision to stay as the deliberate action of the head of a patriarchal family resolved to stand in the breach but rather as a decision arrived at during the course of a casual conversation with his wife.

Ottoman, English, Israeli: We Know Nothing

A further tragedy of which Abu-George speaks concerns the death of his two children: "I have two children. The daughter died of an illness at age 15—the doctor was an ass—and the son died in Jordan at age 20." He maintains that his son fought in the Jordanian army under Glubb Pasha and died alone in Jordan: "He joined Glubb Pasha and Haj Amin al-Husseini. There was no one there [to look after him]; he would sleep in cafés. In the end he died in Jordan." It appears as though this personal loss steeled him against all other calamities and led him to portray his own fate in a dour light and to describe the relations among the groups that surround him in an optimistic manner. He thus replies categorically to our question of whether he feared the Israeli occupation: "No. I was in Acre and in Haifa and there was no fear. The Jews, the Muslims, and the Christians were good friends, and there was no quarrel between them." The wisdom of the common man protects Abu-George and absolves him of all responsibility. As far as he is concerned, the transformation that took place after 1948 affected those at the top and therefore had no relevance to his life: "It was only government policy that changed. By God, their politics is good for nothing [*al-fadi*]. Our story is like chickens that are shooed away. We know nothing." Thus does Abu-George detach himself from matters and reason of the state and its functionaries and liken its attitude toward the common man to shooing away chickens. The motto of his story, "We know nothing," allows him to lead a separate existence untouched by fateful historical events.

After the war Abu-George worked as a painter and watchman in an Acre monastery and as a janitor at the Greek Orthodox school in Haifa. Upon retiring in 1965, he went to live with his sister, and he now receives state benefits. Like many of his generation, he has only an approximate idea of his age—"I am a hundred years old"—but does not bother to find out his precise date of birth: "I really don't know. My sister has my papers."

Abu-George constantly stresses his lack of involvement.

> BELIEVE ME, since the days of the Turks and the days of the English, I haven't been imprisoned and haven't seen the jail even once. I don't know what a jail looks like. I lived in the days of the Turks: Life was good, a king's life. There were no murders or beatings, nothing. There were no quarrels over inheritance, nothing.

He contrasts this tranquil past to Jaffa's fraught present: "By God, the days of the English were better than life in Israel. Now, anyone who does anything is put in prison. Here there are murders and beatings. Murder, murder and death here. There is no order."

Because of his narrative elusiveness, it proved impossible to unravel Abu-George's conception of national identity or gain any notion of his political position. When asked if he felt himself to be Palestinian or Israeli, he replied simply, "Israeli." His reply led to the following sparse dialog.

Q: Why Israeli? You don't even speak Hebrew.
A: It is Israel that governs us, is it not?
Q: And when the English ruled?
A: In the days of the English we considered ourselves English.
Q: And in the days of the Turks you were an Ottoman?
A: Yes, an Ottoman, of course.
Q: And what do you think of the State of Israel?
A: Goodness, nothing, I don't know a thing about them.

Q: And when they occupied the land, how did you feel, in '48 when they came?

A: I worked on the railroad I did.

Q: Were you not angry?

A: No. I have no daughter, I have no house, I have nothing.

Q: But the Palestinians became refugees?

A: Some went to work, and here they are living in Israel, and some left for a different place, and I stayed here. In the end I stayed in Acre.

Q: Abu-George, have you heard of the Intifada?

A: No. I live the life here, and whatever comes, comes.

Q: Have you heard of Abu-'Amar [Arafat]?

A: We're not interested in that one. We only look for a loaf of bread to eat and that's it.

Abu-George, who claims to be literate in Arabic, Greek, and a little English, told us in a different context that he sometimes listens to the radio and reads stories in Greek and that in his youth he used to read the newspaper *Filastin* (published in Jaffa until 1948). We can therefore conclude that his evasive replies do not stem from sheer ignorance but demonstrate that he has chosen to steer clear of any political matter that might disrupt the private routine of his life. He is thus able to leave the national and family tragedy behind. To Abu-George, like Lucian (see epigraph), all identities are merely masks, and the essential core revealed at the last refuge is his personal survival and the "loaf of bread," next to which everything else fades into insignificance. His attachment to a different place and time exacerbates his alienation toward the place where he currently lives. When he leaves his home, he sits on a bench in the public park but makes it quite clear that those who share the bench with him are not his friends: "We pass the time, but I have no friend in this town."

This Is My Life and That's It

Since moving to Jaffa, Abu-George has failed to settle down.

BELIEVE ME, I have lived with the people of Jaffa, and I've discovered that the people of Haifa are better. I have no friends. My cousins are here, but they are not friends. No one comes to ask after me. If I were in Haifa, the house would be full of people coming to see how I was. The people of Haifa are different. I'm telling you the truth. I lie here at my sister's, sit alone in the room. No one comes, nothing.

The days of his youth, filled with humor and pleasantness—"I would laugh with people and tell jokes"—present a stark contrast to his present predicament. Nowadays he shrouds himself in his isolation and shuns any local social network. When asked what is important to him now, he replies, "Nothing is of importance to me. I merely look after my health. But I have no friends or relatives here. My relatives here treat me like a stranger. That's their nature."

Abu-George likewise refuses to attend the municipal senior citizens club located in the neighborhood. His story has nothing of the sense of personal empowerment conveyed by Subhiya abu-Ramadan (Chapter 6), the support facilitated by the state that affords the elderly a modicum of well-being. Because his welfare allowance is absorbed into his sister's housekeeping expenses, Abu-George does not feel in control of his life and income: "I get 1,800 a month. That's enough for me, but the money goes toward the house here. In the days of the English, if you had children, you would eat, and if you didn't, you would beg, and if you had money, you lived off your money."

Toward the end of our conversation we ask Abu-George what he thinks of politicians, and he uses the opportunity to underscore the recurring theme of his tale: "I have nothing to do with politics. I take nothing from it, neither good nor bad. I like to talk about the time in which we live. The present time, that's what I talk about." His focus on the present shields him from any regret he may feel about the passivity he manifested during his life in general and during the 1948 war in particular and his avoidance of any shred of political engagement.

I HAVEN'T BEEN TO THE ARMY. [In World War I] I was a child; I hid in a monastery. I never joined either the Turks or anyone else. I spent the time in the monastery because there they didn't force people to conscript. Also in '48 I kept working at the school, me and the teachers. I was happy at the school. Many died in the war, many Jews and also many Arabs. Even had the Arabs won, my situation wouldn't have been better or worse. This is my life and that's it. I didn't mingle with anyone. I stayed at the school and that's it.

The Return to Haifa

At the end of our first meeting with him, as though to illustrate the respect he is accorded in Haifa, Abu-George urges us to take him to the fiftieth anniversary celebration of the Orthodox school. As an alumnus, he had been invited to the festivities. "Take me with you to Haifa. In Haifa you'll see that no sooner do I arrive, they straight away begin to ask me, 'How are you Abu-George?' They'll start kissing me with all their heart. Here no one gives me the time of day. It is I who talk to them." We agree. The prospect of this excursion—in all likelihood the last time he will return to his hometown—fills him with vitality and animation.

On the day of the reunion, he wears his finest clothes and happily anticipates the well-deserved recognition. When we arrive at the function, however, only a few of those present remember him, and he, because of his poor eyesight, hardly recognizes the speakers or the people around him. Nevertheless, for Abu-George this is an uplifting and heartwarming experience. We ask to visit his house, but it turns out that he didn't actually have a house of his own and had lived in a small room at the school: "The house is gone but wasn't demolished. When I moved to Haifa from Acre, I had a room at the school, and when my wife died, my sister's son came along, loaded my clothes, and brought me here."

As in Ghassan Kanafani's novella *Returning to Haifa* (*'A'id lla Haifa*), Abu-George returns to his city of origin following a prolonged absence and for the last time. Yet the aura of return in this case does not belong to the "great time" and the national tragedy but rather to the small time and to personal losses. In Kanafani's story, Palestinian refugees Safiyya and Said return from Ramallah to their erstwhile home in Haifa in a journey that merges present and past, memory and migration. Kanafani weaves the components of the tragedy into the moving scene that terminates the novella: the dust of memories, the quest for the lost homeland, and the violent conflict with the Israeli Other. Said takes leave of his son Khaldun and of the Haifa house.

I'M LOOKING FOR THE TRUE PALESTINE, the Palestine that's more than memories, more than peacock feathers, more than a son, more than scars written by bullets on the stairs. . . . For us, for you [Safiyya] and me, it's only a search for something buried beneath the dust of memories. And look what we found beneath that dust. Yet more dust.[7]

Abu-George does not look for Palestine, not even for the house he never had. The comparison between Abu-George's final return to Haifa, an entirely prosaic affair, and Said's dramatic return in Kanafani's novella brings into sharp relief the limits of memory and reminiscing of which Mahmoud Darwish wrote to Samih al-Qasem.

> DOES THIS ACT OF REMINISCING not contain a contradiction? What happens at the edge of reminiscence? What happens when we vacate the repository of memory of what is stored therein? I do not speak here of collective memory or about individual memory, which takes the trouble to select its past in order to understand its history at the moment when the great question is posed, the question of its destiny.[8]

At the end of the day, "at the edge of reminiscence," memory is exposed as a bruised reed that cannot be relied on. This story displays a shattered subject—Abu-George and, to some extent, Amram Ben-Yosef (Chapter 9)—who does not speak unless prompted by random interlocutors or those engaged in research. This position of a subject who lacks active agency, who does not impinge on reality by giving it meaning, bespeaks the presence of a narrative and experiential sphere that transcends the integrative interpreting subject. These men are akin to the scattered splinters of a historical subject unattached to the time and place of contemporary daily life. Whereas both the Zionist and the Palestinian nationalist collective biography seek a poetic unity of time, place, and plot, the fragments of stories that conclude Part III are devoid of any motivating national objective and thus end with a whimper. Abu-George signifies the termination of a movement that might be summed up by a question we will address in the Conclusion: How does the big place of myth and redemption morph into a nonplace?

The shrinking existential space of those who live on the fringes of collective memory is borne out of a pincer movement by the dyad of nationalism and modernity. As part of the modern *Geist*, nationalism is stamped by a messianic teleology that beats a path of pilgrimage for those who follow it unreservedly. When this project loses its substance and purpose

and no longer commands belief and commitment among its pilgrims, it is
exchanged for a nomadic life of destination and intent, which leads its fol-
lowers from one impasse to another,[9] as did Abu-George's wanderings from
Haifa to Jaffa. Consequently, the narrative genre transforms from betrayal
and shattered hopes to a matter-of-fact stoic realism. Whereas Fakhri Jday
(Chapter 1) comports himself in the mode of a tragic-romantic hero figure
lifted from a nineteenth-century novel, Abu-George is but a passing shadow,
a figment of his own imagination, neither alive nor dead. His position on
the boundary between the illusory and the tangible is typical of postmodern
readings. Yet these are essentially unfounded readings, because they are still
decoded and translated according to modernity's search for plot and meaning, which are unavoidably typical of the current discussion as well. This is
indeed a trap from which one can escape only by adopting Abu-George's
style of articulation; only this can do textual justice to the true context of
his life, or as he puts it, "We are stupid, and what has happened is of no
consequence." Thus renunciation of history and therefore of historicity is not
the by-product of any mythical conception of being but stems from the nul-
lification of any suggestion of narrative sequence anchored in circumstances
of any kind. From Abu-George's point of view, and therefore also the point
of view of those who wish to understand him, the modes and expressions of
the space in which he lives are embodied in an existence whose codes can
be deciphered only by those who share it. The anthropological sound box is
not always capable of reproducing the requisite range.[10] Deep old age does
indeed present such a challenge, and Abu-George, who inhabits it, appears
to exist in a space of enunciations that seem to be beyond interpretation.[11]

FROM IDENTITY POLITICS
TO POLITICS OF EXISTENCE

We face the sea
You face the sand
From the sea there's no returning
From the sand there's no uprising

We are the lost cause
Of a stone touching the water
Skimming over it
And the water mocks only the living

Rajaa Natour, "Foolishness"

Chronotopes of Nationalism: City, Home, and Threshold

In *After the Last Sky*, Edward Said searches for a new language that defines the discontinuity of Palestinian experience.

> Most literary critics in Israel and the West focus on what is said . . . who is described, what the plot and contents deliver, their sociological and political meaning. But it is form that should be looked at. Our characteristic mode, then, is not a narrative, in which scenes take place seriatim, but rather broken narratives, fragmentary compositions, and self-consciously staged testimonials, in which the narrative voice keeps stumbling over itself, its obligations, its limitations.[1]

The "staged testimonial" by Samed 'Abd al-Baqi al-Maslub that opens this book exalts "Jaffa, the Bride of Palestine, that is no more." It signals the entry into the forking paths of nationalism, where our protagonists meander. Nation and state, they teach us, are not sui generis but rather contingent on personal reflections and dismembered memories, hailed, defied, dismissed, and forever

negotiated as templates for identity formation. Escaping the mythscape, the
elders of Jaffa tell a story of resistance and resilience: for the creative chaos of
the city and against the destructive order of nationalism. Living as strangers
in the Mother of the Stranger (*umm al-gharib*), theirs is a saga of multiple
marginality coupled with a struggle for survival. Rather than seeing like a
state, they see like a city, thus recognizing that "it is not a miniature state, but
rather an order of an entirely different type."[2]

Life stories of Palestinian and Jewish elderly in Jaffa invoke three
major chronotopes, defined as "the intrinsic connectedness of temporal and
spatial relationships."[3] In each chronotope nationalism reveals a simultaneously emergent set of potentialities and constraints. The root chronotopes
for these potentialities are the city, the home, and the threshold (the buffer
zone between domestic and public space). As a narrative configuration of
the time-space nexus, the chronotope is not static but dynamic, because it
defines changing relations between time, place, and script: Time morphs
from mythical into fragmented time;[4] space proceeds from sacred landscape to the small place; the frame of reference moves from the imagined
community (nation, religion) to the primary group (family, neighborhood)
and to the individual self; and ultimately the genre ranges between utopia and irony.

The metaphor of the setting sun highlights the orbit of dissipation: from
the identity politics of territorial nationalism at large to the personal politics
of individual existence; and from the sphere of a besieged imagined community to the arena of identity play and pragmatic interplay.[5] In light of life's
contingencies, the storytellers forebode the dissolution of nationalism as a
coherent cultural ethos and ideological manifesto.

Distinct instantiations of twilight nationalism—sunset, dusk, and nightfall—chart a further gradation of withdrawal from the mythical and mobilizing
chronotope toward a iconoclastic, skeptical, and somewhat stoic chronotope.
In the crepuscule of their life the twelve storytellers emerge as narrators who
are well aware of nationalism's terminal state. Through their lifestyles and very
being, they demonstrate that the urban force field is a meandering trail of
experience. The struggles and negotiations over the boundaries of this field
are an important component in the lives of the protagonists and the urban
ambience around them.

Through the tragic story of loss and despair they share, men of stature still cling to the fading glow of nationalism under which they used to bask. Faced with a diminishing generational cohort and vanishing hopes, the first three storytellers are part and parcel of Jaffa's national history, which to them has also spelled disaster. Their masculinity draws its essence from the patriarchal national order, and as this wanes, they become a symbolic relic or a nostalgic figure shrouded in romanticism and yearning. From this state of being they cherish the chronotope of modern urbanism manifested in the bourgeois Bride of Palestine and the lost community. Their experiences expose the chinks in the armor of national narrative as an ideological auxiliary of an imagined community. These dents are formed by class- and ethnicity-related factors that undermine the façade of total nationalism. To the former pillars of their community, despite their divergent class and ethnic origins, nationalism is still a source of pride embedded in a big place and a mythical time, even though, to a varying degree, they have all reached a dead end by now, personally and inextricably—and nationally.

From the security of their chosen domestic citadel, the women storytellers unfold a different account of the relationship between nation, time, and place, revealing gender's critical role in the performance of nationalism. Whereas the men illuminate the twilight zone and the shattering of the nationalist dream, the women, who have been excluded from the public sphere, paradoxically reveal a vantage point for encountering old age: The chronotope of the home endows them with strength and provides alternative resources that generate and facilitate a more complex set of loyalties. Although the migration and displacement experienced by these women have undone previous social networks and even though they now face decrepitude, their loyalties have replaced the imagined community and help to fill the void opened up by the disintegration of the local community with meaningful activity and personal empowerment. In their different ways, which are a function of their personal bargain with patriarchy,[6] the women overshadow nationalist hegemony or suspend it, thereby deliberately drawing out its sting.

The final accord in the dissipating representation of the master narrative of nationalism is struck by the unadulterated liminality of the last three protagonists. Unencumbered by any collective frame of reference, they place themselves on the threshold, in a small place devoid of myth, glory, pride, or redemption, and in a temporal enclave that is out of sync with the tenor of the times. This liminal chronotope emerges through the way in which their life stories are told, through the location where the interviewees chose to share them, and through their uncanny contents. The threshold takes on various forms: a place of playfulness, a no-man's land, and a space of in-betweenness where one chooses to lie on an outdoor mattress that will become his final resting place.

These "broken narratives" identified by Edward Said thus reveal a field of potentially coexisting modes of nationalism, a cultural realm of opportunity that sprouts from a given sociopolitical breeding ground. The three parts represent three facets of the narrating subject, which are linked in a relation of dissipation: the bourgeois-national subject, the family-domestic subject, and the private-liminal subject. Presented in descending order of their measure of stability, the stories trace various positions of the subject's disintegration: starting with the strategic essentialism of the nationalist subject[7] and concluding with a chinked subject who refuses to kowtow to a linear narrative framework, as though seeking to renounce the modern figure of a coherent subject that possesses a uniform and sequential identity.[8] Among other things, the storytellers reconstruct their biography and arrange their lives around axes of motherhood, authenticity, entrepreneurship, and so forth, which do not play by the conventional rules of the nationalist game. This diversity of positions illustrates the conceptual progression by which the national body offloads its baggage, making way for the domestic body and, in the most extreme case, culminating in the bare life of the body literal. Rather than affirming the social order, these narratives either pragmatically accept it or criticize it harshly.

In this book we raise questions about the life story as an analytical unit and a narrative genre in its own right. In our analysis we have attempted to trace the dynamics of narration within a particular cultural and political context and to decipher the complexities that reveal themselves at the crossroads of gender, ethnicity, age, and nationality. Following Said, one can configure the relations between these categories on two levels: form and content.

First, regarding the arrangement of the narrative and the story's direction, one of our findings is that the categories of gender, class, and age are more significant than nationalism (either Jewish or Palestinian). In other words, the similarities and differences between the life stories of elderly Jews and

Arabs are shaped by their socioeconomic class, age, and gender more than by their national identity. The stories of Fakhri Jday (Chapter 1) and Avraham Bachar (Chapter 2), for example, run along parallel lines from a mythical past of personal and communal prosperity to a present dominated by a sense of devastation, devaluation, and withdrawal, whereas the stories of Subhiya abu-Ramadan (Chapter 6) and Nazihah Asis (Chapter 5) proceed from a past of patriarchal subordination to a present of autonomy and control. The nostalgia evoked by the men in Part I contrasts with the counternostalgia[9] evoked in the narratives of most of the women in Part II and with the discourse of an individual existence devoid of a collective frame of reference in Part III.

With regard to content, the subjects allude to an either harmonious or tense relation between the official nationalist narrative and their own experience. Many studies of the life stories of the elderly underscore the coherence of the narrator's ego, the story's flow, and the "illusion of wholeness."[10] This emphasis becomes all the more important when the discussion focuses on a nationalist subject perceived to represent the collective story. We, however, seek to turn this construction on its head by claiming that the story's frame of reference determines the degree of its plotted coherence. The stories illustrate a number of alternative frames of reference that range from community, to class and gender, to the family and the twists of the self. In these renditions, even if the individual self remains intrinsically coherent, the stories reveal missing links in the chain binding that selfhood with the collective frame of reference, which tends to widen, thereby facilitating greater reflexivity as one approaches old age.

Identity, Betrayal, and Victimhood

Most studies of Jewish-Arab relations in mixed cities underscore the power relations that reproduce the Palestinians' dispossession, alienation, and deprivation.[11] These power relations are formally manifested by mechanisms of spatial separation, discriminatory planning policies, and economic dependence. Yet, contrary to theories of inequality that portray the "mixed city" as the result of an ethnocratic regime and a one-sided economy of identity, the elderly emphasize that the interface it enables makes room for diverse identity zones and perceptions of place that establish political and cultural city lives.

From the point of view of the struggle over the domestication of space as an ongoing project that nurtures a binational third space,[12] rather than use dichotomous categories set in stone (such as the "white" versus the "black" city),[13] Jaffa can be seen as the alter ego of both the Zionist *and* the Palestinian urban projects. From this perspective, the Israeli city and the project of gentrification and Judaization are not a fait accompli but rather a dialectical process that is still playing out, with the conclusion not at all foregone. From the vise that clamps colonizer to colonized, citizen to subject, employer to employee, and bourgeois to proletarian, the mixed city emerges as a third space that is home to diverse conceptions of otherness and identity. In terms of Zali Gurevitch's thick and thin boundaries,[14] this hybrid urbanism blurs the neat thick boundary that fences off the parties who profess to possess complete entities, delineates and segregates worlds (Arab Jaffa and Jewish Tel Aviv), and defines nationalist-urban identity in terms of an essentialist distinction between self and Other. And where this boundary dissolves, we arrive at a faithful description of a more complex reality.

In our analysis of the binational city, the respective Other of the place is seen as an active player, despite having played a subordinate role in the cultural process of the creation of local identity in Israel. Jaffa thus emerges from its ambivalent representation in Jewish and Palestinian imagination not as an object of ultimate otherness or as a nationalist object of yearning, but as a hybrid no-man's land, which generates, through the struggle over the boundary's definition, novel modes of agency and cultural evocations of urban identity. Jaffa's otherness is couched in terms that combine negation and affirmation, distance and proximity, which have coexisted in a constant state of tension and flux at least since 1948. Starting out from Jaffa's dualistic image, a variety of social actors use a range of strategies of representation, yet they fail to reconcile them. The relations among the city's indigenous and migrant residents manifest the tension between national distinctiveness and institutional integration and, through two interrelated processes, express a growing trend toward Palestinization in response to Israelization and segregation that grows out of integration.[15] As a result of this development, the thick boundary that protects the apertures of the collective body (be it Jewish or Arab) is gradually converted into a series of thin boundaries that internalize the Other, draw him or her toward the phenomenological horizon of relevance, and unravel the fringes of urban self-identity to the point that the boundary dissolves.

Jaffa's stories exist in the semantic triangle whose points connect and connote images of strangeness, betrayal, and victimization. These concepts provide evidence of the rupture that Homi Bhabha characterizes as a recurring pattern in the postcolonial experience.[16] However, strangerhood as an existential condition is not merely destructive;[17] it also serves as a source of identity and a spur to action. It enables the storytellers to create a critical distance and allows them to shift across a range of local identities, to choose a particular discourse of zeitgeist according to circumstances, and to take up a position in the national discourse as they interpret it. Like strangerhood, betrayal by the agents of oppressive nationalism releases its victims from political accountability and even goes some way toward explicating the strangeness to which they are subjected. At the same time, a different type of discourse of victimhood enables the individual to identify with the nation and belong to it, despite its perfidy.

The experience of strangerhood, betrayal, and victimhood is dependent on context, gender, and class. The differences between Fakhri Jday's stories of patriarchal bourgeoisie (betrayal by Arab rulers) and the critique voiced by the lower-class women (betrayal by men) that emerges from Subhiya abu-Ramadan's story, for example, undermine the outward impression of unified national hegemony. All the relations between the intervening variables of the personal-nationalist story—the cohort that positions people on a disruptive life track, the ambivalent state that takes but also gives, the channel of cultural memory, the collective representation that dictates patterns of recollection, the family, and one's gender—constitute the repertoire from which the storytellers borrow segments in constructing their identity and positioning themselves along the national-mythical and urban-pragmatic axis.

The storytellers' expressive freedom and articulation of strangerhood originate from the coalescing of a torrent of traumas: migration, the Nakba, and the collapse of the imagined community. These formative events have created populations that perceive themselves to be marginal and that relate their story through the experience of exclusion. This collective marginality allows the storytellers freedom of expression, loosens the straps of collective memory, and opens up an alternative sphere of recollection. Given the absence of centralized social control in the city, the national testimony confined to the field of memory[18] breaks out and stimulates a latent polyphony. Contrary to the classical studies of symbolic construction of community,[19] one discerns among the elderly residents of Jaffa a process of symbolic disintegration that shatters collective memory into fragments. The regime of nationalist justification is thus abandoned in favor of a repertoire of discursive practices that facilitate critical construction of the present, thereby also rewriting the past.

Modes of Nationalism in Everyday Life

How, then, can one conceptualize the Jaffaite interplay between the politics of identity and the politics of existence as embedded in a matrix of contrived coexistence? Since 1948 the dialectical relationship between society and space in Jaffa has continuously spawned Jewish places within Arab spaces and reproduced Palestinian spaces within Israeli ones. These processes have disrupted the congruence between class and nation and between the spatial boundaries that define neighborhoods and the social boundaries that define communities. These boundaries are clearly discernible, for instance, in the division between East and West Jerusalem and divided Belfast. In other words, contrary to the basic assumption of the nation-state, in Jaffa and in other mixed cities one commonly finds a mismatch between space and identity. Demographic and planning processes, whether deliberate or unintended, have continuously constructed Jaffaite space in the form of a system that fails to comply with a hegemonic ethnic- or class-oriented organizing principle. Jaffa is an instance of spatial heteronomy.[20] It challenges the Jewish nation-state and the ethnonationalist logic that regulates it.[21] The concept indicates an urban dynamic that rejects the territorial logic that constitutes well-defined, constant, and mutually exclusive cultural and national units.

Set against the ruling paradigm of methodological nationalism[22] that operates by chaining sociological analysis of ethnically mixed towns to the category of the nation-state and thus conceals much of their interstitial complexities, we shift toward a dialectical theory of sociality and spatiality. Over the past decade, social scientists have become increasingly aware of the potential conceptual problem of reification of the nation-state category.[23] Sociologist Mustafa Emirbayer voices this criticism as part of the theoretical framework he calls relationalism, which takes issue with the concept that he terms substantialism.[24] Following in the footsteps of numerous scholars, from Georg Simmel and Norbert Elias to Michel Maffesoli and Pierre Bourdieu, Emirbayer shows that "relational theorists reject the notion that one can posit discrete, pre-given units such as the individual, class, minority, state, nation or society as ultimate starting points of sociological analysis."[25] Emirbayer goes on to explain, "What is distinct about the relational approach is that it sees *relations* between social units and actors as preeminently dynamic in nature, as unfolding ongoing processes rather that as static ties among inert substances or structures."[26]

According to Emirbayer, this approach enables one to reinterpret several basic concepts of social science, such as power, individual, and community. Thus, as Rogers Brubaker shows, the concept of nation-state is transformed, and instead of describing a sovereign and well-defined territorial unit, it indicates a configuration of power and a complex organizational network— in short, a relational field.[27]

One can similarly conceive of the city not as a receptacle for ethnic communities but as a space of mediation and a site that produces dialectical relations between form, function, and structure, a place that generates social processes and creates urban objects.[28] One can thus reconceptualize the dialectical relations between majority and minority in the mixed city and the identities they mold in terms of a spatial dynamic and political process that are not merely reflections of government policy, national identity, or any other specific cultural script.

In the heteronomous space the laser beam of nationalism is broken into myriad colors and disperses in many directions. Nationalism in this sense does not operate as a functionalist generative order[29] but rather manifests ongoing disorder, creative destruction,[30] and a chronic state of emergency. In the heteronomous space, where parallel and contradictory logics of place, class, ethnicity, and neighborliness operate alongside one another, the regime of narrative mediation is heteronational.

In everyday life the national order is mediated by a series of sociological variables and by the current situation of the local context. We propose a novel perspective of nationalism as a pragmatic and reflexive performance of urban identity forged in Jaffa's urban space. This enabling narrative environment remains loosely attached to national hegemony and animates the city and its aged citizens. By anchoring each performance in the storyteller's national condition, we shift the focus of nationalism to a narrative that is a personal performance of the existential present and that does not consist of scripted ideological testimonials. The poetics of nationalism, including the chronotopes that depict it (city, home, threshold), reveal the dissipation of the nationalist subject and its different metamorphoses. In spatial terms, this is the process that marks the transition from the big place to the small place and from there to a nonplace.

Through this conceptual kaleidoscope nationalism is laid bare: It is not a metanarrative, nor can it be adequately portrayed as banal[31] or as a conventional institutional field.[32] Nationalism spells a malleable narrative performance set on the horizons of relevance of the individual's life. The disparity between the kind of nationalism perceived as "imaginative horizons"[33] and nationalism as experienced in everyday life underscores the indeterminacy that renders it ambivalent.[34] Its fringes are unraveled because processes of identity and identification reformulate a cultural repertoire that defines the conditions of accessibility to the national discourse and blocks access to a sense of belonging.

This approach offers a theoretical alternative to the two discursive trends: constructed nationalism, which errs on the side of primordial identity and collective memory;[35] and methodological nationalism, which conclusively establishes modern bourgeoisie and indigenous ruralism as exclusive spheres of activity.[36] By contrast, situational nationalism conceptually liberates our understanding of nationalism from historical determinism or narrative linearity. It thus turns nationalism on its head: The social situation and self-positioning of actors generates nationalism rather than the other way round. Having been born into a given social class toward the end of a particular historical period characterized by specific cultural constraints, the Jewish and the Palestinian storytellers have all experienced the shattering of their respective generational dream. Faced with this impasse, the very imperative to choose engenders a pragmatic form of strangerhood that impels the social actors to play according to the structural conditions in which they find themselves. Thus a political bane is turned into an existential boon.

EARTH TO EARTH

Posthumous Nationalism

Old people no longer talk
and they talk so slowly when they do.
They are rich, they are poor, their illusions are gone.
They share one heart for two . . .
Though you may live in town, you live so far away
when you've lived too long . . .
Old people no longer dream,
their books get sleep, their pianos are closed . . .
Old people don't die,
they fall asleep one day and sleep too long.

Jacques Brel, "Old Folks"

Half a generation has passed since we first embarked on this project. Many of our protagonists are no longer with us. Nazihah Asis died from a stray horse's kick while she was strolling on Jerusalem Boulevard; she is survived by her longing husband. Subhiya abu-Ramadan departed following an illness and is buried in the Tasso Muslim graveyard. Fakhri Jday was buried in grand ceremony in the Catholic graveyard in Jaffa; his son now manages the family pharmacy. Rabbi Bachar passed on in an old age home in Rishon LeZion miles away from the city he loved. And, finally, Abu-George Hamati died at the age of 102, remaining to this day the oldest person recorded in the post-1948 chronicles of Jaffa.

In recent years Jaffa has seen the rise of a new, young generation of heightened political awareness whose national aspirations are coupled with their passion for city life. Facing creeping gentrification, challenges of survival, and hopes for communal belonging, the Palestinian Generations X and Y also seek a place in the contemporary global world. Jaffa, resilient as always, is still an enabling hub for such contradictory dreams and wishes.

The renewed city that these younger generations face, however, is marked by the eclipse of community. How does one live in a zombie city? How do Palestinian citizens survive in a town marked by communal destruction, which is at the same time a bustling center of urban renewal and Jewish gentrification as well as a site of memory of Palestinians in exile? Although the lived experience in Jaffa cannot be reduced to deathly tropes haunted by an original sin, memories and traces of calamity do not dissolve under conditions of marginality and exclusion. Such a narrative of decline and despair, though forming the main discursive frame for Palestinian Jaffa, does not exhaust other key aspects of community life and the political struggles taking place on a daily basis.

Fueled by new blood running in its veins, the city is nevertheless a sounding board for both cosmopolitan echoes and the fading whimpers of nationalism. In the poetic anthology *The Language of Jaffa: A Load of Jaffaite Creations*,[1] the first-ever collection of works by young Jewish and Palestinian poets living in Jaffa, the editors write:

> Fragments of innumerable tunes and songs, stories and legends, tongues and dialects reverberate in its belly, seep into its life and generate its creations. And the heavy hand of the past continues to strum the chords of Jaffa's present, with fingers that are well acquainted with the scale along which the city's painful refrain slowly ascends . . . a thin seam that runs among the patchwork of neighborhoods, languages, and historical narratives that make up contemporary Jaffa.[2]

Jaffa's transition from the center of Palestinian and Zionist national life to the margins of Israel's White City exacerbates the challenges confronted by its residents and scholars as they try to articulate the city's language, namely, the symbolic code that mediates one's experience of place in a unique way that speaks for itself rather than for the nation or the state. This protean language of the city is articulated by two entwined paroles that produce an incoherent polyphony.

> Jaffa's Arabic and Hebrew stand on a frontline that comprises more than one barrier of the national and cultural war of identities waged between

their speakers. . . . The two languages stand in the middle, locked together like a pair of experienced but exhausted wrestlers.[3]

This exhaustion is magnified in the stories of the third and fourth generations. Indeed, in the new nationalist discourse, elderly Arabs, the Nakba generation of Israel's Palestinian citizens, appear above all as a generation of survivors. Their passive victimhood is contrasted in this discourse with the doughty resistance of their contemporaries who became refugees and freedom fighters. Dan Rabinowitz and Khawla abu-Baker refer to those who were forced to go as intergenerational "living repositories of Palestinian destiny" and depicts them as the keepers of memory.

> For their children and grandchildren, members of the generation of 1948 are living links to history and national identity. The human shadows of that war—those missing from their old communities, those living miserably and harshly in Lebanon, Syria, the West Bank, the Gaza Strip, and Jordan—still haunt the memory. Not surprisingly, the refugees of 1948 have become living repositories of Palestinian destiny. Keepers of the material and symbolic keys of homes they locked in haste, their broken hearts claim the right to return with a persistence that is not easily swayed. They stubbornly refuse to vanish.[4]

The iconography of the elders as the guardians of the key and conversely the empowerment of the "stand-tall generation" encompass a sociological premise that is prevalent in the scholarship on social movements. According to this premise, the agency of the young generation of political activists takes precedence over the tragic choices made by their elders. The emphasis placed on university graduates, social activists, and organizers of demonstrations casts the young in the role of agents of nationalism, blurring and in some cases denying the city's elders the right to act upon memory, because they are neither the champions of lost nationalism nor its latter-day agents. The shadow of their internal exile as refugees in their own homeland renders them politically irrelevant and relegates them to a purely survivalist identity.

Contrary to the mural depicted by the middle-age and stand-tall generations, who boldly portray nationalism as a strategic goal and object of yearning, the pessoptimist elderly assume the unsolicited yet historical and political position as the generation that broke up that monochromatic picture of nationalism. In a crumbling community, the state of crisis paradoxically drives them to draw up a new personal, subversive, and enduring life scheme that challenges both the Zionist and the Palestinian narratives, which consigns them to oblivion and renders them voiceless and feckless. In the binational city, the absence of mechanisms of centralized social control brings about a transformation that unfolds in their stories. Jaffa as a disabling environment for national identity formation transforms into an enabling environment of alternative emergent subjectivities and resistance. This state of affairs allows the individual agents to manage their identity while remaining undetected by national sensors and institutional mouthpieces. The newly found voice of our storytellers is in fact the voice of a city that eschews master narratives and throws into relief the nooks and crannies of the ramshackle edifice of the toils and chores of daily living.

NOTES

Introduction

1. *Samed* is the active participle form of *sumud* (steadfastness, particularly in the context of holding on to one's land), a major theme in the ideology of Palestinian indigenousness. See Shehadeh (1984).

2. The performance cited here took place on Nakba Day (May 15), 2005, in the building of the Association of Jaffa's Arabs, of which Gabi 'Abed is a leading member.

3. In *The Crucified Nation*, Alan Davies (2008) reveals the roots of posttraumatic national discourse in the Christian discourse of sacrifice. Roger Abrahams uses the term *dolorism* to indicate a major component of the politicization of suffering: "Projections of nostalgia become politically potent when the story of loss is converted into narratives of victimization . . . supporting and justifying our cause by retrospectively enlisting the dead" (Abrahams, 2003: 215).

4. Furani (2012: 3).

5. Edward Said, quoted in al-Jarrah (2001). Addressing the search for adequate concepts that describe the Palestinian experience, Said explains: "In Arabic I use the word *shatat* (dispersion) despite my continuing caution and criticism of many terms based on myths of imagination. I naturally reject the term "diaspora." But nothing can prevent the term being used. The Jews used it to fulfill their own imagination, but we are talking about a different situation for the Palestinian. The Palestinian situation and the society Palestinians desire is peculiar to that nation" (Jarah 1999, n.p.).

6. See Pratt (1991) and Monterescu (2015).

7. The term *mixed cities* was first coined by the British colonial regime in the Peel Commission (1937) and subsequently became part of the Israeli and Palestinian post-Nakba discourse. Some Palestinian critics reject this term and propose instead *targeted cities* (*mudun mustahdafa*) or the more optimistic *shared cities* (*mudun mushtarka*). On the evolution of the discourse and ethnic relations in these cities, see Rabinowitz and Monterescu (2008).

8. See, for example, Gur-Ze'ev and Pappé (2003), Massad (2005), Rotbard (2015), and Yiftachel (2006).

9. See Tamari (2008) and LeVine (2005).

10. See Ram (1996).

11. See Rabinowitz and Monterescu (2008: 202 and 218) for an analysis of the effect of Ottoman and British rule on urban mix. Urban spaces in the Ottoman Middle East during the early modern era were predicated on the logic of religious communalism. Although some public spaces were ethnically neutral, residential patterns corresponded by and large to the administrative *millet* system of patronage and classification. Under Ottoman administration, communities, which were vertically subordinate to regional Ottoman rulers and, through them, to the metropole in Istanbul, conducted their affairs largely independent of one another. People living in these communities had neither a common municipal organizational framework of which they were subjects nor a coherent concept of local identity as or affiliation with a unified body of local citizenry. This is understandable once we recall that this era had yet to see territorial nationalism as a defining element of identity and that communities of natives and immigrants alike were defined along ethnoreligious lines. The late nineteenth century saw the old *millet*-based correspondence between spatial boundaries and social grouping blurred; a new form of public space emerged that was exceedingly informed by a new national, rather than denominational, awareness. Ethnonational competition between Jews and Arabs was clearly feeding an exclusionary demand for spatial segregation. Before World War I, urbanism in Palestine was thus exhibiting patterns of modernization and spatial differentiation that clearly diverged from patterns that had guided the old sectarian Ottoman towns. Resonating with an ever-growing logic of nationalism, politicized urban space was about to assume a dramatic role under British rule. In the first half of the twentieth century, a new heteronomous urban form emerged from the collusion of the old Ottoman sectarian urban regime and the new national, modernizing, and capitalist order (both Palestinian and Zionist). Bearing traces of the old system, the new one was in fact a fragmented amalgam of various city forms.

12. See Goren (2004), Bernstein (2007), de Vries (2007), and Monterescu and Rabinowitz (2007).

13. Portugali (1993).

14. LeVine (2005); Monterescu (2015).

15. For example, Yacobi (2009) and Yiftachel and Yacobi (2003).

16. The term "Mother of the Stranger" (*umm al-gharib*) was historically assigned to Jaffa because of its liberal cosmopolitanism, which characterized it as a flourishing city that hosted labor migrants and other foreigners from the region during the heyday of Palestinian urban modernity in the first part of the twentieth century. The term is now used either nostalgically or with bitter irony by local Palestinians who lament the sense of strangeness the city evokes. For instance, in an interview after the release of his 2009 Oscar-nominated film *Ajami*, Skandar Copti said, "Jaffa is called *Umm al-gharib*, the 'Mother of the Stranger,' and people are indeed strangers to each other. Almost nothing brings them together" (quoted in Monterescu, 2015: 93).

17. Minns and Hijab (1990: 156).

18. The High Follow-Up Committee for the Arab Masses in Israel (Lajnat al-Mutaba'a al-'Ulya lil-Jama'ir al-'Arabiyya fi Isra'il) was established in 1982 as an extra-parliamentary umbrella organization to represent Arab citizens of Israel at the national level. It is consistently criticized for excluding Arab communities in mixed towns, such as Lydda, Ramle, Jaffa, Haifa, and Acre.

19. *Madrikh Yafo* (1949: 41). All translations of Hebrew and Arabic are mine.

20. Haskell (1994).

21. See Birenboim-Carmeli (2000).

22. Sociologist Ulrich Beck regards methodological nationalism as one of the greatest threats to critical sociology: "Much of social science assumes the coincidence of social boundaries with state boundaries, believing that social action occurs primarily within and only secondarily across, these divisions. . . . Methodological nationalism assumes this normative claim as a socio-ontological given. . . . To some extent, much of social science is a prisoner of the nation-state" (Beck, 2003: 453–54).

23. Shamir (2000).

24. Lockman (1996: 12).

25. See, for instance, Rotbard (2015), Yiftachel and Yacobi (2003), and Kanaaneh (2002).

26. Soffer (2004); Yiftachel and Yacobi (2003); Zureik (1979); Rotbard (2015); Yacobi (2009).

27. Soffer (2004).

28. Yiftachel and Yacobi (2003).

29. For example, Spivak (1996) and Herzfeld (1996).

30. The most prominent example of this trend at the national level is the founding of the association Zochrot in 2002, whose aim is "bringing knowledge of the Nakba to Israel's Jewish public." Zochrot (which means "remembering") seeks to restore the repressed Palestinian memory and place it on the contemporary political and cultural agenda. Its political project is couched in narrative terms. Through projects such as tours in destroyed Palestinian villages and towns (including Jaffa), the Nakba Map, and the iNakba application, Zochrot seeks to reveal a voice that speaks of Nakba and return, "a voice that seeks recognition for injustice and new paths toward change and redress" (www.nakbainhebrew.org). Another, more local project that offers narrative redress is Autobiography of a City. This organization was started in 2000 "as a direct response to the events of October 2000" and promotes "multicultural public discourse [on] the untold story of the various sections of the population, as part of a future process of reconciliation and healing. . . . The complexity of memory and narrative and the manner in which they are constituted are among Autobiography of a City's major areas of interest" (https://thejaffaproject.com). See also www.campusincamps.ps/projects/autobiography -of-a-city/ (accessed November 7, 2017).

31. Bhabha (1990: 1).

32. Bhabha (1990: 1).

33. For a critique of this trickle-down effect, see Comaroff (1990), Colvin (2008), and King (2007).

34. For a comparable "bargaining with patriarchy," see Kandiyoti (1988).

35. Weiss (2011); Monterescu (2015).

36. Gur-Ze'ev and Pappé (2003); Slyomovics (1998).

37. Appadurai (2000).

38. Trouillot (1995).

39. Bell (2003).

40. In *Number Our Days*, an ethnography of a Jewish American senior citizens' center, Barbara Myerhoff characterizes the human species as a storyteller (*Homo narrans*) (1978: 272). As an existential category of being, old age is a lens through which the interviewee relates time and meaning (271). See also Niles (2010) and Bruner (2003).

41. Quoted in Myerhoff (1978: xv).

42. Myerhoff (1978: xv).

43. See Swedenburg (1995) and Schely-Newman (2002).

44. See Trouillot (1995).

45. Stoler (1992: 183).

46. Stoler (1992: 184).

47. In semiotic anthropological terms, metanationalism can be defined as an array of metapragmatic statements that address the context in which nationalism is presented by the interpreting subject. In this context nationalism as an ideology is merely one component in the field of the creation of political meaning, alongside interaction, position, and the actors' narrative. See R. Bauman (1986) and Silverstein (2001).

48. Rabinowitz (2001).

49. Bourdieu (1987); Ewing (1990); Gubrium et al. (1994).

50. For Dan McAdams, a personal myth is an "act of imagination that is a patterned integration of our remembered past, perceived present and anticipated future" (McAdams, 1993: 12).

51. Bourdieu (1987: 2).

52. Vincent Crapanzano highlights the performative and creative nonrepresentational aspect of a life history as a result of a complex self-constituting negotiation: "The life history is usually constituted from a transformation—the transformation from an oral production to a written product. It becomes text and carries with it all the ontological and epistemological burdens of the text" (Crapanzano, 1984: 957).

53. Hazan (1994).

54. Shield and Aronson (2003).

55. Savishinsky (2000: 43).

56. See Said (2004): "What of the last or late period of life, the decay of the body, the onset of ill health (which, in a younger person, brings on the possibility of an untimely end)? These issues, which interest me for obvious personal reasons, have led me to look at the way in which the work of some great artists and writers acquires a new idiom towards the end of their lives—what I've come to think of as a late style."

57. Kassem (2011); Hasan (2009).

58. Bhabha (1994).

59. Silverstein (2001); Parmentier (2016).

60. Holstein and Gubrium (1995).

61. In *The Poetics of Military Occupation*, Smadar Lavie writes: "Precisely at that moment of decomposition, the moment of recomposition through emergence became possible. Each character, while still just a plain person, rose up and, by temporarily fusing him- or herself with his or her folkloric persona, became the interlocutor, in the fold genre, between the tribal collective memory of the past and its present circumstances. When these characters transformed themselves from ordinary persons into dramatic personae, they conjoined their living selves with the tribal pantheon . . . as allegorical types belonging to tribal folkloric genres that differentiate the history of the tribe from the histories of its occupiers" (Lavie, 1990: 330).

62. Handler (1988); Kapferer (1988).

63. Brubaker et al. (2006); Portugali (1993).

64. Eriksen (1993).

65. Parker et al. (1992); Yuval-Davis (1997).

66. Thaiss (1978).

67. Anderson (1991).

68. Hobsbawm and Ranger (1992).

69. Zali Gurevitch writes: "The big place is more than a particular site and even more than all the sites put together; it is the idea itself. The place ('the land') is a notion that precedes the actual location. The precedence of the notion with regard to the location means that the two are not identical. This is the dialectical element within the Jewish notion of location, which is a source of constant ambivalence because the precedence of the notion impedes the process whereby the place becomes something that is taken for granted, or indigenous as it were" (Gurevitch, 2007: 25).

Chapter 1

1. We conducted the interview with Fakhri Jday in 2003 together with Moussa Abu-Ramadan.

2. Al-Ard (The Land) movement was active between 1959 and 1965 and was the first Arab nationalist political party in post-1948 Israel. It differentiated itself from the communist parties that sought to represent the Arab community and adopted the innovative tactic of contesting the Jewish state in the High Court of Justice. The party's platform did not recognize Israel as a Jewish state, and its actions focused on the struggle against land expropriation and for the crystallization of Palestinian national identity among Israel's Arabs. The movement's attempt to run in the 1965 national election was thwarted when the Central Electoral Committee banned it and its appeal to the High Court was subsequently rejected.

3. Founded in 1979, the Association of Jaffa's Arabs (al-Rabita li-ri'ayat shu'un 'arab yaffa) was the first organization to promote the rights of Jaffa's Palestinian community. The association's founders belong to the first generation of Palestinian intellectuals born in Jaffa after 1948. Based on a nationalist, secular, and nonsectarian platform, the Association seeks to bridge the internal splits within the community and to preserve Jaffa's Arabness in the face of the Tel Aviv municipality's Judaization policies.

4. Rabinowitz and Abu-Baker (2005) distinguish between three generational constellations of Palestinian citizens of Israel: the generation of survivors, the worn-out generation, and the current stand-tall generation.

5. Lustik (1985). See also Rabinowitz and Abu-Baker (2005).

6. Sewell (1996).

7. Colin Powell was the U.S. secretary of state at the time of the interview.

8. Khoury (2002).

9. Khoury (2002: 40–41).

10. Khoury (2002: 41).

11. Khoury (2002: 41).

12. Nora (1989).

13. Nora (1989: 7–19).

14. Gurevitch and Aran (1991); Hazan (2001).

15. In a video display by Re'ut-Sadaqa, screened at an event to mark the Nakba's sixtieth anniversary in July 2008, Jday said, "They say there are 20,000 Arabs in Jaffa today. But we should do well to find among them ten who are not hypocrites."

Chapter 2

1. We conducted the interview in 2003 in the presence of Hicham Chabaita, who also took the photos.

2. The Jews of Bulgaria take pride in 1,500 years of communal life and distinct

identity. Haskell notes that as Sephardic Jews from Europe, the Bulgarians in Israel belonged to an intermediate category in the system of ethnic stratification. The Ashkenazic establishment thus regarded them as urban, educated, and Western, and they were spared the stigma attached to the Mizrahi immigrants from Islamic countries. This also meant that they were allocated houses vacated by Palestinians in Jaffa rather than settled in peripheral areas in the Negev. See Haskell (1994).

3. Haskell (1994: 149).

4. Haskell (1994: 149).

5. Maccabi Jaffa was founded in 1949 by Bulgarian immigrants. In 2000 it was disbanded because of financial and legal issues. The club has recently been reformed by its supporters, and efforts to revive it are under way.

6. Lior Ben Ami's article "Avramiko the Great's Last Performance" (2004) provided a rich source of additional biographical detail.

7. Deshen and Shokeid (1974).

8. Liebman and Don-Yehiya (1983); Almog (2000).

9. See Sorek (2000).

10. Emanuel (1988: 15).

11. Weiss (2011).

12. For an example of the denial of the Palestinian presence on the part of Haifa's Jews, see Rabinowitz (2007).

13. Hazan (1980).

14. Haskell (1994: 94).

15. Herzfeld (1996).

16. Herzfeld (1996: 3).

17. Spiritual Zionists believed in spiritual revival through the creation of a Jewish spiritual center in Palestine that would serve as a counterweight to the threat of assimilation in liberal European societies. Ahad Ha'am believed that the Land of Israel should not be expected to resolve the Jews' existential or economic issues and was not intended to be a physical refuge from exile but rather a cure for the nation's cultural problems. This ideology is antithetical to the political-territorial Zionism espoused by Theodor Herzl. Indeed, as early as 1891, Ahad Ha'am criticized political Zionists for ignoring the Arab presence in the country and for regarding all Arabs as "primitive men of the desert, and as a donkey-like nation" (quoted in Segev, 2001: 104). In so doing, he became one of the first to discern the root of the dispute that has dogged territorial Zionism ever since.

18. On patriotism in a migrant society, see Golden (2004).

19. Hadas and Gonen (1994).

20. See Monterescu (2015).

21. The Arab residents who cannot afford to purchase apartments in heavily gentrified neighborhoods are those who are moving to the Jerusalem Boulevard area and to the Bulgarian housing projects.

22. Haskell (1994: 150).

23. Haskell (1994: 150).

24. Haskell (1994: 151).

25. Hazan (1990).

26. Rabinowitz and Abu-Baker (2005); Shokeid (2009).

27. Turner (1995).

Chapter 3

1. "Yafa kanat biyara wahda" (in Arabic).

2. Abu-Subhi's grandson and Moussa Abu-Ramadan were present during the interview, which took place in 2013.

3. "Illi bishuf mish zai illi bisma'" (in Arabic).

4. Bell (2003).

5. According to Lehi's accounts, this attack severely demoralized Jaffa's Arabs (Milstein 1998: 51). In a statement issued the very same day, Lehi boasted, "This attack will serve as a demonstration and warning that the Jewish fighter is able not only to defend and to repulse attacks by Arab marauders. He will also seek out those responsible for the atrocities and for shedding Jewish blood" (51). The incident, which was one of the first car-bomb attacks in world history (Davis 2008), marked a new escalation in the fighting for the city. In response, British forces sealed off the entrances to Jaffa and left only one exit open to the rest of the country. Jaffa's isolation sealed its fate. While the Haganah waited for an opportune moment to capture the beleaguered city, the Etzel decided to attack Jaffa on April 25, 1948, and in a matter of days, it conquered and leveled Manshiye, a northern neighborhood of Jaffa that borders Tel Aviv. This was followed by the surrender of Jaffa's remaining Arab community to the Haganah on May 13, 1948, one day before Israel's independence was declared in Tel Aviv.

6. On the morning of April 9, 1948, a joint force of Etzel and Lehi fighters that numbered some 110 men attacked the village of Deir Yassin. According to the accounts given by the underground organizations, the objective of the operation was to capture the village and to vacate its population. However, a violent confrontation rapidly developed, the circumstances of which are disputed, during which 100–120 villagers were killed, including women and children. The rumors that rapidly began to spread—to the effect that the Jewish forces were massacring the civilian population and raping the women—generated general anxiety and contributed to the air of panic that spurred people to flee. In Chapter 6 of this book Subhiya Abu-Ramadan reports on the fear of rape and plunder.

7. Lustik (1980).

8. Rabinowitz and Abu-Baker (2005).

9. Ian Lustik (1980) explains the passivity and absence of political violence among Israel's Palestinian citizens (before October 2000) by referring to the state security apparatus designed to prevent the Arab public in Israel from organizing independently and achieving effective political representation.

10. Habiby (1985).

11. See Bardenstein (1998) and Swedenburg (1990).

12. For another case of "relational pluralism," see Kanafani-Zahar (2000) on relations between Christians and Muslims in Lebanon. Kanafani-Zahar argues that pluralism is fashioned through multiple ritual exchanges, which create a "neutral" space of relative laicization.

13. Literally, "the cannon vineyard." Legend has it that a man was riding his donkey when a demon (*'afrit*) possessed it and propelled it and the rider with the speed of a cannonball. The rider eventually pricked the donkey with a pin and thus exorcised the demon. The story became widely known, and the intrepid rider's surname has ever since been known as *Madfa'* (cannon). Karm al-Madfa' is the orchard where Abu-Subhi's family lived.

14. The kibbutz was founded by members of the Gordonia group from Bessarabia,

who were subsequently joined by groups from Argentina, France, and North Africa and by local youth movements.

15. Said (2000).

16. This assertion is often made by Palestinians in exile who are visiting their hometown. See, for instance, the documentary *Disappearances* on the Palestinian neighborhood Manshiyya in Jaffa (the documentary was directed by Anat Even and produced by Jean Bigo and Anat Even; Israel/France, 2017).

17. Another of Abu-Subhi's grandsons maintains that his grandfather has only recently begun to speak about the Nakba, a resurfacing of repressed memory as it were. Abu-Subhi further maintains that he became a part of the local elite without choosing to, owing to the disappearance of the old elite, and that if it hadn't been for the Nakba, he would have remained a tenant farmer shackled to his land. Abu-Subhi is renowned for his religious Islamic knowledge.

18. Harvey (1991).

19. Golan (2001).

20. On the walking dead in the nationalist mythology, see Hever (2001: 50).

21. Felman and Laub (1992).

22. LaCapra (2014: 118).

Chapter 4

1. "Ma kuntu ahsidu sayyidan fi mulkihi, wa-asbahtu ahsidu 'abd 'abdi al-sayyid" (in Arabic).

2. The interview took place in September 2006 with the assistance of Mai Chabaita-Massalha. A number of the biographical details in this chapter are taken from Adam LeBor's *City of Oranges* (2007). In an additional meeting held in September 2010, the sisters read the manuscript of the chapter and made corrections. They also provided us with a collection of historical documents that testify to their father's activity.

3. Ranin here turns to Mai Chabaita-Massalha, whose sister-in-law lives close to the Hakim sisters.

4. Schutz (1971).

5. The agreement between the National Emergency Committee and the Haganah commanders was signed on May 13, 1948, as part of the negotiations over the city's status in the wake of the fighting. The next day, May 14, the British governor left the city and attorney Laniado was appointed governor in his stead. The document (written in English) dryly stipulates as follows:

> AGREEMENT Between the Commander of the HAGANA, Tel Aviv District . . . ; and The Arab population of the area enclosed by Tel Aviv, Mikve Israel, Holon and Bat-Yam. Signed on 13th May, 1948, at Headquarters, Hagana, Tel Aviv District.
>
> WHEREAS the undersigned are the Emergency Committee of Jaffa; and WHEREAS they are in Jaffa in order to direct the affairs of the Arab [*sic*] in the area above defined, following their declaration that Jaffa is an undefended area; AND IN ORDER TO preserve and maintain the peace and welfare of the Arabs in the area above defined; THEY THEREFORE HEREBY solemnly declare and affirm that all Arabs in the area above defined are represented by them; AND THAT they will carry out all the instructions given and to be given by the Commander of the Hagana, Tel Aviv District.

A copy of the original document was handed to us during the conversation and is cited in Arikha (1957: 254).

6. According to the surrender document cited in note 5, the committee included Ahmad Abu-Laban, Salah Nazar, and Ahmad 'Abd al-Rahim. Hassan Barakat was not a member of the committee.

7. Cf. Kassem (2011).

8. See Rabinowitz (1997).

9. Rema Hammami, currently an anthropologist at Bir Zeit University and a resident of Jerusalem, portrayed the experience of visiting Jaffa: "I always go to Jaffa with a sense of emotional trepidation and leave with diffuse anger and resignation. My final feeling on the way home to Jerusalem is generally that I don't want to go back. Going to Jaffa for someone who grew up with it as an iconic myth, a place that no other place can ever measure up to, is bound to bring disappointment. My feeling of being burdened by Jaffa, this place that exists only in the world of lost paradises, is no different from that of any other child of a Jaffaite. For there are no 'former' Jaffaites—they never really left in 1948 but still carry it around with them everywhere and always. I would love to be able to walk through the city without being weighed down by its past and my duty to that past—just to be able to be fascinated by the architecture and the people who live there now, to be able to call them *Yaffawiin* in some meaningful way instead of referring to them as 'the present inhabitants.' Alas, to do so would mean being burned at the stake for collaborating with a reality built on the demolition of dreams" (Tamari and Hammami 1998: 67).

Chapter 5

1. According to the National Insurance Institute of Israel, "A Prisoner of Zion [is] recognized as a disabled person as a result of imprisonment, detention or deportation due to his Zionistic activities, with a disability degree of at least 10%" (National Insurance Institute, 2001: 36).

2. The interview was conducted in 2003 by Daniel Monterescu and Hicham Chabaita, who also photographed Nazihah Asis.

3. A literal translation of this sentence is, "I will be a *kapara* [atonement] for the government."

4. Sered (1992).

5. Yuval-Davis (1997).

6. Melamed (2004).

7. Kanaaneh (2002).

8. Melamed (2004).

9. Bird-David (1990).

10. Forte (2006: 50).

Chapter 6

1. The conversation was held in 2003 with the assistance of Moussa Abou Ramadan, Subhiya's nephew. Abu-Ramadan is Subhiya's maiden name, and she asked us to use it.

2. Atran (1989).

3. Before the end of the British Mandate, political and military considerations dictated the decision not to attack Jaffa directly but rather to capture its surrounding villages, which served as a bridge between Jaffa and other Arab regions of the country. Among these villages were al-Khayriah, Saqia, Yahudia, Azur, and Salameh (for a description of the capture of Salameh, see the Zochrot website (zochrot.org/he/village /49897). These actions were part of the Haganah's Plan D and were founded on the as-

sumption that encirclement would in any event lead to the surrender of Jaffa's residents and its fall. This was likewise the objective of Operation Hamets during Passover 1948. Dozens of the villagers and Qauqji's Salvation Army troops were killed in the heavy fighting, as were twenty-six Haganah fighters, seven of whom were buried as unknown soldiers. The battle was decided on April 30, and the Salvation Army's commander in the town escaped by sea. This defeat accelerated the mass flight from Jaffa, during which 70,000 of its Arab inhabitants escaped. As mentioned, on May 13 Jaffa's Arab leaders signed a surrender agreement with the Haganah. The village of Tel al-Rish subsequently became the Tel Giborim neighborhood, named after the "heroic conquerors" (*giborim*) of the city of Holon during the war.

4. According to the testimony of Abed al-Aziz Saqer, who fought in the village of Salameh in April and May 1948, the secretary-general of the Supreme Arab Committee, Hussein Fakhri al-Khalidi, sought to expose the ugliness of the Zionist enemy by displaying photos from Deir Yassin of severed limbs and murdered men and women. Yet this propaganda backfired. The reports circulated by all channels of communication sowed fear and led to the removal of the women, children, and old people from areas of conflict (interview conducted by Raneen Jeries on March 5, 2007, zochrot.org/he/testimony/52782, [accessed July 12, 2016]).

5. Swedenburg (1995).

6. Swedenburg (1995: 138).

7. Cf. Bishara (1992).

8. Bhabha (1994).

9. For example, Butler (1963), Kaufman (1986), and Tornstam (1999).

10. Sharabi (1988).

11. Kandiyoti (1988).

12. Kamir (2002).

13. Hazan (1980).

Chapter 7

1. Talia Seckbach-Monterescu is Daniel Monterescu's mother. She was interviewed in her house in 2003. She requested to be identified in the text by the combination of her maiden name and her married name.

2. In the 1950s Jewish squatters who had been moved out of the Old City, which was being turned into an artists' colony, known as the Jaffa evacuees (*mefuney Yafo*), were housed in a transit camp in the future Jaffa D.

3. London (1993: 189).

4. Monterescu (2015); Beck (1996).

5. Douglas (1991).

6. Bakhtin (1981).

7. Simmel (1971 [1908]).

8. Berger (1974).

9. Rapport (1995).

10. Clifford (1997).

11. Crapanzano (1985).

12. Bhabha (1994).

13. Hazan (1980).

Chapter 8

1. The interview was held in 2006 in Jaffa's Torsina Café by Daniel Monterescu. It was conducted mainly in Hebrew, but after a while, when Youssef 'Asfur joined in the conversation, Hermosa switched to Arabic. Shabazi is located in south-central Tel Aviv, one of the first Jewish neighborhoods outside the walled city of Jaffa established before the founding of Tel Aviv.

2. Shenhav (2006).

3. In Marxist tradition, Man the Maker—*homo faber*—is a philosophical assumption that human creation is founded on historical development and that the tools of labor manifest man's control over his material environment. Here we use the term in its traditional classical pre-Marxist sense, which underscores the individual's power over his or her destiny.

4. Monterescu (2006).

5. Lieblich and Josselson (1997).

6. At this point in the conversation Hermosa mistakes the interviewer for an Arab and thus says that the conventional code of engagement is "like yours."

7. Eliyahu Sasson (1902–1977) was born in Damascus and occupied senior positions in government, including Minister of Post and Minister of Police. Because of his stature, Hermosa mistakes him for the mayor of Tel Aviv.

8. Simić (1978).

9. Spector-Marsel (2006).

10. Kaufman (1986).

11. Hobsbawm and Ranger (1992).

12. Shenhav (2006: 7).

13. Shenhav (2006: 140).

14. Portugali (1993); Bernstein (2007).

15. Jacobson and Naor (2016).

16. Rotbard (2015).

Chapter 9

1. In his early days, the artist Nahum Guttman was employed by the British administration as a doorman at Jaffa's brothels (1918) and subsequently turned them into an object of aesthetic study. In his renowned series of oil and aquarelle paintings created in 1926, titled *A Brothel in Jaffa*, Guttman documents lascivious acts in the brothels and the ambience generated around them in the Large Area, north of the Old City.

2. Weiss (2011).

3. In the art exhibition "The Large Area" (Agora Gallery, June 2008), the place is presented as the epitome of "the black city" and "the Wild West" of the Middle East. The curator, Sari Golan, wrote about the exhibition as follows: "*The Large Area* is the artistic occurrence that takes place in between historical and political consciousness and the imagined contemporary space. The moniker 'the large area' was originally created to denote a territory in 1950s Jaffa surrounding *The Peak Park* [Gan HaPisga]. The name sprung from the demolition of many of the buildings of the old city of Jaffa, ostensibly for security reasons. As a result, the remnants of the demolished buildings remained strewn in the area and turned into empty plots. The buildings that survived were populated by immigrants from the Balkan countries and North Africa" (quote from the exhibit description at the gallery).

4. Monterescu (2009).

5. According to its website, the Old Jaffa Development Company was founded in 1961 "with the goal of constructing and renovating the Tel Jaffa area (also known as the 'Large Area'), a zone which was a breeding ground for crime, prostitution and drugs. . . . The guiding approach was to renovate and repair the structures in the Old City while preserving their nature and harmonizing it with the scenery. The intent was to attract a new population and transform the area into a center for tourism, recreation, and art. Another stipulation of the plan was that only artists would be eligible to reside in the area" (www.oldjaffa.co.il [accessed January 2, 2016]).

6. Harvey (1991).

7. Menahem Talmi, *Ma'ariv* (May 5, 1967).

8. The interview with Amram Ben-Yosef took place in 2003 at his favorite café in the Large Area. Hicham Chabaita assisted in the interview and photographed the conversation.

9. Brandes (1980); Monterescu (2007).

10. Herzfeld (1996).

11. Wilson (1990); Wacquant (2007).

12. Gurevitch and Aran (1991).

13. Featherstone et al. (1991).

14. Golan (1999: 163).

15. Turner (1975; 1995).

16. Steinberg (1995: 85).

17. Handelman (1977: 191).

18. Steinberg (1995: 85).

19. Baudrillard (1988).

Chapter 10

1. The interview with Abu-George was conducted in 2003 by Daniel Monterescu and Moussa abu Ramadan.

2. Bakhtin (1986: 170). The full quote reads: "There is neither a first nor a last word, and there are no limits to the dialogic context (it extends into the boundless past and the boundless future). Even *past* meanings, that is, those born in the dialogue of past centuries, can never be stable (finalized, ended once and for all)—they will always change (be renewed) in the process of subsequent, future development of the dialogue. At any moment in the development of the dialogue there are immense, boundless masses of forgotten contextual meanings, but at certain moments of the dialogue's subsequent development along the way they are recalled and reinvigorated in renewed form (in a new context). Nothing is absolutely dead: every meaning will have its homecoming festival."

3. Bourdieu (1987).

4. Hazan (2009); Baltes and Smith (2003).

5. The figure of Abu-George is the direct opposite of the national figure of the Palestinian writer Emile Habiby, who asked to be buried in Haifa and for his headstone to bear the inscription "He remained in Haifa" (*baqi fi Haifa*).

6. Kassem (2011).

7. Kanafani (2000: 186–87).

8. Darwish and al-Qasim (1991: 89).

9. Z. Bauman (1992).

10. Fabian (2002).

11. Hazan (1996; 2015).

Conclusion

1. Said (1986: 14).

2. In *Politics of Urbanism: Seeing Like a City*, Warren Magnusson writes: "The sovereign is not so much the rock on which the city is built, as a part of the rubble the city transforms into the structures of urban life. . . . To see like a city is to accept a certain disorderliness, unpredictability, and multiplicity as inevitable, and to pose the problem of politics in relation to that complexity, rather than in relation to the simplicity that sovereignty seeks. To put it bluntly: to see like a city is to grow up politically. . . . To see like a city is to recognize that political order is not something that can be fixed in any simple way. A political order is always in the process of being overcome, and the challenges to it may arise from any quarter" (Magnusson, 2011: 119).

3. Bakhtin (1981: 84). Our choice of the chronotope as a key concept is designed to avoid giving the mistaken impression that our discussion suggests a historically based developmental approach of individual or collective identities. As elaborated later, our perspective is structural rather than historical, synchronic rather than diachronic.

4. Gurevitch (2007).

5. Steinberg (1995).

6. Kandiyoti (1988).

7. Herzfeld (1996: 171); Spivak (1996: 214).

8. Bourdieu (1987); Ewing (1990).

9. Schely-Newman (2002).

10. Ewing (1990). See also Gubrium et al. (1994), McAdams (1996), and Schely-Newman (2002).

11. See Rabinowitz (1997), Yiftachel and Yacobi (2003), and Rotbard (2015).

12. Monterescu (2009).

13. Rotbard (2015).

14. Gurevitch (2007).

15. Monterescu (2011).

16. Bhabha (1994).

17. Z. Bauman (1991); Beck (1996); Monterescu (2015).

18. Lomsky-Feder (2004).

19. Cohen (1985).

20. We make a theoretical distinction between our concept of heteronomy and Michel Foucault's (1986) heterotopia. The sociological development of the concept of heteronomy rests on Ruggie's (1993) discussion of the boundaries of the modern state and space. Following Meinecke (1970), Ruggie contrasts modern territorialism with the political systems of the Middle Ages, which allowed various territorial loyalties to coexist without attempting to exclude one another. Overlapping territorial systems constituted heteronomous shackles that impeded the development of the modern sovereign state, which thus opposed them. The antithetical homonymic order defines the state's borders as discrete territorial spheres. For discussions of heteronomy in other contexts, see Kemp (1999) and Shenhav (2006).

21. Monterescu (2015).

22. Beck (2003); Shenhav (2006).

23. See Abrams (1988 [1977]) Brubaker (1996), Appadurai (2000), and Wimmer and Glick-Schiller (2000).

24. Emirbayer (1997).

25. Emirbayer (1997: 287).

26. Emirbayer (1997: 289; emphasis added).
27. Brubaker (1996).
28. Lefebvre (1996); Harvey (1997).
29. Portugali (1993).
30. Harvey (1991).
31. Billig (1995).
32. Brubaker (1996).
33. See Crapanzano (2003).
34. Bhabha (1990); Bakhtin (1981).
35. See Anderson (1991) and Smith (1991).
36. Swedenburg (1990).

Epilogue

1. Granowski et al. (2009).
2. Granowski et al. (2009: 9).
3. Granowski et al. (2009: 11).
4. Rabinowitz and Abu-Baker (2005: 59).

BIBLIOGRAPHY

Abrahams, Roger. 2003. "Identity." In Burt Feintuch (ed.), *Eight Words for the Study of Expressive Culture*. Urbana: Illinois University Press, 198–222.

Abrams, Philip. 1988 [1977]. "Notes on the Difficulty of Studying the State." *Journal of Historical Sociology* 1(1): 58–89.

al-Jarrah, Nouri. 2001. *Bait baina al-nahr wa-l-bahr: Muhawarat haula al-Falastiniyin wa-l-'awda* [House Between the River and the Sea: Dialogues Regarding the Palestinians and Return]. Beirut: al-Mu'assasa al-'Arabiya li-l-Dirassat wa-l-Nashr.

Almog, Oz. 2000. *The Sabra: The Creation of the New Jew*, trans. Haim Watzman. Berkeley: University of California Press.

Anderson, Benedict. 1991. *Imagined Communities: Reflections on the Origin and Spread of Nationalism*. New York: Verso.

Appadurai, Arjun. 2000. "The Grounds of the Nation-State: Identity, Violence, and Territory." In Kjell Goldmann, Ulf Hannerz, and Charles Westin (eds.), *Nationalism and Internationalism in the Post-Cold War Era*. London: Routledge, 129–43.

Arikha, Yosef. 1957. *Yafo: Miqra'a historit-sifrutit* [Jaffa: A Historical-Literary Reader]. Tel Aviv: Tel Aviv Municipality Press.

Atran, Scott. 1989. "The Surrogate Colonization of Palestine: 1917–1939." *American Ethnologist* 17: 719–44.

Bakhtin, Mikhail. 1981. *The Dialogic Imagination*, trans. Caryl Emerson and Michael Holquist; ed. Michael Holquist. Austin: University of Texas Press.

———. 1986. *Speech Genres and Other Late Essays*, ed. Caryl Emerson and Michael Holquist; trans. Vern W. McGee. Austin: University of Texas Press.

Baltes, Paul B., and Jacqui Smith. 2003. "New Frontiers in the Future of Aging: From Successful Aging of the Young Old to the Dilemmas of the Fourth Age." *Gerontology* 49: 123–35.

Bardenstein, Carol. 1998. "Threads of Memory and Discourses of Rootedness: Of Trees, Oranges, and Prickly-Pear Cactus in Israel-Palestine." *Edebiyat* 8: 1–36.

Baudrillard, Jean. 1988. "On Simulacrum and Simulation." In Jean Baudrillard, *Jean*

Baudrillard: Selected Writings, ed. Mark Poster; trans. Sheila Faria Glaser. Stanford,
    CA: Stanford University Press, 166–84.
Bauman, Richard. 1986. *Story, Performance, and Event: Contextual Studies of Oral Narra-
    tive*. Cambridge, UK: Cambridge University Press.
Bauman, Zygmunt. 1991. *Modernity and Ambivalence*. Ithaca, NY: Cornell University
    Press.
———. 1992. *Intimations of Postmodernity*. London: Routledge.
Beck, Ulrich. 1996. "How Neighbors Become Jews: The Political Construction of the
    Stranger in an Age of Reflexive Modernity." *Constellations* 2: 402–20.
———. 2003. "Toward a New Critical Theory with a Cosmopolitan Intent." *Constella-
    tions* 10: 453–68.
Bell, Duncan. 2003. "Mythscapes: Memory Mythology and National Identity." *British
    Journal of Sociology* 54: 63–81.
Ben-Ami, Lior. 2004. "Avramiko the Great's Last Performance." *Tel Aviv* (October 8).
Berger, Peter L. 1974. *Homeless Mind: Modernization and Consciousness*. Millers Falls,
    MA: Vintage.
Bernstein, Deborah. 2007. "Contested Contact: Proximity and Social Control in Pre-
    1948 Jaffa and Tel-Aviv." In Daniel Monterescu and Dan Rabinowitz (eds.), *Mixed
    Towns, Trapped Communities: Historical Narratives, Spatial Dynamics, Gender Rela-
    tions, and Cultural Encounters in Palestinian-Israeli Towns*. London: Ashgate, 215–42.
Bhabha, Homi K. 1990. *Nation and Narration*. London: Routledge.
———. 1994. *The Location of Culture*. London: Routledge.
Billig, Michael. 1995. *Banal Nationalism*. Thousand Oaks, CA: Sage.
Bird-David, Nurit. 1990. "The Giving Environment: Another Perspective on the Eco-
    nomic System of Gatherer-Hunters." *Current Anthropology* 31(2): 189–96.
Birenboim-Carmeli, Dafna. 2000. *Tzfonim: 'Al ma'amad benoni be-Yisra'el* [Northsiders:
    On the Middle Class in Israel]. Jerusalem: Magnes.
Bishara, 'Azmi. 1992. "Between Space and Place." *Studio* 37: 6–9.
Bourdieu, Pierre. 1987. "The Biographical Illusion." In *Working Papers and Proceedings
    of the Center for Psychosocial Studies*, Richard J. Parmentier and Greg Urban (eds.).
    Chicago: Center for Psychosocial Studies, 1–7.
Brandes, Stanley. 1980. *Metaphors of Masculinity: Sex and Status in Andalusian Folklore*.
    Philadelphia: University of Pennsylvania Press.
Brubaker, Rogers. 1996. *Nationalism Reframed: Nationhood and the National Question in
    the New Europe*. Cambridge, UK: Cambridge University Press.
Brubaker, Rogers, Margit Feischmidt, Jon Fox, and Liana Grancea. 2006. *Nationalist
    Politics and Everyday Ethnicity in a Transylvanian Town*. Princeton, NJ: Princeton
    University Press.
Bruner, Jerome. 2003. *Making Stories: Law, Literature, Life*. Cambridge, MA: Harvard
    University Press.
Butler, Robert. 1963. "The Life Review: An Interpretation of Reminiscence in the
    Aged." *Psychiatry* 26: 65–76.
Calvino, Italo. 1974. *Invisible Cities*, trans. William Weaver. San Diego: Harcourt Brace
    Jovanovich.
Clifford, James. 1997. *Routes: Travel and Translation in the Late Twentieth Century*. Cam-
    bridge, MA: Harvard University Press.
Cohen, Anthony P. 1985. *The Symbolic Construction of Community*. London: Routledge.

Colvin, Christopher J. 2008. "Purity and Planning: Shared Logics of Transitional Justice and Development." *International Journal of Transitional Justice* 2: 412–25.

Comaroff, John L. 1990. "Bourgeois Biography and Colonial Historiography." *Journal of Southern African Studies* 16: 550–62.

Crapanzano, Vincent. 1984. "Life Histories." *American Anthropologist* 86: 953–60.

———. 1985. *Waiting: The Whites of South Africa*. New York: Random House.

———. 2003. *Imaginative Horizons: An Essay in Literary-Philosophical Anthropology*. Chicago: University of Chicago Press.

Darwish, Mahmoud. 2002. *Halat hissar* [State of Siege]. Beirut: Riyad al-Rayyis li-l-Kutub wa-l-Nashr.

Darwish, Mahmoud, and Samih al-Qasim. 1991. *Between the Two Halves of the Orange*, trans. Hannah Amit-Kochavi. Tel Aviv: Mifras Books.

Davies, Alan. 2008. *The Crucified Nation: A Motif in Modern Nationalism*. Eastbourne, UK: Sussex Academic Press.

Davis, Mike. 2008. *Buda's Wagon: A Brief History of the Car Bomb*. New York: Verso.

Deshen, Shlomo, and Moshe Shokeid. 1974. *Predicament of Homecoming: Cultural and Social Life of North African Immigrants in Israel*. Ithaca, NY: Cornell University Press.

de Vries, David. 2007. "Cross-National Collective Action in Palestine's Mixed Towns: The 1946 Civil Servants Strike." In Daniel Monterescu and Dan Rabinowitz (eds.), *Mixed Cities/Trapped Communities: Historical Narratives, Spatial Dynamics, and Gender Relations in Jewish-Arab Mixed Towns in Israel/Palestine*. Burlington, VT: Ashgate, 85–112.

Douglas, Mary. 1991. "The Idea of Home: A Kind of Space." *Social Research* 58: 287–307.

Emanuel, Yitzhak-Moshe. 1988. *The Land of Israel: The Melting Pot*. Jerusalem: Ami.

Emirbayer, Mustafa. 1997. "Manifesto for a Relational Sociology." *American Journal of Sociology* 103: 281–317.

Eriksen, Thomas Hylland. 1993. *Ethnicity and Nationalism: Anthropological Perspective*. London: Pluto Press.

Ewing, K. 1990. "The Illusion of Wholeness: Culture, Self, and the Experience of Inconsistency." *Ethos* 18: 251–78.

Fabian, Johannes. 2002. *Time and the Other*. New York: Columbia University Press.

Featherstone, Mike, Mike Hepworth, and Bryan S. Turner. 1991. *The Body: Social Process and Cultural Theory*. Thousand Oaks, CA: Sage.

Felman, Shoshana, and Dori Laub. 1992. *Testimony: Crises of Witnessing in Literature, Psychoanalysis, and History*. New York: Routledge.

Forte, Tania. 2006. "Scripting for Hollywood: Power, Performance, and the Heroic Imagination in Abu Hanna's 'Real Arabian Nights.'" *History and Memory* 18: 48–85.

Foucault, Michel. 1986. "Of Other Spaces." *Diacritics* 16: 22–27.

Furani, Khaled. 2012. *Silencing the Sea: Secular Rhythms in Palestinian Poetry*. Stanford, CA: Stanford University Press.

Golan, Arnon. 1999. "Zionism, Urbanism, and the 1948 Wartime Transformation of the Arab Urban System in Palestine." *Historical Geography* 27: 152–66.

———. 2001. *Shinui merhavi: Totza'at milhama* [Spatial Change: The Outcome of War]. Beersheba: Ben-Gurion University Press.

Golden, Deborah. 2004. "Patriotism in an Immigrant Society: An Anthropological Perspective." In Avner Ben-Amos and Daniel Bar-Tal (eds.), *Patriotism: Homeland Love*. Tel Aviv, Hakibbutz Hameuchad and Dyonon, 101–33.

Goren, Tamir. 2004. "Separate or Mixed Municipalities? Attitudes of Jewish Yishuv Leadership to the Mixed Municipality During the British Mandate: The Case of Haifa." *Israel Studies* 9: 101–24.

Granowski, Yossi, Yonathan Kunda, and Roman Weter, eds. 2009. *Sfat Yafo: Mit'an yetzira yafo'it* [The Language of Jaffa: A Load of Jaffaite Creation]. Jerusalem: Carmel.

Gubrium, Jaber F., James A. Holstein, and David R. Buckholdt. 1994. *Constructing the Life Course.* New York: General Hall.

Gurevitch, Zali. 2007. *'Al ha-makom* [On Israeli and Jewish Place]. Tel Aviv: Am Oved.

Gurevitch, Zali, and Gideon Aran. 1991. "'Al ha-makom: antropologia yisra'elit" [On the Place: Israeli Anthropology]. *Alpayim* 4: 9–44.

Gur-Ze'ev, Ilan, and Ilan Pappé. 2003. "Beyond the Destruction of the Other's Collective Memory: Blueprints for a Palestinian/Israeli Dialogue." *Theory, Culture, and Society* 20: 93–108.

Habiby, Emile. 1985. *The Secret Life of Saeed: The Pessoptimist,* trans. Salma Khadra Jayyusi and Trevor Le Gassick. London: Zed Books.

Hadas, Orly, and Amiram Gonen. 1994. *Jews and Arabs in a Mixed Neighborhood of Jaffa.* Jerusalem: Floersheimer Institute for Policy Studies (Hebrew).

Handelman, Don. 1977. "Play and Ritual: Complementary Frames of Meta-Communication." In Antony J. Chapman and Hugh C. Foot (eds.), *It's a Funny Thing, Humor.* Oxford: Pergamon, 185–92.

Handler, Richard. 1988. *Nationalism and the Politics of Culture in Quebec.* Madison: Wisconsin University Press.

Harvey, David. 1991. *The Condition of Postmodernity: An Enquiry into the Origins of Cultural Change.* Oxford, UK: Blackwell.

———. 1997. "Contested Cities: Social Process and Spatial Form." In Nick Jewson and Susanne MacGregor (eds.), *Transforming Cities: Contested Governance and New Spatial Divisions.* London: Routledge, 19–27.

Hasan, Manar. 2009. "The Forgotten: Women, Palestinian City, and the Struggle for Memory." PhD diss., Tel Aviv University (Hebrew).

Haskell, Guy H. 1994. *From Sofia to Jaffa: The Jews of Bulgaria and Israel.* Detroit: Wayne State University Press.

Hazan, Haim. 1980. *Limbo People: A Study of the Constitution of the Time Universe Among the Aged.* London: Routledge Kegan & Paul.

———. 1990. *A Paradoxical Community: The Emergence of a Social World in an Urban Setting.* Greenwich, CT: JAI Press.

———. 1994. *Old Age: Constructions and Deconstructions.* Cambridge, UK: Cambridge University Press.

———. 1996. *From First Principles: An Experiment in Ageing.* Westport, CT: Bergin & Garvey.

———. 2001. *Simulated Dreams?: Israeli Youth and Virtual Zionism.* New York: Berghahn.

———. 2009. "Beyond Dialogue: Entering the Fourth Space in Old Age." In Ricca Edmonson and Hans-Joachin von Kondratovitz (eds.), *Valuing Older People: A Humanistic Approach to Aging.* Bristol, UK: Policy Press, 91–104.

———. 2015. *Against Hybridity: Social Impasses in a Globalizing World,* 1st ed. Cambridge, UK: Polity.

Herzfeld, Michael. 1996. *Cultural Intimacy: Social Poetics in the Nation-State.* New York: Routledge.

Hever, Hannan. 2001. *Suddenly, the Sight of War: Nationality and Violence in Hebrew Poetry of the 1940s.* Tel Aviv: Hakibbutz Hameuchad.

Hobsbawm, Eric, and Terence Ranger (eds.). 1992. *The Invention of Tradition.* Cambridge, UK: Cambridge University Press.

Holstein, James A., and Jaber F. Gubrium. 1995. *The Active Interview.* Thousand Oaks, CA: Sage.

Jacobson, Abigail, and Moshe Naor. 2016. *Oriental Neighbors: Middle Eastern Jews and Arabs in Mandatory Palestine.* Waltham, MA: Brandeis University Press.

Jarah, Nouri. 1999. "Edward Said Discusses 'Orientalism,' Arab Intellectuals, Reviving Marxism, and Myth in Palestinian History," trans. Brigitte Caland and Elie Chalala. *Al Jadid* 5(28). www.aljadid.com/content/edward-said-discusses-%E2%80%98orientalism%E2%80%99-arab-intellectuals-reviving-marxism-and-myth-palestinian (accessed November 27, 2017).

Kamir, Orit. 2002. "Honor and Dignity Cultures: The Case of *Kavod* (Honor) and *Kvod ha-Adam* (Dignity) in Israeli Society and Law." In David Kretzmer and Eckart Klein (eds.), *The Concept of Human Dignity in Human Rights Law.* The Hague: Kluwer Law International, 231–62.

Kanaaneh, Rhoda Ann. 2002. *Birthing the Nation.* Berkeley: University of California Press.

Kanafani, Ghassan. 2000. *Palestine's Children: "Returning to Haifa" and Other Palestinian Stories,* trans. Barbara Harlow and Karen E. Riley. London: Lynne Rienner.

Kanafani-Zahar, Aïda. 2000. "Relational Pluralism Between Christians and Muslims in Lebanon: The Emergence of a 'Limited Secularity' Space." *Archives de Sciences Sociales des Religions* 109(1): 119–45.

Kandiyoti, Deniz. 1988. "Bargaining with Patriarchy." *Gender and Society* 2: 274–90.

Kapferer, Bruce. 1988. *Legends of People, Myths of State: Violence, Intolerance, and Political Culture in Sri Lanka and Australia.* Washington, DC: Smithsonian Institution Press.

Kassem, Fatma. 2011. *Palestinian Women: Narrative Histories and Gendered Memory.* London: Zed Books.

Kaufman, Sharon. 1986. *The Ageless Self: Sources of Meaning in Later Life.* Madison: Wisconsin University Press.

Kemp, Adriana. 1999. "Sfat ha-mar'ot shel ha-gvul: Gvulot territorialiyim ve-kinuno shel mi'ut le'umi" [The Janus-Faced Border: Territorial Borders and the Constitution of a National Minority in Israel]. *Israeli Sociology* 2: 319–49.

Khoury, Elias. 2002. *Gate of the Sun,* trans. Humphrey Davies. New York: Picador.

King, Peter. 2007. *Crime and Law in England, 1750–1840: Remaking Justice from the Margins.* Cambridge, UK: Cambridge University Press.

LaCapra, Dominick. 2014. *Writing History, Writing Trauma,* reprint ed. Baltimore: Johns Hopkins University Press.

Lavie, Smadar. 1990. *The Poetics of Military Occupation: Mzeina Allegories of Bedouin Identity Under Israeli and Egyptian Rule.* Berkeley: University of California Press.

LeBor, Adam. 2007. *City of Oranges: An Intimate History of Arabs and Jews in Jaffa.* New York: W. W. Norton.

Lefebvre, Henri. 1996. *Writings on Cities.* Cambridge, MA: Blackwell.

LeVine, Mark. 2005. *Overthrowing Geography: Jaffa, Tel-Aviv, and the Struggle for Palestine, 1880–1948.* Berkeley: University of California Press.

Lieblich, Amia, and Ruthellen Josselson. 1997. *The Narrative Study of Lives.* Thousand Oaks, CA: Sage.

Liebman, Charles S., and Eliezer Don-Yehiya. 1983. *Civil Religion in Israel: Traditional Judaism and Political Culture in the Jewish State*. Berkeley: University of California Press.

Lockman, Zachary. 1996. *Comrades and Enemies: Arab and Jewish Workers in Palestine, 1906–1948*. Berkeley: University of California Press.

Lomsky-Feder, Edna. 2004. "Life Stories, War, and Veterans: On the Social Distribution of Memories." *Ethos* 32(1): 82–109.

London, Yaron. 1993. *Kishon: A Biographical Dialogue*. Tel Aviv: Ma'ariv Press.

Lucian of Samosata. 1905. *The Works of Lucian of Samosata*, trans. Henry Watson Fowler and Francis George Fowler. Oxford, UK: Clarendon Press.

Lustick, Ian. 1980. *Arabs in the Jewish State: Israel's Control of a National Minority*. Austin: University of Texas Press.

Madrikh Yafo [The Jaffa Guide]. 1949. Jaffa: Kanaf Press.

Magnusson, Warren. 2011. *Politics of Urbanism: Seeing Like a City*. Abingdon, UK: Routledge.

Massad, Joseph. 2005. "The Persistence of the Palestinian Question." *Cultural Critique* 59: 1–23.

McAdams, Dan. 1993. *The Stories We Live By: Personal Myths and the Making of the Self*. New York: Guilford.

———. 1996. "Narrating the Self in Adulthood." In James E. Birren, Gary Kenyon, Jan-Erik Ruth, Johannes J. F. Schroots, and Torbjorn Svensson (eds.), *Aging and Biography: Explorations in Adult Development*. New York: Springer, 131–48.

Meinecke, Friedrich. 1970. *Cosmopolitanism and the National State*. Princeton, NJ: Princeton University Press.

Melamed, Shoham. 2004. "Within a Few Dozen Years We Will All Be Mizrachi": Maternity, Fertility, and the Construction of the 'Demographic Threat' in the Minimum Age for Marriage Law." *Theory and Criticism* 25: 69–96 (Hebrew).

Milstein, Uri. 1998. *History of Israel's War of Independence*, Vol. 3, *The First Invasion*. Lanham, MD: University Press of America.

Minns, A., and N. Hijab. 1990. *Citizens Apart: A Portrait of the Palestinians in Israel*. London: I. B. Tauris.

Monterescu, Daniel. 2006. "Stranger Masculinities: Gender and Politics in a Palestinian-Israeli Third Space." In L. Ouzgane (ed.), *Islamic Masculinities*. London: Zed Press, 122–42.

———. 2007. "Heteronomy: The Cultural Logic of Space in Jaffa." In Daniel Monterescu and Dan Rabinowitz (eds.), *Mixed Towns, Trapped Communities: Historical Narratives, Spatial Dynamics, Gender Relations, and Cultural Encounters in Ethnically Mixed Towns in Israel/Palestine*. London: Ashgate, 157–78.

———. 2009. "The Bridled Bride of Palestine: Orientalism, Zionism, and the Troubled Urban Imagination." *Identities: Global Studies in Culture and Power* 16(6): 1–35.

———. 2011. "Estranged Natives and Indigenized Immigrants: A Relational Anthropology of Ethnically Mixed Towns in Israel." *World Development* 39(2): 270–81.

———. 2015. *Jaffa Shared and Shattered: Contrived Coexistence in Israel/Palestine*. Bloomington: Indiana University Press.

Monterescu, Daniel, and Dan Rabinowitz (eds.). 2007. *Mixed Towns, Trapped Communities: Historical Narratives, Spatial Dynamics, Gender Relations, and Cultural Encounters in Ethnically Mixed Towns in Israel/Palestine*. London: Ashgate.

Myerhoff, Barbara. 1978. *Number Our Days: A Triumph of Continuity and Culture Among Jewish Old People in an Urban Ghetto*. New York: Touchstone.

National Insurance Institute, Israel. 2011 (January). *National Insurance Programs in Israel.* Jerusalem: National Insurance Institute. www.scribd.com/document/90990515/Bit uach-Leumi-Programs-2011 (accessed June 1, 2016).

Natour, Raja. 2008. "Foolishness." *Mitaam* 14: 54.

Niles, John D. 2010. *Homo Narrans: The Poetics and Anthropology of Oral Literature.* Philadelphia: University of Pennsylvania Press.

Nora, Pierre. 1989. "Beyond Memory and History: Les Lieux de Mémoire." *Representations* 26: 7–24.

Parker, Andrew, Mary Ruso, Doris Sommer, and Patricia Yaeger (eds.). 1992. *Nationalism and Sexualities.* London: Routledge.

Parmentier, Richard J. 2016. *Signs and Society: Further Studies in Semiotic Anthropology*, reprint ed. Bloomington: Indiana University Press.

Portugali, Juval. 1993. *Implicate Relations: Society and Space in the Israeli-Palestinian Conflict.* Dordrecht: Kluwer Academic.

Pratt, Mary Louise. 1991. "Arts of the Contact Zone." *Profession* 91: 33–40.

Rabinowitz, Dan. 1997. *Overlooking Nazareth: The Ethnography of Exclusion in Galilee.* Cambridge, UK: Cambridge University Press.

———. 2001. "The Palestinian Citizens of Israel: The Concept of Trapped Minority and the Discourse of Transnationalism in Anthropology." *Ethnic and Racial Studies* 24: 64–85.

———. 2007. " 'The Arabs Just Left': Othering and the Construction of Self Amongst Jews in Haifa Before and After 1948." In Daniel Monterescu and Dan Rabinowitz (eds.), *Mixed Towns, Trapped Communities: Historical Narratives, Spatial Dynamics, Gender Relations, and Cultural Encounters in Palestinian-Israeli Towns*, London: Ashgate, 51–64.

Rabinowitz, Dan, and Khawla Abu-Baker. 2005. *Coffins on Our Shoulders: The Experience of the Palestinian Citizens of Israel.* Berkeley: University of California Press.

Rabinowitz, Dan, and Daniel Monterescu. 2008. "Reconfiguring the 'Mixed Town': Urban Transformations of Ethno-National Relations in Palestine/Israel." *International Journal of Middle East Studies* 40: 195–226.

Ram, Hanna. 1996. *The Jewish Settlement in Jaffa: From a Sephardic Community to a Zionist Center, 1839–1939.* Jerusalem: Carmel.

Rapport, Nigel. 1995. "Migrant Selves and Stereotypes: Personal Context in a Postmodern World." In Steve Pile and Nigel Thrift (eds.), *Mapping the Subject: Geographies of Culture and Transformations.* London: Routledge, 267–88.

Rotbard, Sharon. 2015. *White City, Black City: Architecture and War in Tel Aviv and Jaffa.* Cambridge, MA: MIT Press.

Ruggie, John. 1993. "Territoriality and Beyond: Problematizing Modernity in International Relations." *International Organization* 47(1): 139–74.

Said, Edward W. 1986. *After the Last Sky: Palestinian Lives.* New York: Pantheon.

———. 2000. *Out of Place: A Memoir.* New York: Vintage.

———. 2004. "Thoughts on Late Style." *London Review of Books* 26(15) (August 5): 3–7.

Savishinsky, Joel. 2000. *Breaking the Watch: The Meaning of Retirement in America.* Ithaca, NY: Cornell University Press.

Schely-Newman, E. 2002. *Our Lives Are But Stories: Narratives of Tunisian-Israeli Women.* Detroit: Wayne State University Press.

Schutz, Alfred. 1971. *Reflections on the Problem of Relevance.* New Haven, CT: Yale University Press.

Segev, Tom. 2001. *One Palestine, Complete: Jews and Arabs Under the British Mandate.* New York: Picador.

Sered, Susan. 1992. *Women as Ritual Experts: The Religious Lives of Elderly Jewish Women in Jerusalem.* New York: Oxford University Press.

Sewell, William H. 1996. "Historical Events as Transformations of Structures: Inventing Revolution at the Bastille." *Theory and Society* 25: 841–81.

Shamir, Ronen. 2000. *The Colonies of Law: Colonialism, Zionism, and Law in Early Mandate Palestine.* Cambridge, UK: Cambridge University Press.

Sharabi, Hisham. 1988. *Neopatriarchy: A Theory of Distorted Change in Arab Society.* New York: Oxford University Press.

Shehadeh, Raja. 1984. *Samed: Journal of a West Bank Palestinian,* 1st ed. New York: Franklin Watts.

Shenhav, Yehouda. 2006. *The Arab Jews: A Postcolonial Reading of Nationalism, Religion, and Ethnicity.* Stanford, CA: Stanford University Press.

Shield, Renee Rose, and Stanley M. Aronson. 2003. *Aging in Today's World: Conversations Between an Anthropologist and a Physician.* New York: Berghahn.

Shohat, Shmuel. 2008. "I'm Dancing." *Mitaam* 14: 10.

Shokeid, Moshe. 2009. *Three Jewish Journeys Through an Anthropologist's Lens: From Morocco to the Negev, Zion to the Big Apple, the Closet to the Bimah.* Brighton, MA: Academic Studies Press.

Shostak, Marjorie, 2000. *Nisa: The Life and Words of a !Kung Woman.* Cambridge, MA: Harvard University Press.

Silverstein, Michael. 2001. "The Limits of Awareness." In Allessandro Duranti (ed.), *Linguistic Anthropology: A Reader,* 1st ed. Malden, MA: Wiley-Blackwell, 382–401.

Simić, Andrei. 1978. "Winners and Losers: Aging Yugoslavs in a Changing World." In Barbara Myerhoff and Andrei Simić (eds.), *Life's Career–Aging: Cultural Variations on Growing Old.* Beverly Hills, CA: Sage, 177–96.

Simmel, Georg. 1971 [1908]. "The Stranger." In G. Simmel, *On Individuality and Social Forms,* ed. D. Levine. Chicago: Chicago University Press, 143–49.

Slyomovics, Susan. 1998. *The Object of Memory: Arabs and Jews Narrate the Palestinian Village.* Philadelphia: University of Pennsylvania Press.

Smith, Anthony D. 1991. *National Identity.* Reno: University of Nevada Press.

Soffer, Arnon. 2004. *Demography in Israel in Light of the Disengagement Process: 2004–2020.* Haifa: Chaikin Geostrategy Institute, Haifa University.

Sorek, Tamir. 2010. *Arab Soccer in a Jewish State: The Integrative Enclave.* Cambridge, UK: Cambridge University Press.

Spector-Marsel, Gabriela. 2006. "Never-Aging Stories: Western Hegemonic Masculinity Scripts." *Gender Studies* 15: 49–82.

Spivak, Gayatri Chakravorty. 1996. *The Spivak Reader: Selected Works of Gayatri Chakravorty Spivak,* ed. Donna Landry and Gerald M. MacLean. New York: Routledge.

Steinberg, Pnina. 1995. "Identity Play." MA thesis, Department of Sociology and Anthropology, Tel-Aviv University.

Stoler, Ann. 1992. "In Cold Blood: Hierarchies of Credibilities and the Politics of Colonial Narratives." *Representations* 37: 151–85.

Swedenburg, Ted. 1990. "The Palestinian Peasant as National Signifier." *Anthropological Quarterly* 63(1): 18–30.

———. 1995. *Memories of Revolt: The 1936–1939 Rebellion and the Palestinian National Past.* Minneapolis: University of Minnesota Press.

Tamari, Salim. 2008. *Mountain Against the Sea: Essays on Palestinian Society and Culture.* Berkeley: University of California Press.

Tamari, Salim, and Rema Hammami. 1998. "Virtual Returns to Jaffa." *Journal of Palestine Studies* 27(4): 65–79.

Thaiss, Gustav. 1978. "The Conceptualization of Social Change Through Metaphors." *Journal of Asian and African Studies* 13: 1–13.

Tornstam, Lars. 1999. "Gerotranscendence and the Functions of Reminiscence." *Journal of Aging Studies* 4: 155–66.

Trouillot, Michel-Rolph. 1995. *Silencing the Past.* Boston: Beacon Press.

Turner, Victor. 1975. *Dramas, Fields, and Metaphors: Symbolic Action in Human Society.* Ithaca, NY: Cornell University Press.

———. 1995. *The Ritual Process: Structure and Anti-Structure.* New York: Aldine de Gruyter.

Wacquant, Loïc. 2007. *Urban Outcasts: A Comparative Sociology of Advanced Marginality.* Cambridge, UK: Polity.

Weiss, Yfaat. 2011. *A Confiscated Memory: Wadi Salib and Haifa's Lost Heritage.* New York: Columbia University Press.

Wilson, William Julius. 1990. *The Truly Disadvantaged: The Inner City, the Underclass, and Public Policy.* Chicago: University of Chicago Press.

Wimmer, Andreas, and Nina Glick-Schiller. 2002. "Methodological Nationalism and Beyond: Nation-State Building, Migration, and the Social Sciences." *Global Networks* 2(4): 301–34.

Yacobi, Haim. 2009. *The Jewish-Arab City: Spatio-Politics in a Mixed Community.* London: Routledge.

Yiftachel, Oren. 2006. *Ethnocracy: Land and Identity Politics in Israel/Palestine.* Philadelphia: University of Pennsylvania Press.

Yiftachel, Oren, and Haim Yacobi. 2003. "Urban Ethnocracy: Ethnicization and the Production of Space in an Israeli 'Mixed City.'" *Environment and Planning D: Society and Space* 21: 673–93.

Yourcenar, Marguerite. 2005. *Memoirs of Hadrian,* trans. Grace Frick. New York: Farrar, Straus & Giroux.

Yuval-Davis, Nira. 1997. *Gender and Nation.* London: Sage.

Zureik, Elie. 1979. *The Palestinians in Israel: A Study in Internal Colonialism.* Boston: Routledge & Kegan Paul.

INDEX

INDEX

Jerusalem Boulevard, 45, 46, 47, 48, 59, 80, 126, 233, 242n21; Jewish population, 5, 6, 8–9, 18, 58–59, 59–60, 242n2; Large Area, 190, 191–92, 193, 200, 203, 204–10, 247nn1,3, 248n5; vs. Lydda, 140–41; Manshiya neighborhood, 188, 243n5, 244n16; as mixed city, 3, 4, 5–7, 9–10, 14, 19, 56, 62, 108, 138, 162, 227–28, 230, 231, 236, 237n7, 238n18; as Mother of the Stranger, 2, 7, 71, 224, 238n16; National Emergency Committee, 91, 95, 96, 97–98, 100, 106–7, 244n5, 245n6; new Jewish residents vs. long-standing Jewish residents, 6, 8–9; before 1948 war, 5–6, 18, 69–70, 74; during 1948 war, 1–2, 5, 6, 7, 8, 31, 55, 56, 65–71, 75–76, 81, 91, 92, 94, 95–98, 106–7, 126, 129–31, 230, 243n5, 244n5, 245n3; orchards in, 27, 63, 65, 68–69, 74, 105, 160; Palestinian-Jewish relations in, 1, 3–4, 5–6, 8, 13, 34–36, 54–56, 59–60, 59–73, 62, 64–65, 67–68, 93, 98–99, 103, 116–17, 132, 146–47, 164–65, 187, 200–201, 206, 214, 228, 233–35; Palestinian population, 5, 54–56, 59–60; Project Renewal, 61; Ramat Aviv, 190, 203–4; role in Jewish immigration, 5, 8–9, 16, 18, 61; Saraya attack in, 66–67; social vs. spatial boundaries in, 6; as spatially heteronomous, 230, 231, 249n20; Tabitha Scottish School, 91, 92–93, 102–3, 143; and Tel Aviv, 5, 8, 9, 48, 73, 175–76, 184, 188, 189, 191, 204, 207–8, 210, 234, 241n3; Tosina Café, 175, 184, 247n1; as transit city, 8, 57, 58–62
Jday, Fakhri: vs. Subhiya abu-Ramadan, 128, 146; vs. Abu-Subhi, 66, 67, 71, 85, 86–87; on Arabic language, 54, 146; attitudes regarding Arab bourgeoisie, 28; attitudes regarding Arab nationalism, 32, 33, 40–41; attitudes regarding Arab politicians, 28, 32, 33, 39, 40–41, 47, 229; attitudes regarding greed, 37, 40; attitudes regarding Jaffa, 28, 29–31, 34, 36–40, 42, 43–44, 45–46, 47, 62, 66, 67, 106, 177, 241n15; attitudes regarding Palestinian

nationalism, 27, 28, 29, 33–34, 38–44, 62, 213, 229; attitudes regarding the Israeli state, 28, 32, 36, 38–39, 47, 214, 215; vs. Rabbi Avraham Bachar, 45–47, 49, 58, 62, 86–87, 227; at Beirut University, 40–41; class identity of, 36–37, 43, 46; as community representative, 28, 46; death of, 233; on divide and rule, 33–34; as elite, 27, 28; as estranged, 28, 29, 45–46; vs. Hakim sisters, 106; vs. Abu-George Hamati, 213, 214, 215, 222; on journalists, 38; on land expropriation, 31–33; motto "Power cannot suppress free will," 27; as national symbol, 27, 28; on 1948 war, 32, 36, 215, 216; on Palestinian-Jewish relations, 34–36; personal narrative of, 27–44; picture of, 28; on political parties, 37, 38; sense of betrayal in, 27, 29
Jerusalem, 6, 230
Jewish Agency, 116, 119
Jewish attitudes: regarding Arabic, 156, 183, 186; regarding the Holocaust, 13, 86, 152, 162, 163; regarding Israeli culture, 149–50, 151, 153, 175, 176, 186; regarding Israeli state, 149–50, 162, 165, 166, 168–69, 170; regarding Jaffa, 8, 9, 28, 45–49, 54–56, 59–61, 116–17, 118, 119, 124, 151, 159–60, 162–65, 166–67, 168–69, 184–85, 189, 223–24, 225, 228; regarding Jewish nationalism, 14, 27, 28, 45, 62, 120, 121, 123, 155, 166, 170, 182, 210, 223–27, 232, 234–35, 236; regarding Jewish-Palestinian relations, 54–56, 60, 116–17, 124, 164–65, 175, 176, 181–82, 183–84, 200–201; vs. Palestinian attitudes, 45–47, 232
Jewish dietary laws, 155, 186
Jewish immigration, 21, 52, 56, 122, 123, 138, 149, 150, 151, 155–56, 169, 177, 229; from Bulgaria, 45, 47–49, 58–59, 61, 62, 75–76, 93, 103, 161, 241nn2,5; from Iraq, 93, 103; role of Jaffa in, 5, 8–9, 16, 18, 61; from Romania, 75–76, 93, 103, 159, 161; from Syria, 18, 111, 113–16, 118, 119, 120, 121, 123
Jewish National Fund, 32, 69